"This book fills a very important gap in the tra⸍ ⸍ ⸍ ⸍ ⸍th professionals. Carefully researched, well organized, and wonc cian who recognizes the importance of spirituality feels uncertain of how to approach these issues in ⸍

—**Ruth Baer, PhD**, professor of psychc
and author of *The Practicing Happiness Workbook*

"Spiritual and religious competency is a foundational skill for clinicians, but has typically received much less attention than it deserves. This book thoughtfully engages key issues and provides clinicians with up-to-date resources and strategies for building this core skill."

—**Willoughby Britton, PhD**, assistant professor of research in the department
of psychiatry and human behavior at the Warren Alpert Medical School of
Brown University

"If you're a psychologist or clinician, put *Spiritual and Religious Competencies in Clinical Practice* on your list of must-read books. It will be your guide to helping clients access the religious and spiritual resources—like coping skills or social support—available for their treatment or recovery. Keep it close and refer to it often!"

—**Christine Carter, PhD**, author of *The Sweet Spot* and *Raising Happiness*

"If you are unaware of the spiritual dimensions of healing, your competence will be seriously compromised. This is a must-read manual for therapists, healers, doctors, nurses, or anyone in the healing professions."

—**Deepak Chopra, MD**

"This critical resource takes a deep look at the self-insight, knowledge, and skills that clinicians need to have in working with clients of varying spiritual and religious identities. Unlike vague advice to be open and empathic, this book relies on research and provocative clinician experiences to highlight specific recommendations to take seriously psychologists' oft-ignored requirement to respect and take seriously clients' diverse spiritual and religious identities."

—**Adam Cohen**, associate professor of psychology at Arizona State University

"This is a much-needed contribution that significantly raises awareness of religious and spiritual dimensions of clients' lives, highlights client resources that can be drawn upon, and expands the diversity discussion in a thoughtful and inclusive way. I would recommend this book for every therapist."

> —**Brant Cortright, PhD**, professor of psychology at the California Institute of Integral Studies and author of *Psychotherapy and Spirit* and *Integral Psychology* (SUNY Press)

"One of the major developments in psychology and medicine in recent decades is the realization that spiritual and religious practices can have major positive influences on health and longevity. These findings, buttressed by thousands of studies, are now largely accepted as part of the canon of medical science. These practices are not handed down from on high, but can be taught by professionals who are competent to do so. The development of these competencies is what this breakthrough book is all about. *Spiritual and Religious Competencies in Clinical Practice* is a doorway toward a more empathic, compassionate, and effective form of healing. This book is of value not just for mental health professionals, but for practicing physicians as well."

> —**Larry Dossey, MD**, executive editor of *Explore: The Journal of Science and Healing* and author of *One Mind*

"Aimed at clinicians, this is also a quietly profound and transformational book. It draws readers into a heartfelt engagement with their own deepest questions and longings while offering many practical guidelines and suggestions for skillful, effective work with diverse spiritual, religious, and existential issues. Unique, and destined to be a classic in the field."

> —**Rick Hanson, PhD**, author of *Buddha's Brain*

"Grounded solidly in research, Vieten and Scammell do a masterful job of applying general multicultural competence issues involving therapist attitudes, knowledge, and intervention strategies to the spiritual and religious domains. A must-read for all mental health professionals, but especially those who find their commitment to diversity most challenged by clients' spirituality and religiousness."

> —**Peter C. Hill, PhD**, Rosemead School of Psychology, Biola University

"In this revolutionary book, Vieten and Scammell open our eyes to the power of the sacred in the therapeutic encounter, enabling client and clinician to find purpose, healing, and joy in the individual's religious and spiritual convictions."

—**Dacher Keltner**, professor of psychology at the University of California, Berkeley; director of Greater Good Science Center; and author of *Born to Be Good: The Science of a Meaningful Life*

"I love this book. I wish I'd been given this when I first began my clinical psychology studies. Cassandra Vieten and Shelley Scammell have done a masterful job in clearly elucidating the subtle spiritual and religious competencies that we need to understand within ourselves, and with the people we counsel, be they clients, patients, students, or parishioners. *Spiritual and Religious Competencies in Clinical Practice* is a trailblazing book that should be mandatory reading for all of us who intend to be or are already in clinical practice, no matter our discipline. I love how Vieten and Scammell weave together pertinent research, case vignettes, and didactic material to form a beautiful tapestry of understanding for all of us who follow in their footsteps. We truly do great service to our clients and ourselves by understanding and integrating the sixteen core principles that Vieten and Scammell have so skillfully set before us in their book."

—**Richard Miller, PhD**, clinical psychologist, president of the Integrative Restoration Institute, past president of the Institute for Spirituality and Psychology, and author of *The iRest Program for Healing PTSD*

"Building on sound clinical research and practice, Vieten and Scammell have created an excellent, user-friendly book that will guide mental health professionals in the development of the attitudes, knowledge, and skills for competence in spiritually integrated psychotherapy."

—**Kenneth I. Pargament, PhD**, professor in the department of psychology at Bowling Green State University and author of *Spiritually Integrated Psychotherapy: Understanding and Addressing the Sacred*

"Spiritual experiences are among the most powerful influences on the human psyche and the few universals among all human cultures, and yet they've long been addressed only superficially in professional psychological training, leading to an unfortunate 'spiritual illiteracy' among many mental health professionals. Thankfully, with the publication of this excellent, thorough, nuanced volume, that painful gap in psychological training can now be filled."

—**Terry Patten**, coauthor of *Integral Life Practice*

"An extraordinary book weaving together the rigor of science with the wisdom of contemplation. I give it my highest recommendation."

—**Shauna Shapiro**, professor at Santa Clara University and author of
Mindful Discipline and *The Art and Science of Mindfulness*

"Spirituality and religion are subjects of ultimate concern and yet confusing to many people seeking therapy today. These excellent guidelines, well grounded in research and knowledge of best practices, are a valuable resource for all helping professionals and the diverse populations they serve."

—**Frances Vaughan, PhD**, psychologist and author of *Shadows of the Sacred*

"How do we incorporate spirituality into our practice? Deep down, most of us clinicians and therapists know that spirituality is an essential piece of health and healing. Unfortunately, it is rarely addressed. Vieten and Scammell's amazing work walks us through how to bring this forgotten piece back into our practices to truly treat the whole being."

—**Helané Wahbeh, ND, MCR**, assistant professor at Oregon Health and
Science University

"With rare comprehensiveness and clarity, Vieten and Scammell skillfully guide readers through the *whys* and the *hows* of developing clinical competencies in dealing with the spiritual and religious issues that can invisibly trouble patients and derail their well-being. Their sixteen competencies are right on target. The substantive scientific data, case studies, practical tools, and resources for every competency help clinicians venture skillfully into this uncharted but essential domain of psychological healing. An incredible achievement."

—**Linda Graham, MFT**, author of *Bouncing Back: Rewiring Your Brain for
Maximum Resilience and Well-Being*

"Spiritual and religious beliefs to a large extent shape our world view. Without this understanding a therapist can easily miss a crucial element of why someone thinks or acts as he or she does. *Spiritual and Religious Competencies in Clinical Practice* is a groundbreaking work. It not only delivers important information that's been sorely lacking in this area but, even more, provides tools that can help a therapist guide a patient toward true transformation. A real contribution to the field!"

—**James Baraz**, coauthor of *Awakening Joy* and cofounding teacher of
Spirit Rock Meditation Center

SPIRITUAL & RELIGIOUS COMPETENCIES IN CLINICAL PRACTICE

Guidelines for Psychotherapists
& Mental Health Professionals

CASSANDRA VIETEN, PhD
SHELLEY SCAMMELL, PsyD

New Harbinger Publications, Inc.

Distributed in Canada by Raincoast Books

Copyright © 2015 by Cassandra Vieten and Shelley Scammell
      New Harbinger Publications, Inc.
      5674 Shattuck Avenue
      Oakland, CA 94609
      www.newharbinger.com

The graphic "Size of Major Religious Groups, 2010" from the Pew Forum's Global Religious Diversity report, April 4, 2014, appears with permission from the Pew Research Center. http://www.pewforum.org/2014/04/04 /global-religious-diversity/

Cover design by Amy Shoup
Acquired by Melissa Valentine
Edited by Jasmine Star

Library of Congress Cataloging-in-Publication Data on file

FSC
www.fsc.org
MIX
Paper from
responsible sources
FSC® C011935

RAINFOREST ALLIANCE CERTIFIED

Printed in the United States of America

17   16   15

10   9   8   7   6   5   4   3   2   1   First printing

This book is dedicated to Christina Grof and Stanislav Grof, pioneers who advanced our understanding of the intersection of spirituality and psychology, and helped us understand more about being human.

CONTENTS

FOREWORD

I n our fields of mental health, we stand at an important moment in our evolution. From a range of disciplines working with the mind and even those working directly with the body, we devote our professional lives to serving the health and healing of others. Each person brings an inner experience, a "mind," that shapes not only how we feel and think and behave but how the very health of our body unfolds across a lifetime. In this way, any professional concerned with clinical issues can benefit from an understanding of the human mind and a focus on mental well-being. For psychotherapists and other mental health professionals, knowing about the mind and mental well-being are crucial for our work. But what does mental health really mean? And what is the mind whose health we are trying to promote?

In this important and groundbreaking book, you will be offered a rigorous account of one component of mental health: our sense of connection to something larger than our bodily defined "self" and our experience of discovering and creating meaning and purpose in our lives. A range of research, carried out directly by the authors and by other academic investigators, will be systematically presented to offer a set of tested guidelines for clinical practitioners so that an organized, logical, and empirically validated set of data will serve as the foundation for a clear view of how clinicians can explore the religious and spiritual lives of those they serve.

But why, you may ask, should you be interested in adding yet another set of data to accumulate in the evaluation of the clients and patients you see? Isn't simply exploring the various diagnostic criteria of the *Diagnostic and Statistical Manual of Mental Disorders* enough to state that someone has well-being? As so many of us were taught, if a person does not meet criteria for having a formal disorder, don't they then, by default, have "mental health?"

The simple answer is no. The National Institute of Mental Health has recently suggested that we need to move beyond the simple view of the *DSM* as some holy grail of diagnostic accuracy and look more scientifically at what creates mental suffering in our lives. In the field I work in, interpersonal neurobiology (IPNB), we also strive for a new approach for our work in mental health—as well as in education, parenting, contemplative practice, organizational functioning, and our general life as human beings on this precious and fragile planet. In IPNB we offer a view of human life that combines all the fields of science, from math to anthropology, neuroscience to sociology, into one framework. Then we look for the ways to bring their universal, overlapping findings into this "consilient" view of science, and discover ways to apply these scientific principles in practical ways.

From this effort we offer a definition of the mind and then make a scientifically informed proposal about what a healthy mind might actually be.

Though over a hundred thousand mental health professionals surveyed have revealed that about 95 percent of us have never been offered a definition of the mind, we are now in a position to suggest that the mind can be defined and a healthy mind then proposed from this viewpoint. We see that one aspect of the mind—perhaps distinct from the mind's consciousness and its subjective experience, perhaps related—is this: an embodied and relational, self-organizing emergent process that regulates the flow of energy and information. A healthy mind from this perspective would be one that optimizes this regulation, enabling self-organization within us and between us and the world to promote the flexible, adaptive, coherent, energized, and stable flow of energy and information over time. But how does this occur? Through a process involving the linkage of differentiated elements of a system, called *integration*. Integration creates harmony; the lack of integration leads to chaos and rigidity. Each symptom of each syndrome in the *DSM* can be reinterpreted as an example of chaos and rigidity. And what is not included in the *DSM* is the notion that harmony—the result of integration—is the way we experience well-being.

Where does this process of integration occur? Within the brain and its body, and between us, in our relationships with other people and entities outside of these bodies we live in. In this view, the brain within the whole body is seen as the embodied mechanism of energy and information flow; relationships are the sharing of energy and information; and the mind is the self-organizing emergent process that regulates that flow.

And what is the connection of this view of mind to spirituality and religion? Are these separate aspects of human life? Let's look deeply at these questions.

Research reveals that one of the most powerful influences on several dimensions of our lives—how long we live, how happy we are, the health of our minds, and our medical health—is the nature of our social networks of support. How we are connected to a larger set of interpersonal relationships shapes our well-being. From an IPNB view, we see this finding as arising from the relational aspect of mind: our well-being is created within our connections with others. The brain is a social organ, and brain circuits and their functions are influenced directly by our sense of connection to others outside of these bodies we live in.

When it comes to examining a person's well-being, inner processes—like how we feel and regulate our emotions, how we think and understand the world, and how we relate to others and understand their inner lives—are also quite important. When these mental processes are integrated, well-being ensues. Regulation arises from integration in the brain; relationships that support well-being honor differences and cultivate compassionate communication as linkages. Even in studies of the brain, when differentiated areas are linked, optimal self-regulation ensues and mental health is present. When there is impairment in this neural integration, various illnesses are present, from schizophrenia to manic-depressive illness.

Spirituality can be seen as the way in which we find connection to something "larger" than our bodily defined self, and the ways we find purpose and meaning in our day-to-day lives. Spirituality is a human experience involving connection and meaning. This can be seen as finding differentiation and linkage between ourselves and others for connection, and within ourselves for meaning. And at the heart of religious practice, beneath specific institutional practices and customs, we can see the drive to connect and find meaning, too. While some organized approaches leave individuals far from such spiritual meaning and connection, at their heart is often the original intent for such integrative ways of living.

From an IPNB perspective, a narrowly defined sense of self limits our well-being because it limits our state of integration. When we connect with others beyond our bodily selves, we become a part of a larger whole. And when we face issues of life and death, of meaning and purpose, we also can create deeper states of integration by coming to realize how profoundly interconnected we are—not only with other people but with other living beings, with our planet, and with the larger world, coming to sense our place in the universe. Physics and math reveal, and ecology and anthropology support, that we human beings, as individuals and as a species, are part of an interconnected whole. The issue then becomes, as Albert Einstein suggested, that we live with the "optical delusion" of our separateness and how we ought to "widen our circles of compassion" to create more well-being in our lives. What could be more spiritual than that?

For me, spirituality and religion can be seen as how we explore meaning in our lives and come to develop a deep sense of being a part of this larger whole—however it is experienced—and the many ways this opening process can be defined.

And so this book fits well with a scientifically grounded interdisciplinary view of human life that offers a definition of the mind and suggests that a healthy mind is one that promotes integration—within and between.

What struck me in reading this magnificent manual of clinical assessment of religious and spiritual life was how deeply committed and scientifically thorough our guides have been in creating this important book. I learned a tremendous amount, soaking in their years of hard-earned data, absorbing their careful articulation of what could easily have been simply opinion and a narrow point of view. Instead, what you'll discover in these illuminating pages is a beautifully constructed, empirically derived approach to taking a history about how this spiritual and religious integration in a person's life has been shaping his or her development, influencing relationships, molding the mind, and helping, or sometimes hurting, well-being.

Careful discussions of how "spiritual crises" might arise are offered here to prepare us as clinicians for working directly with a range of challenges that may arise on a client's life journey. A developmental perspective is also offered so that we can see how spiritual and religious growth may have been unfolding in the person's life, what factors influence this path, and how a clinician can best invite the sharing of this information in a respectful and helpful way. The authors also thoroughly explore how to distinguish psychiatric disorders from spiritual emergencies and the disorientation that can arise as new senses of self arise with the opening of the mind to an awareness of something larger than our bodily self as being "who we are." And, among the many, many pearls of wisdom and superb suggestions you'll find in your learning journey ahead, there is also a crucial examination of your own state of mind as a clinician and how this influences the interactions with those you'll be seeing. We don't always, or perhaps even often, share the particular spiritual or religious development of others, and so respecting these differences and compassionately communicating in ways that invite further discussion are crucial. In addition, throughout the book you'll find "journal entries" of the direct experiences of clinicians, including the authors themselves, and how they have faced the challenges that can arise with such assessments.

This book is essential reading for new and experienced clinicians, in the field of mental health and beyond, that can create a scientifically based, clinically useful approach to understanding how spirituality and religion have played a role in the development of the mind and of mental health. I hope you'll benefit as much as I have from the opportunity to learn from the wisdom we've been so graciously offered in these illuminating pages. Enjoy!

—Daniel J. Siegel, MD
    Mindsight Institute, California

PREFACE

In 2007, the two of us sat down in Shelley's office with David Lukoff, psychologist and founder of the Spiritual Competency Resource Center, to discuss how we might take action to promote the incorporation of basic spiritual and religious competencies into the field of psychology. At the time, we were all involved in a small nonprofit organization called the Institute for Spirituality and Psychology, the mission of which was to explore how both psychology and the world's spiritual and religious traditions hold important knowledge about promoting mental and emotional thriving. Our thought was that dialogue between the two might offer important insights into ways to reduce human suffering and promote psychological and spiritual well-being.

Our driving hypothesis was that the divide between psychology and spirituality was limiting clinical effectiveness, at times resulting in misdiagnosis and missed opportunities for accessing resources that could contribute to some clients' therapeutic success. As the research committee for the Institute for Spirituality and Psychology, we were interested in understanding what general information about spirituality and religion might help therapists be more clinically effective without them having to become spiritual or religious themselves. We wondered what basic competencies we might be able to identify, through research, that would advance the field of psychology and also provide resources for spiritual and religious issues so that practitioners could provide competent psychological help.

David was the perfect person to work with. He had written over fifty articles relating to the intersection of spirituality and psychology, differential diagnosis between psychosis and religious or spiritual problems, and the role of spiritual and religious practices in psychological well-being. He was also the coauthor, with Francis Lu, MD, of the V code for "Religious or Spiritual Problem" in the fourth edition of the *Diagnostic and Statistical Manual of Mental Disorders* (*DSM-IV*); it appeared within the category "Other Conditions That May Be a Focus of Clinical Attention," which covers conditions that don't reach the level of clinical diagnosis. This condition remains in the most recent version of the manual (*DSM-5*), in the subcategory "Problems Related to Other Psychosocial, Personal, and Environmental Circumstances," and is described thus: "This category can be used when the focus of clinical attention is a religious or spiritual problem. Examples include distressing experiences that involve loss or questioning of faith, problems associated with conversion to a new faith, or questioning of spiritual values that may not necessarily be related to an organized church or religious institution" (American Psychiatric Association, 2013, p. 725).

Getting this condition into the *DSM* was a major advancement because, in a sense, it meant the field recognized that religious and spiritual problems were officially worth paying attention to in clinical practice.

At the time, Cassandra was a scientist studying spirituality and health at the California Pacific Medical Center Research Institute in San Francisco, and was also the director of research at the Institute of Noetic Sciences. Since its inception in 1973, the Institute of Noetic Sciences has focused on bringing objective science together with inner (noetic) wisdom to advance human thriving. She had recently completed studies, funded by the National Institutes of Health and the state of California, on the use of mindfulness meditation to reduce cravings and relapse in alcoholism and other addictions, and was working on a large-scale study, funded by a private foundation, examining health and well-being in relation to engagement in spiritual practices and communities. She had also coauthored a book about studies she and her colleagues had conducted on the psychological effects of experiences of spiritual transformation: *Living Deeply: The Art and Science of Transformation in Everyday Life* (Schlitz, Vieten, & Amorok, 2008).

Shelley was teaching psychology in the master's program at the American College of Traditional Chinese Medicine in San Francisco and in the PhD program at the California Institute of Integral Studies, had an active clinical practice, and also often consulted with her students and with other professionals regarding spiritual experiences and psychological health. She was particularly known in the community as a clinician who could skillfully deal with people who were having distressing experiences with religious or spiritual aspects.

At that point, spirituality and religion had already been recognized as an aspect of multicultural competencies. The American Psychological Association had published *Guidelines on Multicultural Education, Training, Research, Practice, and Organizational Change for Psychologists* (2002) and explicitly defined "culture" as "the embodiment of a worldview through learned and transmitted beliefs, values, and practices, including religious and spiritual traditions" (p. 8). Furthermore, their subsequent *Guidelines and Principles for Accreditation of Programs in Professional Psychology* (2013) stipulated that cultural and individual diversity include religion, and required each program accredited by the American Psychological Association to have and implement "a thoughtful and coherent plan to provide students with relevant knowledge and experiences about the role of cultural and individual diversity" (p. 10). The guidelines also require that all interns "demonstrate an intermediate to advanced level of professional psychological skills, abilities, proficiencies, competencies, and knowledge in the…issues of cultural and individual diversity" (p. 15).

Despite this, we couldn't find much guidance that clinicians could rely on regarding how to work with clients in these realms, or that training programs could use to guide their curricula. Other than a couple of poster presentations (Lopez, Brooks, Phillips, & Hathaway, 2005) and theoretical contributions (Corbett, 1996, 2007, 2011), there did not appear to be research-based guidelines for competently working with clients' religious and spiritual issues.

While research shows that most psychotherapists already recognize religion and spirituality as important aspects of human diversity (Crook-Lyon et al., 2012; McMinn, Hathaway, Woods, & Snow, 2009), the vast majority of work in fostering multicultural competency focuses on ethnic and racial diversity. Attention to spiritual and religious aspects of diversity is inadequate (Frazier & Hansen, 2009). For example, Nagai (2008) found that among clinicians working with Asian and Asian-American clients, self-ratings of spiritual competence were significantly lower than those for ethnic and racial cultural competence. While specific competencies exist or are in development for gender (American Psychological Association, 2007), sexual orientation (American Psychological Association, 2012), aging (American Psychological Association, 2009), and multicultural issues (American Psychological Association, 2002), specific training in competencies for spiritual and religious diversity has been lacking. So we embarked on a project to develop such competencies.

We discussed competence versus proficiency early on. "Competence" refers to the basic attitudes, knowledge, and skills clinicians should possess to conduct effective therapy. "Proficiency," on the other hand, refers to a high degree of expertise or skill. We agreed that we weren't interested in identifying skills needed for clinicians to become proficient in spiritually oriented care or to have a specialty or niche practice in which they explicitly include spiritual or religious interventions in their practice, as discussed in Hathaway (2008). In fact, as we dug deeper into the literature, it became increasingly clear to us that incorporating religious or spiritual *interventions* into therapy for those clients who request them requires not basic competence but proficiency. When religious or spiritual interventions are requested by clients and are appropriate, psychologists should integrate them into therapy only when they have the training to do so. For those who are interested in offering such interventions, there is quite a bit of literature, along with a number of training programs, on actively integrating spiritual and religious approaches into therapy (Barnett & Johnson, 2011; Martinez, Smith, & Barlow, 2007; Potik, 2010).

However, we were interested in identifying the basic attitudes, knowledge, and skills that *all* psychologists and other mental health professionals should possess to be able to work at a baseline level of competence with their clients' religious and spiritual diversity and issues. Drawing from work on other aspects of multicultural competence, and after a thorough literature review, we began by drafting a set of provisional basic competencies.

By March 2010, our research team had grown to include postdoctoral student Ronald Pilato (now a faculty member at Antioch University) and postdoctoral student Ingrid Ammondson (now a psychologist). We invited fifteen clinicians (psychologists, marriage and family therapists, and a physician) with expertise in the intersection of psychology and religion/spirituality to a half-day focus group to review a set of provisional competencies we'd created via our thorough literature review. By consensus, we created a set of twenty-four provisional competencies.

Then, in 2011 and 2012, we conducted an online survey of 184 psychologists and other mental health professionals, 105 of whom were classified as experts in this domain, asking them to comment on the content, clarity, and relative importance of each of the twenty-four items that had been refined by the focus group. At this point, we also enlisted the support of Kenneth Pargament, a well-known expert in the psychology of religion and spirituality, to advise us on the project and review our results. The survey included such questions as "Is this aspect of competency described clearly?" "Do you have any suggestions for changing the content or wording of this aspect of competency?" and "In terms of your own practice of psychology, please rate the extent to which you possess this competency."

When all the responses were in, we first calculated means and standard deviations of the clarity, self-assessment, and importance ratings. We analyzed the open-ended responses that gave feedback on wording of items, using a thematic analysis technique that provided a grouping framework for similar responses. When similar feedback appeared in several of the responses, we incorporated it into the revision process. Through this painstaking process of quantitative and qualitative data analysis, the provisional items were revised, some were combined with others, and others were deleted. This resulted in the sixteen spiritual and religious competencies for psychologists and other mental health professionals you will find in this book: three in the area of attitudes, seven in the area of knowledge, and six in the area of skills. We published the results of this project in the American Psychological Association's journal *Psychology of Religion and Spirituality* (Vieten et al., 2013).

We followed this with a survey of three hundred psychologists and mental health professionals who were selected specifically for *not* being experts in the intersection of spirituality and psychology. This time we wanted to inquire among the general population of clinicians to determine whether they believed clinicians should receive training in and demonstrate each competency, whether they had received formal training in any of the competencies, and to what extent they felt they themselves demonstrated each competency in their clinical practice. We discovered that 80% of the participants believed psychologists should receive training in addressing spiritual and religious aspects of patient's lives. Further, 70% of the respondents stated they had little or no explicit training in how to competently address these areas (Vieten et al., 2014).

Spiritual and Religious Competencies

This book presents sixteen research-based spiritual and religious competencies for psychologists and mental health professionals, along with descriptions, clinical case examples, and strategies for cultivating each of them. Each competency in this book has been carefully constructed and informed by input from hundreds of therapists. We've demonstrated, as previously discussed, that psychologists and mental health professionals believe these competencies are important basic attitudes, knowledge, and skills that should be included in the training of all therapists and that, in general, they had not received such training. The resulting competencies are listed below. Note that these guidelines were developed specifically for psychologists, and our research-based competencies used the word "psychologists." Throughout this book we've generally changed the word "psychologist" to "clinician," since these guidelines should be useful for all mental health professionals.

Attitudes

1. Psychologists demonstrate empathy, respect, and appreciation for clients from diverse spiritual, religious, or secular backgrounds and affiliations.

2. Psychologists view spirituality and religion as important aspects of human diversity, along with factors such as race, ethnicity, sexual orientation, socio-economic status, disability, gender, and age.

3. Psychologists are aware of how their own spiritual or religious background and beliefs may influence their clinical practice and their attitudes, perceptions, and assumptions about the nature of psychological processes.

Knowledge

4. Psychologists know that many diverse forms of spirituality and religion exist, and explore spiritual and religious beliefs, communities, and practices that are important to their clients.

5. Psychologists can describe how spirituality and religion can be viewed as overlapping yet distinct constructs.

6. Psychologists understand that clients may have experiences that are consistent with their spirituality or religion, yet may be difficult to differentiate from psychopathological symptoms.

7. Psychologists recognize that spiritual or religious beliefs, practices, and experiences develop and change over the life span.

8. Psychologists are aware of clients' internal and external spiritual or religious resources, and practices that research indicates may support psychological well-being and recovery from psychological disorders.

9. Psychologists can identify spiritual and religious experiences, practices, and beliefs that may have the potential to negatively impact psychological health.

10. Psychologists can identify legal and ethical issues related to spirituality and religion that may surface when working with clients.

Skills

11. Psychologists are able to conduct empathic and effective therapy with clients from diverse spiritual or religious backgrounds, affiliations, and levels of involvement.

12. Psychologists inquire about spiritual and religious background, experience, practices, attitudes, and beliefs as a standard part of understanding a client's history.

13. Psychologists help clients explore and access their spiritual and religious strengths and resources.

14. Psychologists can identify and address spiritual and religious problems in clinical practice and make referrals when necessary.

15. Psychologists stay abreast of research and professional developments regarding spirituality and religion specifically related to clinical practice, and engage in ongoing assessment of their own spiritual and religious competency.

16. Psychologists recognize the limits of their qualifications and competence in spiritual and religious domains, including their responses to clients' spirituality or religion that may interfere with clinical practice, so that they (1) seek consultation from and collaborate with other qualified clinicians or spiritual or religious sources (priests, pastors, rabbis, imams, spiritual teachers, and so on), (2) seek further training and education, and/or (3) as appropriate, refer clients to more qualified individuals and resources.

The purpose of creating these spiritual and religious competencies is threefold. First, we hope they will help clinicians avoid biased, inadequate, or inappropriate practice when they encounter spiritual or religious issues. Second, they are meant to enable clinicians to identify and address spiritual or religious problems and harness clients' inner and outer spiritual and religious resources, thus improving treatment outcomes. Third, this set of competencies will provide training guidelines for continuing education and professional development of already practicing clinicians, as well as content that can be integrated throughout clinical training and supervision for new therapists.

ACKNOWLEDGMENTS

The authors wish to thank Melissa Valentine, Catharine Meyers, and all of the staff at New Harbinger Publications for seeing the value of this book. Many thanks to Jess Beebe and Jasmine Star for their excellent editing. We extend our deep gratitude to Cary Dakin and Alan Pierce, who helped tremendously with background research, citations, and references for this book. We are also grateful to our collaborators in the research that led to the competencies described in this book, including David Lukoff, Ron Pilato, Ingrid Ammondson, Alan Pierce, and Kenneth Pargament. Thanks to David Hodge, Scott Richards, and Christina and Stan Grof, who generously gave permission to adapt and utilize their work, and to Suzanne Bastear for her excellent illustrations of the lifemap and ecomap. Thanks as well to the many scholars who have inspired us to take the next steps in this work, including Frances Vaughan and Roger Walsh. Thank you also to Michael Sapiro for his excellent contributions; to Tony White and Daphne Crocker-White, who provided valuable feedback on the manuscript; and to Tina Amorok for her infinite wisdom. We appreciate the board members of the Institute for Spirituality and Psychology (ISP), where the spiritual competencies project was birthed, especially Richard Miller, Gary Buck, Janis Phelps, Lindsey Beaven, Sophia Reinders, Sandy McDonald, Matthew Spalding, and David Lukoff. Thanks also to the faculty and staff of the California Institute of Integral Studies, where each of us did our graduate work, who are now helping take ISP to its next stage. In addition, we'd like to thank the Social Relations of Knowledge Institute, the Carl and Roberta Deutsch Foundation, and the members of the Institute of Noetic Sciences for supporting our research. Finally, we thank our families and friends who helped us in myriad ways throughout the writing of this book, especially Indigo Vieten; Courtney Bercut, Taryn, and Ian Mendius; and Richard Mendius, whose invaluable support made this work possible.

INTRODUCTION

A client comes in wearing a traditional Muslim *hijab* (a veil covering the head and chest). She introduces herself as Azizah, and after partially completing your intake form, she looks down and quietly says that she's coming in to discuss problems in her marriage. Once she's seated, you notice she's left most of the intake form blank. You review her address, telephone number, and basic information, then begin to review the rest of the form with her orally. She is very tentative in her responses to your questions, rarely meeting your eyes. You aren't sure if she is shy, fearful, or exhibiting a behavioral style appropriate to her cultural background. As Azizah's story unfolds, she reveals a complex relationship among herself, her husband of fourteen years, and her mother-in-law that appears to be, at the very least, stifling to her and, at worst, abusive. As she explains her situation and her responses to it, she frequently refers to her faith in the principles of Islam as providing a source of support for her own coping. However, she also quotes the Qur'an twice during the session while looking down and shrugging of her shoulders, and in your view, she seems to use these quotes to excuse the unkind and potentially abusive behavior of her husband and his mother toward her. As the session winds down, she bows her head and briefly looks at you directly, seeming to plead for help.

Are you able to help this client? Maybe you're confused and unsure about how to proceed—a bit at sea. Can you challenge some of her less adaptive beliefs without disrespecting her spiritual tradition? Which aspects of her presentation represent cultural norms, which are appropriate to her spiritual tradition, and which might be maladaptive or pathological? To what extent must you learn more about Islam to be clinically competent in this case? Should you consult, and if so, with whom? Would it be better to refer out? Where should you start?

The temptation may be to simply rely on general unconditional positive regard or benign respect when dealing with religious and spiritual issues, taking care to avoid assumptions and stereotypes, just as you would with any other form of diversity. You may believe that clinical sophistication, general cultural competence, or simple common sense will allow you to adequately treat clients with spiritual and religious beliefs and practices that are unfamiliar or very different from your own.

The premise of this book is that clinical acumen, common sense, and general cultural competence are insufficient for adequately attending to the religious and spiritual domains of our clients' lives. Just like the training you receive as a mental health professional to competently attend to racial and gender differences, specific training in spiritual and religious competencies is essential to becoming an adept therapist in today's world.

This book provides you with the attitudes, knowledge, and skills you need to address the spiritual and religious domains of your clients' lives in clinical practice. Reading it will help you:

- Knowing how to sensitively inquire about clients' spiritual and religious beliefs and practices when conducting your initial assessment and taking a history, and doing so as a matter of routine

- Possessing a level of comfort and curiosity about clients' religious and spiritual lives that will make them feel comfortable bringing them up in therapy

- Understanding how individual clients' spiritual or religious backgrounds may have influenced their life, identity, and worldview

- Knowing how to help clients access any inner and outer religious and spiritual resources that may be available to assist in their treatment planning or recovery, such as coping skills or social support

- Being able to identify spiritual or religious problems and either helping clients navigate them or working with clergy and other spiritual advisors to help them do so

All of this will make you not only a more competent clinician, but also a more popular one, in all likelihood. Since many clients would like to address these issues in therapy, cultivating these skills should increase your clients' satisfaction and the effectiveness of your treatment. There will be more meaning and depth in your sessions, and in your relationships with your clients. As you learn to work with clergy and other spiritual advisors in your community, you'll become known as a clinician who is friendly to and able to address religious and spiritual domains, even if you are not at all religious or spiritual yourself, and you may receive more referrals as a result. In short, learning these competencies should enhance your practice on a number of levels.

Definitions

While there are varying definitions of the concepts discussed in this book, such as religion, spirituality, and competence, our research has led us to the following working definitions.

Religion and Spirituality

Although the words "religion" and "spirituality" have historically often been used interchangeably, they are increasingly understood to be distinct yet overlapping constructs (Kapuscinski & Masters, 2010; Piedmont, Ciarrochi, Dy-Liacco, & Williams, 2009; Schlehofer, Omoto, & Adelman, 2008; Zinnbauer et al., 1997). For some, "spirituality" is a broad term that includes but is not limited to religion, whereas for others, "religion" may encompass spirituality. Some people's spirituality is informed by participation in organized religion, while others describe themselves as spiritual but not religious.

We use the term "religion" to refer to affiliation with an organization that is guided by shared beliefs and practices, with members who adhere to a particular understanding of the divine and participate in sacred rituals.

"Spirituality" is less easily defined. We use it to mean an individual's sense of connection to or search for the sacred (Pargament, Mahoney, Exline, Jones, & Shafranske, 2013). It is important to note that the term "sacred" is used here inclusively, to refer not only to concepts of God and higher powers, but also to other aspects of life that are perceived to be manifestations of the divine or imbued with divine-like qualities, such as transcendence, immanence, boundlessness, and ultimacy (Bowling Green State University, 2012).

Pargament and Sweeney (2011) have defined "spirituality" as "the journey people take to discover and realize their essential selves and higher order aspirations" (p. 58–59). P. C. Hill and colleagues (2000) define "spirituality" as referring to thoughts, feelings, and behaviors related to a concern about, a search for, or a striving for understanding and relatedness to the transcendent. "Spirituality" has also been defined as an individual's internal orientation toward a transcendent reality that binds all things into a unitive harmony (Dy-Liacco, Piedmont, Murray-Swank, Rodgerson, & Sherman, 2009).

When they analyzed the existing literature on spirituality and psychology, Kapuscinski and Masters (2010) found that "communion with the sacred, or a search for the sacred" (p. 194) was included in 67% of definitions of spirituality, and that the word "sacred" most commonly referred to God or to the transcendent. These authors propose that it is the focus on the sacred that differentiates spirituality from psychological constructs such as meaning, purpose, or wisdom (we'll discuss this further in chapter 6).

To be as inclusive as possible, throughout this book we will use the acronym SRBPs to refer to spiritual and religious beliefs and practices (acknowledgments to Saunders, Miller, & Bright, 2010, for this helpful term).

Competence

We agree with Kaslow's (2004) conceptualization of "competence" as "an individual's capability and demonstrated ability to understand and do certain tasks in an appropriate and effective manner consistent with the expectations for a person qualified by education and training in a particular profession or specialty thereof" (p. 774). A "competency" is a specific attitude, knowledge, or skill that must be cultivated to become competent. As a subset of multicultural competencies, then, "spiritual and religious competencies" are defined as a set of attitudes, knowledge, and skills in the domains of spirituality and religion that all clinicians should have in order to effectively and ethically practice therapy, regardless of whether or not they conduct spiritually oriented psychotherapy or consider themselves spiritual or religious (Vieten et al., 2013, p. 16).

In this book, the word "attitudes" refers to the implicit and explicit perspectives and biases people hold about spirituality and religion as it relates to the practice of psychology. "Knowledge" refers to information, facts, concepts, and awareness of research clinicians should possess about spirituality and religion as it relates to the practice of psychology. "Skills" refers to therapists' ability to actively and effectively utilize their knowledge of spirituality and religion in their clinical work with clients. From here forward, when we refer to "spiritual and religious competencies," this is what we mean.

Why Spiritual and Religious Competencies?

Three basic activities of general multicultural competence are (1) engaging in the process of becoming aware of one's own assumptions about human behavior, values, biases, preconceived notions, personal limitations, and so on; (2) attempting to understand the worldview of culturally different clients without judgment; and (3) implementing relevant and sensitive intervention strategies with culturally different clients (Arredondo et al., 1996; S. Sue, 1998). These capacities clearly extend to cultural differences involving religion and spirituality. But, one might ask, why should training in multicultural competence explicitly focus on spiritual and religious competencies? Here are five key reasons.

Reason 1: Our Clients Are Spiritual and Religious

The United States is a religious nation. Whereas economic development and national wealth are inversely related to religiousness throughout much of the world (Norris & Inglehart, 2004), the US population remains more religiously affiliated than most other developed countries. Indeed, it is the third-most-religious developed Western nation, preceded only by Italy and Ireland (Ellison & McFarland, 2013). In the United States, 92% of people believe in God (Newport, 2011). Gallup polls from 1992 through 2012 indicate that up to 59% of Americans report that religion is "very important" in their lives, with another 29% reporting that religion is "fairly important" (Gallup, 2012). Further, 40% of Americans consider themselves "very religious," while 29% see themselves as "moderately religious" (Newport, 2012). Clearly, religion holds an important place in the hearts of many of our clients.

According to the research of Ellison and McFarland (2013), the majority of Americans (80%) identify with a religious practice. Half of US citizens participate in a religious community or congregation (J. A. Davis, Smith, & Marsden, 2007; Kosmin, Mayer, & Keysar, 2001, as cited in Ellison & McFarland, 2013, p. 22). The majority of Americans who are religious subscribe to some form of Christianity (Ellison & McFarland, 2013). The approximate breakdown is as follows:

- Conservative Protestant groups that are fundamentalist, charismatic, or evangelical take in 30% of the population (Ellison & McFarland, 2013). These groups adhere to belief structures that subscribe to the tenets of original sin and divine grace as the portal to "individual salvation" (Hempel & Bartkowski, 2008, as cited in Ellison & McFarland, 2013).

- General Social Surveys and the American Religious Identification Survey estimate that 12 to 15% of US adults prefer more liberal Protestant denominations, such as Presbyterian or Methodist (Ellison & McFarland, 2013).

- An estimated 25% of American adults identify as Catholic, even if they currently may not be active members of the church (Ellison & McFarland, 2013).

- Populations of smaller Christian groups, such as the Latter-Day Saints (Mormons) and Jehovah's Witnesses, are harder to determine (Ellison & McFarland, 2013).

- Non-Christian faiths, such as Judaism, Islam, Hinduism, and Buddhism, are followed by 5% of the US population (Ellison & McFarland, 2013).

- An estimated 15 to 20% of US adults express no religious preference at all in surveys (Ellison & McFarland, 2013).

The United States is home to several thousand specific religious denominations and faith traditions, with each region having its own religious or spiritual trend. Religious diversity is greater in major metropolitan areas, especially gateway cities for immigration, including New York, Los Angeles, Miami, Washington, Honolulu, San Francisco, and Houston (Ellison & McFarland, 2013). These cities host large numbers of diverse faiths, including non-Judeo-Christian religions. In the mid-Atlantic and Midwest United States, cities tend to be more homogeneous, with three thousand counties dominated by followers of one or a small number of denominations (Jones et al., 2002).

However, the landscape of SRBPs in the United States is rapidly shifting. At the beginning of this century, Fuller (2001) estimated that almost 40% of Americans were not affiliated with any church or religion, and that approximately 20% identified themselves as spiritual but not religious. A January 2002 Gallup poll showed that as many as 33% of Americans identified themselves as spiritual but not religious (G. H. Gallup, 2003) and predicted an increase in the number of people unaffiliated with religions and a decrease in those affiliated with the Protestant religion. That prediction has been fulfilled (Pew Forum on Religion and Public Life, 2012b).

By 2010, 72% of Millennials (eighteen- to twenty-nine-year-olds) described themselves as spiritual rather than religious (Phillips, 2010). While a majority of Americans (74%) still consider themselves Christian, a growing number (17.8%) identify themselves as religiously unaffiliated (Pew Forum on Religion and Public Life, 2012b). Clearly, in today's world, therapists must be competent to address not only the religious aspects of client experiences, but also the less easily defined spiritual aspects.

We must also be aware that many people do not engage in any religious or spiritual practice whatsoever. Between 15 and 20% of US adults expressed no religious preference at all (Kosmin & Keysar, 2009; Pew Forum on Religion and Public Life, 2012b). Any set of spiritual and religious competencies must also include attention to and respect for lack of religious or spiritual involvement in clients.

So one good reason to learn more about how to attend to religious and spiritual domains is that the vast majority of the clients you will encounter will have SRBPs that are probably important to them. Of course, the mere fact that many people are spiritual or religious does not necessarily indicate that clinicians should attend to this dimension of individual difference. Prevalence alone is insufficient justification. For example, if a large percentage of the population took an interest in stock car racing, it is unlikely that competencies in this area would be required for practicing psychology. There are other good reasons for therapists to prepare themselves to address spiritual and religious domains.

Reason 2: The Role of Mental Health Professionals Is Expanding

In earlier generations, most people attended a local church, temple, synagogue, or other place of worship. The local minister, pastor, priest, rabbi, or other spiritual leader was the go-to person for questions of faith. Often, that leader was also a resource for issues of family, marriage, relationships, work, finances—almost any concern a person might have.

While former generations turned to their religious leaders for the answers to life's questions, our current culture has largely shifted its expectations. Many traditional churches are witnessing dwindling congregations, and an entire generation is growing up with no religious affiliation. So to whom are people turning for life guidance, for help with their most private existential struggles, and even for resetting their moral compass? Very often, they turn to mental health practitioners.

Increasingly, people turn to therapists for guidance in how to handle issues that arise in work and relationships, in everyday life, and in their hearts, minds, and souls. While most therapists receive thorough and careful training in the mental and emotional aspects of psychological well-being, very few receive adequate training in the domains of human existence that hold the deepest meaning for the majority of our clients: spirituality and religion.

Reason 3: Clients Want to Talk About Their Spirituality and Religion

There is consistent evidence that clients would prefer to address spirituality and religion in therapy. Twenty years ago, studies showed that clients prefer a therapist with spiritual values (G. H. Gallup & Bezilla, 1994; Lehmann 1993), and over a decade ago, most clients of university counseling centers reported a desire to have religion or spirituality discussed during counseling (Rose, Westefeld, & Ansley, 2001). However, what actually occurs is different. Psychologists report discussing spirituality and religion with only 30% of their clients, and less than half address clients' SRBPs during assessment or treatment planning (Hathaway, Scott, & Garver, 2004).

Clients' desire to discuss religious and spiritual issues in therapy can also present a dilemma for some clinicians. While therapists generally report being open to discussing spiritual and religious issues (Post & Wade, 2009), as a group we are considerably less religious than the clients we serve (Bergin & Jensen, 1990; Delaney, Miller, & Bisono, 2007; Shafranske & Cummings, 2013). For example, whereas 92% of the general population believes in God, only 66% of psychologists do. And while 75% of the public agrees with the statement that their approach to life is based on religion, only 35% of psychologists do (Delaney et al., 2007). Because spirituality and religion are less personally important to psychologists overall than to their clients, these realms may be neglected in the general practice of therapy. Whether or not you are spiritual or religious yourself, your therapeutic acumen will be enhanced by being comfortable and curious when inquiring about these aspects of clients' lives, and by being able to do so ethically and effectively.

Reason 4: Spirituality and Religion Are Linked to Psychological Functioning

SRBPs are important in the psychological functioning of most adolescents and adults (Hathaway et al., 2004) in many ways:

- Contributing to identity development (Fukuyama & Sevig, 2002; Magaldi-Dopman & Park-Taylor, 2010)

- Informing worldview (Arredondo et al., 1996; Leong, Wagner, & Tata, 1995)

- Helping them avoid risky scenarios (McNamara, Burns, Johnson, & McCorkle, 2010)

- Helping them cope with difficulties (Arredondo et al., 1996)

SRBPs provide meaning and support in times of stress (Oman & Thoresen, 2005; Park, 2005), and positive religious coping has been shown to contribute to successful stress management (Ano & Vasconcelles, 2005; Cornah, 2006; Pargament, Ano, & Wachholtz, 2005; Pargament & Raiya, 2007). Further, over 80% of severely mentally ill patients report using religion to cope (S. A. Rogers, Poey, Reger, Tepper, & Coleman, 2002; Tepper, Rogers, Coleman, & Malony, 2001), and spirituality has long been recognized as a core component of recovery from substance use disorders (Delaney, Forcehimes, Campbell, & Smith, 2009).

Spirituality has also been linked to an increased sense of meaning, purpose, resilience, satisfaction, and happiness (Fredrickson, 2002; Fry, 2000; Pargament, 2011; Pargament et al., 2013). Overall, a robust body of empirical evidence has demonstrated beneficial relationships between various dimensions of SRBPs and psychological health (for example, Green & Elliott, 2010; Koenig, King, & Carson, 2012; W. R. Miller & Thoresen, 2003; Oman & Thoresen, 2005).

In addition, interventions that have roots in spiritual traditions are being increasingly employed for treatment of depression and anxiety, as well as for enhancing psychological well-being. For example, mindfulness-based therapies have demonstrated effectiveness for improving anxiety and mood symptoms (Hofmann, Sawyer, Witt, & Oh, 2010; Toneatto & Nguyen, 2007). Dialectical behavior therapy (DBT; Linehan, 1993) and adaptations of it have shown promise and efficacy for treating borderline disorder, substance abuse, eating disorders, and depression (Robins & Chapman, 2004). Acceptance and commitment therapy (ACT; Hayes, Strosahl, & Wilson, 1999) has demonstrated robust effect sizes compared to control groups across a number of difficulties (Powers, Zum Vörde Sive Vörding, & Emmelkamp, 2009; Ruiz, 2010). Various forms of spiritually informed cognitive behavioral therapy have demonstrated success, in particular with clients to whom religion is important (Waller, Trepka, Collerton, & Hawkins, 2010).

Knowing how SRBPs are related to psychological well-being can help you tap into those resources when appropriate for your clients. At the same time, religion and spirituality are not always positive influences on clients' psychological well-being. While the vast majority of clinicians regard religion as beneficial (82%) rather than harmful (7%) to mental health (Delaney et al., 2007), the relationship between religious or spiritual involvement and well-being is not consistently positive (Powell, Shahabi, & Thoresen, 2003; Rosenfeld, 2010). As a therapist, it will be helpful for you to be able to identify aspects of SRBPs that may be exacerbating a client's symptoms or becoming maladaptive in some way.

In fact, there is evidence that some forms of SRBPs can have negative effects on psychological well-being (Exline & Rose, 2005; Exline, Yali, & Lobel, 1999; Pargament, 1997). Certain forms of SRBPs have also been associated with higher mortality and morbidity (Exline & Rose, 2005; Pargament, 1997), and negative spiritual coping can have a detrimental impact on mental and emotional health (King et al., 2013; Lindeman & Aarnio, 2007). As one example, scrupulosity and hyperreligiosity are characteristics of some obsessive-compulsive and psychotic disorders (Brewerton, 1994; Greenberg, Witztum, & Pisante, 1987). For instance, one of Shelley's clients developed an elaborate daily ritual based on his fear of being stalked by his mother's former boyfriend. In hopes of keeping the boyfriend away while his single mother was still at work, the client, then nine years old, started setting up icons and crosses from his Catholic background in a certain order, which took up nearly forty minutes. This later evolved into a time-consuming ritual he felt compelled to complete before leaving the house, contributing to the onset of agoraphobia by the time he was in his twenties.

The term "spiritual bypassing" (Welwood, 1984) has been used to describe another problematic factor with SRBPs: unhealthy misuse of religious or spiritual practices or terminology to avoid dealing with important psychological issues or problems with relationships or global functioning (Cashwell, Bentley, & Yarborough, 2007; Cortright, 1997; Welwood, 2000). Finally, religious and spiritual struggles in and of themselves may require informed interventions (Exline, Grubbs, & Homolka,

2014; Exline & Rose, 2005; Lukoff, Lu, & Turner, 1992; Lukoff, Lu, & Yang, 2011). Clearly, both positive and dysfunctional forms of religious and spiritual involvement are important for psychologists to recognize and address. (We'll address this topic in detail in chapter 9.)

Reason 5: Mental Health Professions Are Behind

Psychology as a whole is lagging behind other health care fields in establishing basic spiritual and religious competencies. For over a decade, the Association of American Medical Colleges (1999) has recommended that training programs "incorporate awareness of spirituality, and cultural beliefs and practices into the care of patients in a variety of clinical contexts…and recognize that their own spirituality and [their] cultural beliefs and practices might affect the ways they relate to, and provide care to, patients" (p. 25).

The Joint Commission on the Accreditation of Healthcare Organizations, which provides health care accreditation to over nineteen thousand health care organizations in the United States, requires that medical professionals perform a spiritual assessment as a standard element of patient care (2014). Similar movements to establish spiritual and religious competencies have been active for nurses (McSherry, Gretton, Draper, & Watson, 2008; Pesut, 2008; van Leeuwen, Tiesinga, Middel, Post, & Jochemsen, 2008).

Some progress has been made in social service and mental health professions. The American Psychiatric Association began to require training in spiritual competencies during residency (Campbell, Stuck, & Frinks, 2012), and religious and spiritual competencies for psychiatrists have been partially established (Josephson, Peteet, & Tasman, 2009; Verhagen & Cox, 2010). There have been efforts to create guidelines for social workers (Hodge, 2007) and professional counselors (Council for Accreditation of Counseling and Related Educational Programs, 2009; Robertson, 2010; J. S. Young, Cashwell, Wiggins-Frame, & Belaire, 2002). However, psychologists in particular have had no research-based competencies that we are aware of until now.

Why Don't Spiritual and Religious Competencies Already Exist?

You may wonder why therapists aren't already covering this realm. If so many clients are interested in God or spirit, why isn't it a subject in the therapy room? As clinicians, we are enthusiastic about discussing our clients' marriages, divorces, family life with children, work lives, friendship problems, health issues, sexual proclivities, losses, traumas, and just about every possible problem, but we are less inquisitive about their beliefs and experiences on the religious or spiritual level. Why is that?

An emphasis on establishing psychology as a scientific discipline may have led to a reluctance among many psychologists and mental health professionals to acknowledge the relevance of spirituality and religion in psychological functioning (Coon, 1992; W. R. Miller & Thoresen, 2003; Plante, 2008). This is particularly true in psychology training programs and among academic psychologists who chafe at psychology being considered a "soft" science. Psychologists often hesitate to acknowledge or investigate domains of human existence that could potentially be viewed as metaphysical or supernatural, resulting in what Saunders, Miller, and Bright (2010) have called "spiritually avoidant care" (p. 355).

Psychologists have even been described as antagonistic to religion and spirituality (J. Hill, 2000; Plante, 2008). There is evidence that psychologists hold explicit and implicit negative biases based on perceived client religiosity, for example, appraising religious clients as more mentally ill or having a poorer prognosis (S. O'Connor & Vandenberg, 2005; Ruff, 2008). Perceptions of psychologist bias or prejudice against religion and spirituality may prevent utilization of their services by clients who find these domains important, while also limiting referrals from clergy or spiritual directors who fear the spiritual or religious domain might be ignored, misunderstood, or pathologized in therapy (Richards & Bergin, 2000; Worthington & Sandage, 2002). Therefore, becoming more competent as a therapist will not only improve the quality of your own clinical practice, but also advance the field as a whole.

Another reason that spiritual and religious competencies may not have been developed previously is that most clinicians have little education or training in how to ethically and effectively attend to the religious and spiritual domains in clinical practice (Brawer, Handal, Fabricatore, Roberts, & Wajda-Johnston, 2002; Hage, 2006; Schafer, Handal, Brawer, & Ubinger, 2011; Schulte, Skinner, & Claibom, 2002). A decade ago, only 13% of clinical psychology programs accredited by the American Psychological Association included any formal coursework in religion or spirituality (Brawer et al., 2002), and 90% of psychologists reported that SRBPs were not discussed in their academic training (W. R. Miller & Thoresen, 2003). Though incorporation of spirituality and religion into supervision and coursework in graduate training programs accredited by the American Psychological Association has increased since that time, at this point only 25% of psychology training programs provide even one course in religion or spirituality (Schafer et al., 2011). A recent study of 292 faculty members and students in psychology training programs accredited by the APA indicated that doctoral programs and predoctoral internships were relying on informal and unsystematic sources of learning to provide training in religious and spiritual diversity (Vogel, 2013). In contrast, 84 to 90% of medical schools offer courses or formal content on spirituality and health (Koenig, Hooten, Lindsay-Calkins, & Meador, 2010).

Due to lack of exposure to the literature, the fields of psychology and mental health care simply may not have recognized the importance of these arenas to our clients' psychological and emotional functioning, and therefore have not prioritized them in training. This book is intended to provide guidelines so that training in spiritual and religious competencies can be easily integrated into coursework, internships, supervision, and continuing professional education.

Conclusion

To summarize, most of our clients are religious, spiritual, or both, and they are increasingly widely diverse in their spiritual and religious beliefs and practices. These beliefs and practices are very meaningful to many clients and are often important aspects of their psychological functioning and well-being. Our clients have every right to demand religious and spiritual competence from us, as a subset of multicultural competence. Just as there are guidelines for our colleagues in psychiatry, nursing, and medicine, we too require training and support to feel comfortable navigating these realms in the therapy room.

More and more of peoples' lives are coming into the therapy room these days. No subject is taboo anymore; our role has expanded. We must not avoid religious and spiritual issues in clinical practice. Rather, we need to prepare ourselves to competently address them.

With this book, it is our intention to help you include spirituality and religion in psychotherapy, making them topics you can work with comfortably and effectively. Our premise is that developing spiritual and religious competence will enhance your treatment outcomes and increase client satisfaction, and also may enrich your experience of the work you do, whether or not you personally are spiritual or religious or interested in becoming so. If you are able to effectively engage with these domains of your clients' lives, you will be better equipped to harness the religious and spiritual inner and outer resources that may assist in clients' recovery, wellness, and psychological development.

Each of the chapters in this book presents one of the competencies, describing it in detail, discussing why it's important for practicing good therapy, and providing ways to cultivate that competency. We also discuss complexities, nuances, or exceptions to the rule. The competencies are organized into three categories: attitudes, knowledge, and skills. In the appendix, we provide training guidelines; and in the resources section, we suggest recommended readings, as well as videos and websites, for further exploration of each competency.

Part 1

ATTITUDES

Chapter 1

DEMONSTRATING EMPATHY, RESPECT, AND APPRECIATION

The first three competencies are attitudes: stances you take toward the religious and spiritual domains of clients' lives when engaging in clinical practice. Often, attitudes are implicit, meaning they function under the surface of conscious awareness. This chapter and the next two encourage you to consciously examine the attitudes you currently hold and to cultivate a few attitudes that are crucial to spiritual and religious competence, beginning with the most foundational spiritual competency of all: demonstrating empathy, respect, and appreciation for clients with diverse spiritual and religious backgrounds and beliefs.

COMPETENCY 1: Psychologists demonstrate empathy, respect, and appreciation for clients from diverse spiritual, religious, or secular backgrounds and affiliations.

You might read this foundational spiritual and religious competency and say to yourself, "Of course! Isn't that obvious? I have no problem demonstrating empathy, respect, and appreciation for those who hold diverse perspectives. It comes with the territory." However, in our own practices and research on this issue, we've found that clients often experience a lack of empathy, respect, and appreciation regarding their spiritual or religious beliefs and practices (SRBPs), even from otherwise very compassionate and skilled clinicians.

In fact, Shelley has had well over one hundred clients seek her out after experiencing thoughtlessness, a lack of sensitivity, or outright prejudice regarding their religious or spiritual experiences or beliefs in therapy—often without awareness on the part of the therapist. Many clients have told her that their previous therapists ignored or dismissed their spiritual or religious beliefs and practices, misunderstood them, or, in some cases, even pathologized them for their beliefs. At first Shelley assumed these were unique cases, but over time she began to see a trend. It seemed that many people with strong spiritual or religious experiences, beliefs, or practices were being inadvertently deprived of competent treatment by well-meaning but inadequately trained mental health practitioners.

The research literature provides further evidence for a perceived lack of empathy, respect, and appreciation among therapists with respect to clients' spiritual and religious beliefs and practices (Cox, Campbell, & Fulford, 2007; Cragun & Friedlander, 2012). Some people resist seeking psychological treatment because they fear their religious beliefs will be judged, minimized, or ignored (Buckholtz, 2005; Leong et al., 1995). Some members of a congregation or spiritual community won't go to a therapist because they anticipate that their religious beliefs or traditions may be weakened (Mayers, Leavey, Vallianatou, & Barker, 2007). Clergy may refrain from recommending that parishioners seek psychological treatment for the same reason (Bledsoe, Setterlund, Adams, Fok-Trela, & Connolly, 2013; Lish, Fitzsimmons, McMinn, & Root, 2003; VanderWaal, Hernandez, & Sandman, 2012).

Indeed, historically the field of psychology has at times demonstrated a marked lack of empathy, respect, and appreciation for people's spiritual and religious beliefs and practices. Freud (1930/1961) famously reduced religion to a mass delusional pathology, saying, "The whole thing is so patently infantile, so foreign to reality, that…it is painful to think that the majority of mortals will never be able to rise above this view of life" (p. 22). The father of cognitive psychology, Albert Ellis (2001), scorned religion, not only calling it "childish dependency," but going so far as to claim, "Spirit and soul is horseshit of the worst sort. Obviously there are no fairies, no Santa Clauses, no spirits. What there is is human goals and purposes as noted by sane existentialists. But a lot of transcendentalists are utter screwballs." John Watson, one of the fathers of behaviorism, advocated the outlaw of religion, which he said excused "failure and weakness" (Buckley, 1989, p. 165).

Today, psychologists may generally be more open-minded and measured in how they express their views, but they remain unusually nonreligious in comparison to the general population and are far less religious than the clients they serve (Shafranske, 1996). The history of the major movements in psychology, the generally less religious worldview of psychologists as a group, and the lack of specific training in religious and spiritual issues (as there is in other aspects of diversity) all put many therapists at risk for unintentional failures in empathy, respect, and appreciation when it comes to religion and spirituality. Even among mental health professionals who are themselves spiritual or religious, having empathy, respect, and appreciation for people with SRBPs different from their own is not a given, but an attitude that must be cultivated.

Defining Empathy, Respect, and Appreciation

At its most rudimentary level, spiritual and religious competence in psychology entails avoiding prejudice based on SRBPs. Here, however, we are talking about moving far beyond lack of prejudice and into actively empathizing with, respecting, and appreciating clients' spiritual and religious beliefs, experiences, and practices. This involves paying attention to the spiritual and religious domains of clients' lives, being curious about them, harnessing their positive aspects, and addressing clients' struggles around these domains. This is done in much the same way we attend to the other important aspects of their lives related to their psychological and emotional functioning, such as their families, work, thoughts, emotions, and physical health.

Numerous studies, reviews of the literature, and reviews of those reviews show that, without question, therapists' ability to be empathic, respectful, warm, genuine, and appreciative of their clients is strongly correlated with positive treatment outcomes (Decker, Nich, Carroll, & Martino, 2014; Messina et al., 2013; Neukrug, Bayne, Dean-Nganga, & Pusateri, 2013; Patterson, 1984; J. C. Watson, Steckley, & McMullen, 2014). The power of what Carl Rogers (1961) called "unconditional positive regard" (p. 283) seems to reach far beyond therapists' technical abilities, the sophistication of their case formulation, and the content of their interventions in predicting treatment success. This makes it tremendously important to identify places where we may be challenged in our ability to manifest this essential ingredient of successful therapy.

What is empathy? Simply defined, "empathy" is the ability to feel or imagine another person's emotional experience (McDonald & Messinger, 2011). The online Merriam-Webster dictionary (2014) defines empathy more loquaciously as "the action of understanding, being aware of, being sensitive to, and vicariously experiencing the feelings, thoughts, and experience of another without having the feelings, thoughts, and experience fully communicated in an objectively explicit manner." In other words, you don't have to have gone through what your client is going through, you don't have to agree with her perspective or worldview, you don't even need to understand all the components of her situation—but you must be able to feel for her, and feel *with* her to a certain extent, to be effective.

We are using the term "respect" to refer to the understanding that our clients are important and valuable and deserve to be treated that way. Their spiritual and religious—or secular, nonreligious—beliefs, experiences, and practices deserve to be valued and acknowledged just as their thoughts and feelings, their hopes and dreams, and their successes and struggles do. This is true in every relationship, but as professionals, we are called upon to demonstrate consistent and genuine respect, even in the face of beliefs or behaviors that we may not understand or agree with. Some of our clients may have seldom had the experience of being treated this way, so doing so is, in itself, therapeutic.

Appreciation goes one step further. We use the term "appreciation" to describe an ability to not only respectfully tolerate clients' beliefs, but to actively attend to them and express their essential worth, quality, or importance. If we appreciate what is offered to us in the room, whether or not we agree with it or believe in it ourselves, clients can feel valued and seen—an important aspect of the therapeutic process. In this case, appreciating clients as whole beings, with minds, emotions, bodies, and, for some, rich religious or spiritual lives, is essential to competent care.

Said another way, *not* attending to the spiritual or religious domains of clients' lives, *not* asking about SRBPs while taking a history, and *not* demonstrating curiosity about spiritual experiences are all ways in which we can fail to show empathy, respect, and appreciation for clients. The same is true of responding to spiritual or religious content that is unfamiliar or unusual by either letting it pass, dismissing or disregarding it, or quickly pathologizing it.

When Empathy, Respect, and Appreciation Are Challenged

No matter how skilled you are as a therapist, when confronted with religious and spiritual, or even secular beliefs and practices that are very different from your own, your capacity to demonstrate empathy, respect, and appreciation may be challenged, and your clinical competence threatened. Consider this case example.

✳ Clinician's Diary

A number of years ago, Shelley was working for a large outpatient hospital system in California. Prior to seeing new clients, she had little information about them, so all she knew about this case was that she was meeting a couple. She expected to find a couple in distress, but upon greeting them she noticed that they were holding hands and laughing. Both were dressed casually but presentably. *This will be an easy case,* she thought to herself. After Shelley and the clients discussed the initial guidelines of therapy, they shared that they were planning to get married and were seeking premarital counseling, leading to the following dialogue.

Joe: I've got two children, ages nine and eleven, and Nancy's got one, age fourteen. I think the kids get along fine. They're good kids, good students, but getting married will be a big adjustment for all of us. Nancy and I have been dating a year, and I've been widowed a year and a half. They need a new mom, and Nancy's terrific. She's a natural at parenting. It would probably be easier, in a way, to just live together. But since my wife passed away and Nancy's ex-husband lives in another state, we will be raising the kids as a couple.

Shelley: How did you meet?

Nancy: We met at church; Joe just showed up one day, and I noticed him immediately. His girls were so cute and well-behaved, and he seemed like such a great dad. I soon found out that he was widowed.

Joe: I had to relocate quickly after my wife died. The mortgage was too high for my income alone. We moved to an apartment across town, and there was this church next door, so I just went there soon after moving. I met Nancy on our second visit there, and that's that.

Shelley: That's wonderful. So what brings you here today?

Nancy: Well, my pastor thought we should come in. I've been a member of our church for many years, and he wanted someone different to work with us. He's too close to me, he said. He's a bit worried, because he feels Joe should have joined our church by now and gotten more involved. It's not such a big church, and we all need to pull our weight. I volunteer every week at the church, but Joe's not gotten very involved. He comes on Sundays for services with the girls, of course, but my pastor feels he's not committed…not pulling his weight. I think it will all come in time; I'm not too worried.

Shelley: So your church means a lot to you?

Nancy: Oh, yes, my faith means everything to me and to my daughter; it saved us during a hard time when I was divorcing my former husband. I don't know where we'd be without it.

Shelley: Joe? What's going on for you and your girls?

Joe: Well, you know, I think Nancy's terrific, and I'm fully committed to getting married soon. But, honestly—and don't get mad at me, Nance—I just can't buy everything your church believes in. I mean, I was raised in a very different style of Christian church, and I'm not sure I can quite swallow what they go for in this one.

Nancy: Wow, you've never said that before, honey. What do you mean? I thought you liked our church. You're there every week.

Joe: I love you, and I appreciate how nice and welcoming everyone's been. You all care so much for each other, and it's a fine place and all, but I don't always agree with everything in the church itself.

Nancy: Like what?

Joe: Well, as I mentioned to you, the girls were very upset that we couldn't celebrate their birthdays this year. Their mom was big into birthdays, with home-
made cake and a party with friends and all. She made a big deal of them. And
now they're not supposed to celebrate their birthdays, or even Christmas. It's
hard on them. I don't care about mine, but this is a hard thing for them to
change. They're upset. It's just that they're kids, and this church is pretty
serious about all this.

Nancy: I didn't know it was bothering you that much.

Joe: Well, this year I secretly held a birthday party for both girls. I had to.

Nancy: What? That's against our rules! We're getting married in my church. How
could you do that?

Joe: My girls just lost their mom, Nance. How could I not? They need some traditions to continue…

Nancy: I'm not trying to be mean! You told me that you and the girls understood all
the reasons why we don't use symbols outside of our worship… And you were
okay with it!

Joe: I know, I know. It's just all too much sometimes. Doctor Scammell, what do
you think?

As a therapist who had attended church growing up, Shelley found herself a bit taken
aback during this session with Joe and Nancy. She had heard of a church not celebrating
major Christian holidays or birthdays, but had never directly encountered one. At the
moment in the therapy room, she was able to hold her reaction in check. But internally
and after the session, having children herself, she couldn't imagine not celebrating their
birthdays. It seemed punitive and harsh to deprive children of joyful occasions, make
them different from their classmates, and put them outside the mainstream culture.
She couldn't understand the rationale underlying such a stance and even found herself
feeling anger. She also realized it might be hard for her to show the same level of empathy,
respect, and appreciation for Nancy as she did for Joe.

Take a moment to self-reflect on how you would handle this case. Joe's family traditions are deeply meaningful to him, as well as to the majority culture, while Nancy's
religious beliefs are sacred to her and represent a religious minority perspective. If this
couple came to you, would you find yourself leaning toward the position of one partner
or the other? Would you experience judgment? Would you have difficulty respecting,
appreciating, or empathizing equally with both people? How does your own personal

background affect your view of birthday celebrations? What is your view of religious beliefs that restrict people from engaging in common cultural activities and encourage them to restrict their children from engaging in such activities? Could you competently provide services to this couple? If you do disagree with Nancy's religious beliefs, could you still demonstrate empathy, respect, and appreciation for her? If so, how? These were the questions that Shelley faced. And while this example is a bit extreme, when you begin to inquire about SRBPs you may encounter situations that challenge your capacity for empathy, respect, and appreciation.

Ways to Cultivate Empathy, Respect, and Appreciation

Let's look into how this foundational attitude can be developed and sustained. The first steps toward cultivating this competency are to become aware of and then actively explore any judgments or reactions that might impair your ability to demonstrate empathy, respect, and appreciation. While overt bias against certain worldviews or belief systems can certainly impair therapists' ability to be empathic, respectful, and appreciative toward clients, problems often originate in biases therapists hold that they aren't aware of. With awareness of any of your own challenges in this area, you can choose to work on cultivating these qualities in yourself, or to make referrals in instances where you just can't work effectively with a client. Let us be clear: Making a referral when you know you cannot demonstrate these qualities in yourself is, in itself, a demonstration of competence in this arena.

Awareness

People typically aren't aware of their own biases or behaviors that are difficult for them to accept in themselves. We each hold implicit biases that have been conditioned by our upbringing, region, class, and culture and by the media. To explore this, you might find it interesting to visit https://implicit.harvard.edu/implicit and take a few of the implicit association tests you will find there. These tests use reaction time to assess biases with respect to race, gender, sexual orientation, and even religion. Most people are chagrined to find that they have a harder time quickly associating an image of a woman with an office, work, or leadership role than a man, and a harder time associating a man with a home or kitchen, despite being consciously egalitarian in their views about gender roles. These tests don't imply hidden racism or sexism, but instead point to a certain level of conditioning that we may not be aware of.

As a therapist, you may sometimes find it difficult to admit that you simply cannot muster empathy or respect for a client or for his beliefs or practices. So a key aspect of cultivating awareness is to give yourself permission to hold significant judgments about certain SRBPs. Almost everyone does. For each of us, there are certain kinds of beliefs and practices that seem immoral, harmful, or just plain wrong. Sometimes this is experienced viscerally rather than mentally; for example, you might want to be an open-minded person who can rise above your biases, but at a gut level, you feel a deep sense of unease when a client shares certain beliefs, experiences, or practices.

Mindful awareness is a process by which you allow whatever you are experiencing to be present, and explore it with curiosity, rather than trying to change it. Mindfulness, or moment-to-moment nonjudgmental awareness of your experiences, is a practice that has been shown to enhance empathy in therapists (Baer, 2010; S. L. Shapiro & Carlson, 2009). You can start by simply noticing when you have thoughts, feelings, or body sensations in response to a client sharing a belief, experience, or practice he engages in. In the moment, in session, allow your responses to be as they are and note them. Then, when you have time for reflection afterward, explore them. (For more details on how to use mindfulness when dealing with spiritual or religious material as a clinician, see chapter 11.)

Exploration

After sessions that contain religious or spiritual material that makes you feel uncomfortable, take some time to examine your own reactions. You can do this through contemplation, by writing case notes or in a practice-related diary you may keep, or by investigating your responses in supervision or consultation. Be gentle with yourself—in other words, demonstrate empathy, respect, and appreciation for your own responses. You might ask yourself the following questions:

- *When in the session did I start to feel uncomfortable?*

- *What did I feel uncomfortable about?*

- *How did my discomfort manifest in my thoughts, my emotions, or my body?*

- *Why might I have felt uncomfortable with what was being shared or what I noticed?*

- *Who did I feel uncomfortable about: myself, my client, someone my client shared about, or all three?*

Also reflect upon whether you had difficulty accepting or feeling empathy for the client because of something she said or did related to her religion or spirituality.

Another important consideration is whether, looking back on it now, you wish you had known more or done something differently.

After devoting awareness and exploration to the situation, you may find that you need to refer the client to another professional. If this is the case, don't hesitate to do so. Although referring the client to another clinician may be interpreted as a rejection, it is the most skilled thing you can do if you know you can't genuinely produce the empathy, respect, and appreciation that will lead to treatment success.

Learning More

When therapists encounter challenges to their ability to manifest empathy, respect, and appreciation in response to religious or spiritual material, they often engage in what Saunders, Miller, and Bright (2010) have termed "spiritually avoidant care" (p. 355). Rather than risk being actively disrespectful, they take the safe route and ignore the issue completely. We recommend that you do just the opposite: address the spiritual and religious content your client is bringing up, and the responses that arise within you, with openness and curiosity. In addition to asking clients themselves, you can do something proactive to increase your knowledge about the spiritual or religious beliefs or practices they are sharing. For example, you could look up the philosophy or doctrine of their church or spiritual practice online or at the library, seek out a colleague who might know more about a specific SRBP, contact a religious scholar or local expert who's familiar with the religious or spiritual group and its doctrines, or even visit a temple, church, or place of worship to find out more.

Inquire Respectfully and Listen

Beyond simply gathering information, investigate the *meaning* of the belief or practice for the client, and actively listen with real curiosity. For example, in the case above, Shelley might have asked Nancy about her church's traditions: "Nancy, I'm sorry to say I haven't had any experience with your church or its practices. Could you help me by explaining what it means to not celebrate birthdays or Christmas from your perspective? That would help me understand." Exploring the meaning or purpose of the practice, ritual, or belief, rather than the content, may make it easier for you to cultivate empathy and compassion.

Take the Client's Perspective

Another powerful approach you might consider is actively engaging in perspective taking: putting yourself in the client's shoes. If you were your client, with his unique constellation of life experiences, family upbringing, and socioeconomic status, and had lived in the same regions he had and the culture he's been most familiar with, what would you believe, experience, or practice? Consider what psychological, existential, or emotional purpose the client's SRBPs might serve, for the moment putting aside whether that purpose is adaptive or maladaptive. Allow yourself to imagine in detail what the client's SRBP brings to him at this point in his life, as if you were looking at the world through his eyes. These approaches can help you develop a degree of empathy, respect, and appreciation that you may not have had before.

Attend to Nonverbal and Environmental Cues

There are many aspects of expression and perception, and verbalization is only one. To imbue your practice with empathy, respect, and appreciation, you must pay attention not only to what you say, but also to how you convey your perspective nonverbally. In the course of your training, you may have learned about nonverbal communication, such as body language, facial expression, eye contact, physical closeness, and other unvocalized cues. People are sensitive to these, often on a subconscious level. When you're listening to a client discuss SRBPs that are unfamiliar or distasteful to you, you may say the right things but belie the meaning of your words by narrowing your eyes, looking away, physically pulling back, and so on. Let's say, for example, that a client shares about a daylong practice of doing prostrations that left him exhausted and weak, and you find this practice quite unnecessary and perhaps harmful. You may say, "I'm glad you found meaning in that," but convey disapproval with your eyes, tone of voice, or facial expression. It would be unreasonable (and futile) to attempt to control every one of your nonverbal cues. However, you can become more aware of them and be thoughtful about your responses, both verbal and nonverbal, particularly when you notice that you're reacting negatively.

You also may need to consider respect for spiritual and religious diversity in your office space and practice-related materials. Your clients will notice not just your responses, but also environmental cues such as your clothing, mannerisms, pictures, or graphic elements on your stationery, website, and business cards. Even colors and furniture can serve as subtle cues. Ignoring this aspect of nonverbal communication is unwise, as Shelley found out the hard way.

✳ Clinician's Diary

Years ago Shelley had a client, Barbara, who had converted to a very conservative Christian sect before they began working together. This was not the focus of the therapy; rather, the therapy centered on work-related issues. As they worked together over the course of a year, Barbara repeatedly mentioned going to church and attending special classes related to her Bible study. Shelley was happy that Barbara was connected to this community, especially because Barbara was somewhat isolated and estranged from her family of origin.

One day, however, Barbara came in furious. Shelley had a statue of Quan Yin (a Chinese goddess) in her office, and Barbara said it deeply disturbed her. She felt that Shelley was "putting idolatry in front of Jesus" and wanted it removed. She then chastised Shelley for putting false gods in front of the one and only savior.

Shelley removed the statue immediately and listened to Barbara rage. Unbeknownst to Shelley, Barbara's anger about this statue had been building over time. To Shelley it was simply an object of beauty that represented a feminine aspect of the sacred, but by displaying it, she had unintentionally upset Barbara, who nearly left her as a therapist because of it.

What would you have done in Shelley's shoes? Would you also have removed the statue, or would you have discussed its value to you and insisted on keeping it in your office? What would help you decide how to respond? Has anything similar ever occurred in your practice, or in your life experience? Removing the statue was one of many possible responses Shelley could have chosen. The important part was choosing a response that conveyed empathy, respect, and appreciation for the particular client's spiritual or religious beliefs.

Empathy Isn't the Same as Enabling

Sometimes demonstrating empathy, respect, and appreciation for clients from any spiritual, religious, or secular background will be enhanced by, and in fact dictate, a well-thought-out clinical intervention that runs counter to a client's spiritual or religious beliefs and practices. When you feel uncomfortable, sometimes it's for good reason, such as a client becoming a member of a harmful cult or engaging in practices that are detrimental to herself or others. (See chapter 9 for more on harmful involvement.)

When clinical needs call for an intervention that isn't in alignment with a client's SRBPs, the client may perceive you as lacking in empathy, respect, or appreciation. In such cases, the need to protect the client's safety may outweigh your desire to understand the client's perspective. For example, you may find it necessary to intervene if a client is engaging in intense spiritual or religious practices to the detriment of global functioning, such as neglecting schoolwork, hygiene, or nutrition. But even then, you can conduct the intervention in a way that demonstrates empathy, respect, and appreciation for the client.

Conclusion

Although positive regard for clients is obviously a key element of successful clinical work and should extend to the domain of spiritual and religious diversity, as therapists we can sometimes be challenged in our ability to demonstrate empathy, respect, and appreciation for worldviews that are unfamiliar or distasteful to us. Rather than avoiding the religious or spiritual aspects of clients' lives, however, you can actively cultivate a warm and curious stance toward your clients and their beliefs and practices, even when you don't necessarily agree with them. Mindfully paying attention to your own responses, including what you say, nonverbal communication, and environmental cues, can help you choose responses that are clinically effective and respectful of religious and spiritual diversity. On that note, the next chapter will emphasize seeing religious and spiritual beliefs and practices as important aspects of clients' diversity.

Chapter 2

Appreciating Religious and Spiritual Diversity

The American Psychological Association (2002), along with most other mental health professional associations, has recognized religion and spirituality as an essential aspect of multicultural diversity: "Multiculturalism, in an absolute sense, recognizes the broad scope of race, ethnicity, language, sexual orientation, gender, age, disability, class status, education, religious/spiritual orientation, and other cultural dimensions" (p. 380). Nonetheless, as therapists, we sometimes pay less attention to religious and spiritual diversity than to other forms of multicultural diversity.

COMPETENCY 2: Psychologists view spirituality and religion as important aspects of human diversity, along with factors such as race, ethnicity, sexual orientation, socioeconomic status, disability, gender, and age.

Why do we not pay more attention to religious and spiritual diversity? One key reason is that many of us simply weren't trained to do so. As mentioned in the introduction, while multicultural courses are required in most training programs, many programs de-emphasize religious and spiritual diversity or don't include any training in this area.

Attending to religion and spirituality as a form of diversity may be seen as less important than attending to race or ethnicity because of how racism and discrimination have harmed our society. Well-organized and much needed social movements, along with powerful films, books, and popular figures in politics and the media, have made us keenly aware of the far-reaching negative consequences of prejudice, violence, abuse, and discrimination based on race and ethnicity. It is important to remember, however, that religious persecution has globally and historically wrought as many ill effects as racial prejudice, and can give rise to as many psychological issues as the persecution of any other form of diversity.

Of all the aspects of multiculturalism mentioned above, spirituality and religion may be one of the most invisible, despite how essential it is in many clients' lives. While we can often guess (though still should explicitly ask about) socioeconomic status, race, ethnicity, gender, age, disability, and sometimes even sexual orientation, unless a new client is wearing some sort of clothing or other items that indicate a religious or spiritual affiliation, like a yarmulke or veil, upon meeting that client we have no idea what sort of belief system lies within. What people believe in, what lies in their hearts regarding the sacred, where their moral compass lies—all are hidden. Because religious and spiritual diversity is often invisible, clinicians must directly ask about this realm.

The Importance of Recognizing Religious and Spiritual Aspects of Diversity

You may wonder how recognizing religion and spirituality as important aspects of human diversity can help clinicians be effective. It does so in very much the same way as recognizing other aspects of diversity.

Attending to the multiple aspects of human diversity we encounter in our clients helps us better understand who they are and what motivates them—both as unique individuals and as part of societal groups. In general, recognizing diversity allows us to avoid making overgeneralizations about how "people" are. For example, we know that some cultures value eye contact as a sign of intimacy and trust, while others avoid eye contact as a matter of respect. In the same way, clients from some religious groups may wear very conservative clothing as an expression of their values, whereas in other clients this could be a sign of shame or excessive self-consciousness about the body. It's essential that clinicians avoid making snap judgments and instead investigate the specific meanings of these kinds of behaviors for each individual client. Some behaviors may be more related to clients' SRBPs than to psychological issues.

Recognizing SRBPs as aspects of diversity also helps us be aware of prejudices—especially those that we as clinicians may hold about certain groups or people. There is some evidence that psychologists hold explicit and implicit negative biases based on perceived client religiosity—for example, appraising religious clients as more mentally ill or having a poorer prognosis (S. O'Connor & Vandenberg, 2005; Ruff, 2008). And even if we ourselves do not hold prejudices about our clients based on religion or spirituality, we can recognize how they may have experienced prejudice or discrimination from others based on their SRBPs throughout their lives. The religious or spiritual group they are affiliated with may have experienced these things in current generations, or it may have occurred historically, such as repeated persecution of Jewish people or bias against those of Muslim or Christian faith over the years. All of these experiences, even if they happened in previous generations, can affect clients' views of the world, their responses to situations, and their overall schemas or worldview.

✳ Clinician's Diary

Several years after Shelley finished teaching at a college of traditional Chinese medicine in San Francisco, a former student, whom we will call Alicia, came to Shelley for help with her marriage. Alicia loved her husband but was quite unhappy with the institution of marriage itself and what the role of a wife was turning out to be for her. Although she enjoyed aspects of being married, such as sharing her daily life with a loved one and having been free to go to graduate school while her husband supported her, Alicia was uncertain about staying married. As having children was the next logical step, this possibility was looming over her marriage. In addition, her husband's job situation had recently shifted and she now had to work to pay off her student loans.

Having just finished graduate school, Alicia was unsure about her ability to work with patients; her training had left her feeling inadequate for treating the many varied illnesses she encountered. Still, she was able to sustain an office and had several ongoing clients, so she had some stability and income. Nevertheless, she felt unable to move forward in her life.

After over a year of working with Alicia, Shelley began to feel frustrated. They had definitely made inroads into Alicia's issues, including exploring how her minority status had influenced her life, and the therapy had helped her in many ways. Alicia had learned how to maintain more appropriate boundaries with her overbearing mother and insensitive workmates. She was more able to express her needs to her husband and as a result felt more in tune with him and supported. She had started group supervision with some fellow students to overview ongoing cases, so she gained more professional support. Yet Shelley couldn't help feeling that some element was missing—until the following interchange occurred after Alicia showed up ten minutes late for a session.

Alicia: Sorry I'm late.

Shelley: That's okay. It's so unlike you to be late. I was a bit worried.

Alicia: I was fine; I just got caught up.

Shelley: Oh, no problem. Caught up with work?

Alicia: No, I was praying.

Shelley: Oh, is everything okay? Is somebody hurt?

Alicia: No, I go to the church a few blocks away.

Shelley: Oh, you never told me.

Alicia: Yes, I visit the church on my way here. It makes me feel calm and peaceful.

Shelley: How wonderful. Do you go often?

Alicia: Yes, I go to church to pray daily, sometimes twice a day.

Shelley: Oh, I'm sorry I never even asked you about that part of your life. Your faith must mean a lot to you.

Alicia: Yes. My husband and I met there. He attends too, but usually just on Sundays.

Shelley: Is that a problem for you? That he doesn't go more?

Alicia: Sometimes. Honestly, I feel most at home in the church. I love to just be there, sitting with God, praying. I sometimes feel I was a nun in a past life, if you believe in those kinds of things. The world is just too much for me, really. I enjoy studying Chinese medicine, but I don't want to practice it. But I have to. I have to make a living.

Shelley: Have you thought of becoming a nun?

Alicia: Yes, many times. It seemed like the best option for me in my early twenties, but part of me wanted to try being married. Now I have, and even though my husband is a nice man, I think I may have made the wrong choice.

Shelley: Oh, I never knew this was part of your life story. Please tell me more about this—this is so important.

This discussion continued over the next few sessions, and then Alicia suddenly stopped coming to therapy. Despite a follow-up call, Shelley wasn't quite sure what had happened. Alicia declared that her decision was a financial one (despite being a low-fee client). But it may also have been that, through therapy, Alicia had reached a decision point that she wasn't yet ready to face.

Alicia, among other clients, sparked Shelley's interest in working on this book. In therapy, they'd explored issues related to gender and racial and ethnic diversity, but for an entire year, Shelley had missed Alicia's deeply religious nature, which had a great bearing on her worldview. By not exploring this avenue earlier on, Shelley missed an opportunity because an important part of Alicia's psyche had been missing in the therapy room.

Ways to Cultivate Respect for Religious and Spiritual Diversity

A key step for increasing your recognition of religion and spirituality as important dimensions of multicultural diversity is to explore within yourself how you currently address these elements in clinical practice. To do so, spend some time considering the following questions:

- *Do I believe that spiritual and religious diversity is as important as other aspects of diversity, like race or ethnicity, in the clients I work with? Why or why not?*

- *Is my own religion or spirituality, or lack thereof, an important aspect of my own diversity? Would knowing about my SRBPs both now and in the past help someone else better understand who I am and what I may have experienced in life that is different from others? Has anyone ever treated me differently because of my religion or spirituality?*

- *Do I typically ask my clients about their spiritual or religious beliefs and practices? Why or why not?*

- *If I were in therapy, would I want my clinician to ask me about my spiritual and religious beliefs and practices? Why or why not?*

You can contemplate these questions, write your responses to them in your journal, or discuss them with a partner or a small group.

One action you can take to experience firsthand the importance of religion and spirituality as an aspect of multicultural diversity is to explore how that diversity, perhaps just as much as race, ethnicity, gender, or other aspects of diversity, has influenced people who have been affiliated with different forms of religion and spirituality. Here we've listed some lines of inquiry you might pursue. (Also see the resources section at the end of the book for materials that might aid your inquiry.)

- Learn more about how various religious and spiritual groups may have experienced persecution and discrimination historically.

- Explore how these groups may still be discriminated against or persecuted for their beliefs.

- Notice how these groups are portrayed in popular culture, and reflect upon how being portrayed in this manner may affect their experience.

- On a more subtle level, investigate how people with certain religious affiliations are viewed by the more intellectual, scientific, materialist, or psychoanalytic cultures that have influenced the practice of psychology and mental health.

- Talk to spiritual or religious leaders to learn more about how they've experienced either support or a lack of support from mental health professionals.

With clients, remember to inquire respectfully and listen. You might ask directly, "Do you think that being [Jewish, Christian, Muslim, pagan, atheist, or whatever the case may be] has influenced your view of the world or how you've been treated by others? If so, how?" Don't hesitate to ask clients about their religious or spiritual background, beliefs, and practices, and when they reply, listen carefully.

By engaging in such inquiry, you'll increasingly view religion and spirituality as fundamental aspects of diversity—aspects that should be explicitly explored rather than ignored. You should find that attention to this important element of diversity enhances your clinical practice.

Going Further

The points in this chapter may seem obvious, but not all psychologists agree that spirituality and religion are aspects of multicultural diversity. In a survey of 340 psychologists, Crook-Lyon and colleagues (2012) found that 77% strongly agreed that religion and spirituality are multicultural issues, but 10% were neutral and 13% disagreed. One comment by a respondent, which was representative of participants who agreed that religion and spirituality should be addressed as a form of multicultural diversity, was "I am amazed that people who advocate multiculturalism resist consideration of religion. Is this bias maybe the last bastion of prejudice in psychology?" (Crook-Lyon et al., 2012, p. 177). Another said that "to study multiculturalism without serious examination of religious/spiritual issues would be asking to study sailing without a study of the wind" (Crook-Lyon et al., 2012, p. 178).

Among those who disagreed, one respondent said that spirituality and religion are simply too loaded and shouldn't be included in multicultural training because "it's too difficult for practitioners of a faith to remain dispassionate in teaching and discussion" (Crook-Lyon et al., 2012, p. 178). As you might guess, we disagree with the stance that avoiding issues that evoke strong feelings in training or the therapy room is a good approach. Yes, religion and spirituality are topics that evoke passion, but so are race, ethnicity, sexual orientation, class status, and even age or disability.

Also, some who disagreed were concerned about the definition of multiculturalism becoming too broad. One respondent noted, "If religion (organized or not) were to be included in multiculturalism, then where would we stop—should we also include political affiliation?" (Crook-Lyon et al., 2012, p. 178). We propose that in clinical practice it is helpful to explore any individual differences, variables, or aspects of worldview that carry a set of biases, assumptions, or historical or societal prejudices for either the client or clinician.

Having said all this, when you learn about how any form of multicultural diversity has influenced large numbers of people, whether through prejudice, discrimination, assumptions, or unfair generalizations, you may be tempted to assume a given client has experienced these influences. This is just another form of potentially harmful generalization that could cause a lack of attunement in the clinical arena.

Making generalizations based on any aspect of diversity can be just as harmful to the therapeutic alliance as ignoring potentially important elements of diversity. For example, if you've learned that people who are atheist are considered by some to be amoral, you might immediately assume that an individual client who is atheist has experienced these perceptions. She may not have. In fact, she may have found that this aspect of her worldview has been tremendously helpful and garnered respect from her friends and colleagues. Alternatively, if you have a client who belongs to a religious group that has traditionally been persecuted and assume that he has experienced such prejudice, you might treat him as though he has a chip on his shoulder. But his lived experience of his membership in this religious group may have brought him nothing but psychological support and enhanced well-being. It's important to find out what the actual experience of any particular client has been.

Conclusion

The purpose of considering religion and spirituality to be equal to the host of other multicultural diversities is not to encourage assumptions. Rather, it is to build the understanding that this aspect of clients' lives may set them apart from others, may link them to others due to a shared understanding, or may have had no profound effects whatsoever on their mental and emotional well-being. Your job as a competent clinician is to learn more about how clients' multicultural diversity—whether racial, ethnic, socioeconomic, or a matter of gender, sexual orientation, age, disability, religion, or spirituality—has influenced their lives, and how it can inform assessment, diagnosis, treatment planning, and therapeutic interactions.

Just as clients' religious or spiritual background, beliefs, affiliations, and practices have probably influenced how they've been viewed and treated by others and how they view the world, so have your own. In the next chapter, we explore the third and final competency in the category of attitudes: gaining a deeper understanding of how *your* religious and spiritual diversity may influence your clinical practice.

Chapter 3

Being Aware of Your Own Beliefs

Everyone has some background in relation to spirituality and religion, whether it involves being brought up in a religious or spiritual tradition (which may still be present or may have changed), simply having a devoutly religious nature, or having no religious or spiritual upbringing, beliefs, or practices whatsoever. No matter what your religious and spiritual beliefs and practices have been or currently are, they may affect everything from what you eat and what you wear to what you assume about the nature of reality and how you view psychological phenomena.

These beliefs are conveyed to some extent to your clients—if not explicitly then implicitly—by how you dress, how you decorate your office, how you talk to them, and how you respond to the material they present. Your own beliefs may even influence your assessment, diagnosis, and treatment planning. Therefore, the third competency focuses on cultivating an awareness of how your own religious and spiritual background, beliefs, and practices might influence your competence as a clinician.

COMPETENCY 3: Psychologists are aware of how their own spiritual or religious background and beliefs may influence their clinical practice and their attitudes, perceptions, and assumptions about the nature of psychological processes.

Why would you, as a clinician, need to explore your spiritual and religious beliefs? What do they have to do with therapy? First, your SRBPs, or lack thereof, have probably tinted your worldview in ways that you may or may not be aware of. Worldviews function like sunglasses. They filter our perceptions. Evidence indicates that different religious affiliations, or types and levels of religiousness, influence our ideas about free will, locus of control, and forgiveness versus punishment, as well as about more obvious issues, such as abortion, the death penalty, and adultery (Adamczyk & Hayes, 2012; Cochran, Chamlin, Beeghley, Hamden, & Blackwell, 1996; Espinosa, 2008; Lindsey, Sigillo, & Miller, 2013).

For example, if you believe in a benevolent God, it changes your perspective on and therefore your response to life's greatest challenges. Similarly, the meaning you make of the experiences your clients encounter will be affected by your worldview.

Second, in the therapy room you might avoid things that are important because of your discomfort with specific issues. For example, if your religious or spiritual beliefs are in direct conflict with actions your client takes, such as gambling or going to a strip club, you may unintentionally avoid addressing those topics. Another possibility is that clients share an aspect of their religious or spiritual life that is very important to them, but you don't adequately attend to it.

Third, you might inadvertently demonstrate a lack of attunement with a client. You may express a "truth" about life that's a given for you, based on your religious or spiritual background or beliefs, whereas your client holds a completely different truth. For example, you may believe that people are essentially good but can sometimes be misled by circumstances and that the world is generally a safe place. Your client, on the other hand, may participate in a religious or spiritual tradition, such as Vodun, Santería, or some forms of shamanism, that holds that certain people and forces in the world are evil and will attack. Your beliefs may prevent you from fully comprehending the terror your client experiences at times.

Fourth, you might make unintentional gaffes. For example, you could wear a piece of jewelry or clothing or have an office decoration that offends a client. You may unconsciously use phrases like "Let's meditate on that" or "Oh my god." You may say, "I'll keep you in my prayers" after the death of someone close to a client, not realizing that this kind of religious language may not be a part of your client's life, and may even be offensive to the client. Wearing a necklace with a cross may be a simple way you express your beliefs to the world, but for a client, it could make you seem self-righteous or judgmental. Or you may have a Buddha displayed in your office as a reminder to stay peaceful, but for a client it may indicate that you're out of touch with mainstream values, or could even seem like idolatry.

In chapter 1, we shared a story about how this fourth issue played out in Shelley's practice. The following story, taken from Cassandra's experience, illustrates broader challenges posed by this third competence: being aware of your own beliefs and how they may impact the therapeutic alliance.

☀ Clinician's Diary

Cassandra was raised in an essentially agnostic household, where religion wasn't an important part of life. Her father was a scientist who believed that organized religion was, at best, a benign way for people to deal with the uncertainties of life and, at worst, a divisive influence that led to conflict, schisms between people, and sometimes violence.

When Cassandra was in her late teens and twenties, she began to discover within herself an intense interest in spirituality and religion. She studied world religions in all their variety and developed a personal spirituality and set of practices that helped her explore the mysteries of life. She had deep commitment to her spiritual principles and practices while also appreciating the role of science and the secular viewpoint in exploring the nature of reality. And ultimately, she thought of herself as someone who had equal appreciation for the gamut of religious perspectives. But that latter self-concept was challenged in her work with one particular client, whom we will call Steven.

Steven worked at a blue-collar job by day but spent much of his free time participating in a very conservative evangelical Christian group that frequently conducted public demonstrations against abortion. Steven came to therapy for substance abuse problems, which seemed to be rooted in both biological addiction issues and clinical levels of depression and anxiety. He approached life with an attitude of fear, anger, and suspicion. His religious life and community offered him a number of resources, including social support, a sense of meaning and purpose, and a set of activities that helped keep him from being isolated. The group seemed to provide Steven with a direction in life. However, it also seemed to exacerbate his fear, anger, and suspicion. He had frequent nightmares about abortion, fantasies about harming or killing doctors who performed abortions, and vague intentions to vandalize or terrorize abortion clinics.

In contrast, Cassandra's upbringing and spiritual views leaned toward compassion, empathy, and support toward women who chose abortion, and she had a hard time separating her own strong beliefs from what might be appropriate in clinical practice. She wrestled with many questions:

- Would it be best to try to enhance the positive aspects of Steven's religious group and its activities and to de-emphasize the negative aspects that seemed to be leading to increased distress and negative consequences for him?

- Should she avoid Steven's religious life in therapy and only focus on his feelings and experiences, somehow carefully avoiding the context of those feelings and experiences?

- Should she directly share her misgivings about Steven's activities with him?

- Should she refer out to a clinician from a more like-minded religious tradition, who might be able to help Steven while maintaining fidelity to the essential tenets of his faith?

While Cassandra had solid skills for treating substance abuse, depression, and anxiety, her own spiritual views and her reactions to Steven's views obscured her ability to see the next steps in treatment clearly. When she became aware of these prejudices, she sought supervision. She ended up continuing to treat Steven for substance abuse and mood issues but referred him to a therapist who shared his faith to discuss issues related to his religious practices.

Has anything like this happened to you? Reflect on a time when your spiritual or religious beliefs may have influenced your clinical practice. Alternatively, imagine a time in the future when they might. How would you gauge whether or not your spiritual or religious worldview was getting in the way of competent care? And it if was, how might you handle it?

Exploring Your Own Beliefs and Practices

The first step to understanding how your own current and past SRBPs might influence your clinical work is to reflect on them. In chapter 12, we'll discuss several ways to explore clients' spiritual and religious history. You can use those same approaches to explore your own beliefs.

Here are a few questions, drawn from the material in chapter 12, that you might ask yourself (adapted with permission from Hodge, 2013, pp. 102–103). Set aside some quiet time to reflect on these questions, whether in contemplation, by writing in your journal, or in discussion with a small group:

- Describe the spiritual or religious tradition you grew up in. How did your family express its spirituality or religious beliefs?

- What sort of religious or spiritual experiences stood out for you when you were growing up?

- What do you hold sacred in your life?

- What spiritual or religious beliefs do you find especially meaningful?

- To what degree has your spirituality been a source of generally positive emotions and experiences, such as strength, pleasure, meaning, joy, intimacy and connectedness to others, closeness with God, hope for the future, confidence in yourself, or compassion for both others and yourself? How has this affected you?

- Has your religion or spirituality been a source of more difficult emotions or experiences, such as pain, frustration, guilt, anger, confusion and doubt, anxiety, fear, feelings of personal insignificance, or feelings of alienation from others? How has this affected you?

You might also draw a timeline or map of your religious and spiritual history (as will be described further in chapter 12). Start with your early childhood and consider the major periods of your life, chronologically, focusing on the primary events that exemplify your religious and spiritual history. Pay particular attention to aspects of your religious and spiritual history that might influence your ability to work effectively with clients.

As you look at your own history in this area, you're likely to feel a sense of things that went right and others that went wrong. Spend some time pondering or reflecting on those experiences. Do you wish something different had happened? Is there some wounding that would benefit from professional help? Are you left with a sense of peace, anger, curiosity, or even bafflement? Often, what we experience is part of a larger cultural zeitgeist—a social norm at the time. Putting your spiritual and religious experience into the larger social context can be helpful.

Once you've explored this aspect of your history, you may feel a need to take action in some way. You might decide to share about this with another person or a group, do some more writing about your spiritual and religious background, draw or make a collage to represent your history or express your feelings, or speak with a therapist, spiritual advisor, or clergyperson about it. You might choose to visit a grave or sacred spot, create a ritual outdoors, set up an altar, reacquaint yourself with the religion of your family, explore religions or forms of spirituality that aren't familiar to you, or study some aspect of religion or spirituality more deeply. Some people simply recommit to whatever helps them reach a sacred space inside. The idea here is to openly and compassionately examine your own spiritual and religious history and current beliefs as an important part of who you are and how you see the world.

Investigating How Your Beliefs Affect You Professionally

Once you've explored your religious and spiritual background in depth, investigate how it may affect the biases and assumptions you take into your clinical work. Here are a few questions to help you get started on this process; as you'll see, these foundational beliefs can have a bearing on a wide variety of situations in the therapy room:

- Did your religious or spiritual tradition teach that there is a reason for everything or that "God doesn't give you more than you can handle"? Or did it lead you to believe that life can be random and unfair? How might this impact your response to clients' difficulties, such as those of a client who has been in a major car accident?

- Does your spiritual and religious background lead you to perhaps believe a client's assertion that she can communicate with someone who died, or would you see this as wishful thinking or delusional?

- What do you think happens after death? What are your beliefs about heaven, hell, and the existence of a soul? If you believe in a soul, does it move into another phase after death or disappear completely? Is the body's death the end of life? Does this set of beliefs affect your ideas about clients who are dealing with the death of a loved one or what you might say to them?

- Do you believe that life should be preserved at all costs? How might this affect your treatment of a patient with a terminal illness who's deciding whether or not to engage in another round of chemotherapy?

- In your religious tradition, is abortion always immoral or sometimes understandable? How might this affect your feelings about a client who reports having had two abortions?

There are no right or wrong answers to these questions. They are designed to help you understand how your religious and spiritual beliefs, or lack thereof, might influence your response to clients. You may not be able to change your beliefs, but by building awareness of your biases, you'll be in a better position to choose a clinically appropriate response when these issues arise.

Be aware that your religious and spiritual background, or lack thereof, may also *positively* influence your clinical work. For example, your beliefs and practices may have helped you cultivate an enhanced capacity for compassion and forgiveness. You may have practiced mindfulness as a part of your spiritual life, allowing you to be curious, present, and attentive in the face of discomfort. So also inquire into what you're better at as a clinician because of your religious and spiritual background.

What to Do Once You're Aware of Your Biases

The approaches outlined above will help you explore your religious and spiritual background, how it may have influenced your overall worldview, and how this influences your clinical practice. Just being aware of these effects and continuing to explore them will probably result in more competent clinical care because you'll be more thoughtful about how you frame and respond to each case.

In addition, when seeing clients, actively use this awareness to assist you in conducting effective therapy. There may be times when you notice a red flag—some sort of bias or assumption arising. You can take this as a signal to be attentive to your own reactions and, if warranted, refrain from interpretation and move to a more client-centered approach. Rather than sharing what the material brings up for you, you might focus on what the client is experiencing and how you can help him with that. Depending on your theoretical orientation, at times it might be appropriate for you to share your curiosity or lack of familiarity about what clients are sharing, perhaps saying something like "I'm not familiar with that tradition. Tell me more."

Of course, there might be times when your own worldview, biases, or assumptions prevent you from being able to conduct effective therapy. Even if you think that you can separate these aspects of yourself from your professional approach, old beliefs may come forward when you least expect them. These are times to get supervision, consult with a clergyperson or spiritual teacher, or make a referral to another practitioner. It's okay and understandable if you feel uncomfortable with something that arises in the room; just seek supervision and get help. This doesn't mean you aren't competent. On the contrary, it's the competent response.

Conclusion

In this chapter, we've reviewed how your own spiritual and religious background and beliefs, or lack thereof, can influence your worldview and perspective on life. This can have a profound effect on your clinical practice, in everything from how you formulate cases to your choice of interventions to the language you use, the clothes you wear, and how you decorate your office. You may not be able to change your worldview, perspective, or religious or spiritual background. But you can build awareness of how your spiritual or religious background and current beliefs and practices can create biases and assumptions in your work. The more awareness you have, the more conscious you can be in making decisions about how to effectively deal with each client, and about any reactions you may have toward the material clients present. You'll also be able to draw upon your spiritual and religious background for strengths that can assist you in being an effective therapist.

In part 1 of this book, we described three competencies in the domain of attitudes and beliefs. These competencies have to do with the general ways that competent clinicians think about or view the religious and spiritual aspects of human experience in clinical practice. Now we move on to part 2, which presents seven competencies in the domain of knowledge—in other words, what you need to know or learn to be a clinician who is competent in the arena of religious and spiritual diversity. This starts with knowing that many diverse forms of spirituality and religion exist and taking the time to actively learn about those that are important to your clients.

Part 2

KNOWLEDGE

Chapter 4

Exploring Diverse Beliefs and Practices

The first three competencies fall into the category of attitudes, or beliefs. The next seven are in the domain of knowledge. Therapists' approaches to clients are guided by attitudes, but case formulation, treatment planning, and intervention choices are also influenced by knowledge. For example, an inexperienced clinician may misdiagnose some disorders simply due to lack of exposure. Ten years later, that same clinician may be able to spot those same disorders within minutes. Also crucial is staying abreast of current research and theoretical advances, which is why continuing education is required in our field. And whatever your level of experience, you can actively seek knowledge about aspects of your clients with which you are unfamiliar.

COMPETENCY 4: Psychologists know that many diverse forms of spirituality and religion exist, and explore spiritual and religious beliefs, communities, and practices that are important to their clients.

As the world has become increasingly connected, initially through trade and the printing press, then by ease of travel and mass media, and now via the Internet, global religious and spiritual diversity has grown in tandem and has now skyrocketed to unprecedented levels.

Today, there are an estimated 41,000 Christian denominations worldwide (Pew Forum on Religion and Public Life, 2011), with over 2,500 in the United States alone, and new forms of spirituality seem to be emerging almost daily. Meanwhile, the number of people in the United States who claim "none" for religious affiliation has risen to a record 19.6% in 2012. Yet many of the unaffiliated hold some religious or spiritual beliefs, such as belief in God or a universal spirit, even though they may not identify with a particular faith (Pew Forum on Religion and Public Life, 2012b).

Nevertheless, many people lack exposure to this diversity unless they live in a large city where they encounter many cultures, races, and orientations. Many people live in relatively homogeneous areas, amidst neighbors who may have more or less the same outlook as they do. And even when diversity exists within a community, some people may be familiar only with the particular faith or tradition they follow or in which they were raised.

Size of Major Religious Groups, 2010
Percentage of the global population

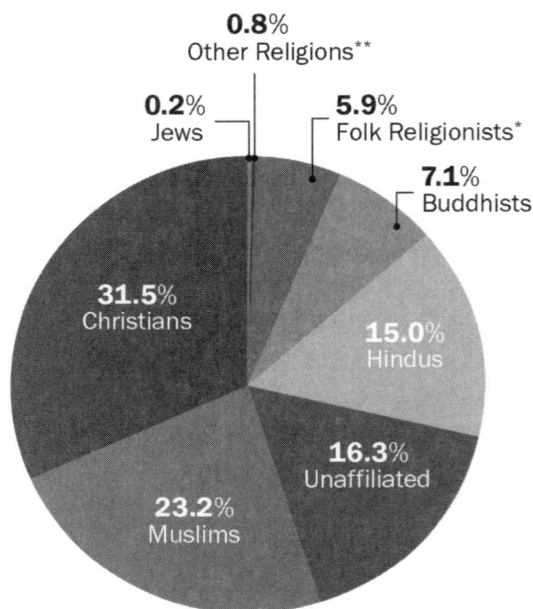

0.8% Other Religions**

0.2% Jews

5.9% Folk Religionists*

7.1% Buddhists

31.5% Christians

15.0% Hindus

16.3% Unaffiliated

23.2% Muslims

*Includes followers of African traditional religions, Chinese folk religions, Native American religions and Australian aboriginal religions.

**Includes Bahai's, Jains, Sikhs, Shintoists, Taoists, followers of Tenrikyo, Wiccans, Zoroastrians and many other faiths.

Percentages may not add to 100 due to rounding.

For example, Shelley grew up in a rural farming community. Most people living there were Christian and attended church regularly, so it was a Christian majority culture and relatively homogenous. As a child, Shelley had vague ideas about the differences between various Christian doctrines because she sometimes went to different churches with friends and their families. In general, people attended a church close to their home; it was a way to socialize with neighbors and stay connected in an ongoing way.

You may share a similar background, having little experience with religious diversity. Yet these days, it's likely that the clients you'll encounter in your clinical practice will be more religiously and spiritually diverse than in the past. This is particularly true if you're practicing in an urban area. However, even in regions that are relatively homogeneous, it's imperative to not make overgeneralized assumptions about clients' SRBPs, but instead to ask about their specific beliefs.

✳ Clinician's Diary

An attractive twenty-four-year-old female client we will call Stacey came in to see Shelley, presenting with a weight control issue and a history of sexual abuse that she was ready to confront. Stacey and her boyfriend of the previous few years had broken up, and she was anxious to lose weight and gain enough courage to date again. Initially, Shelley worked with Stacey in a standard way, taking her family history and learning about her psychosocial circumstances. Stacey had friends, was gainfully employed, and was looking forward to a full life. What arose, however, was that every aspect of her life was tinted by her conflicting feelings about her Mormon upbringing and her current status as single. Within a few sessions, it became clear that if Shelley didn't understand more about Mormonism and what Stacey's faith meant to her, they couldn't proceed effectively with the therapeutic process.

Cultivating Awareness of Religious and Spiritual Diversity

Shelley has noticed that over the years, she's sometimes been caught unaware of a client's religious or spiritual background, as in the preceding example. Not having inquired about the history and current status of their spiritual and religious beliefs, she has stumbled into sessions unprepared. Perhaps you've had similar experiences. To boost therapist effectiveness and client satisfaction, it's essential to learn more about clients' spiritual or religious background. Here are some specific ways of doing so.

Asking the Question

Before you can learn more about a client's SRBPs, you must find out what those SRBPs are. When approaching this subject, you are at a delicate stage in opening the dialogue. You can start with a simple question, such as, "Do you mind telling me about your religious or spiritual beliefs? Would that be helpful to our work together? If not, that's fine too."

While research shows that the majority of clients want to be asked about their SRBPs (Blanton, 2005; Diallo, 2013; Knox, Catlin, Casper, & Schlosser, 2005; Oxhandler & Pargament, 2014; Post & Wade, 2009), some clients may be sensitive about this and choose not to discuss it during the course of therapy with you. This is perfectly acceptable. If a client isn't interested in speaking about this and it isn't part of the reason she entered therapy with you, then let it be. However, in some situations you may wish to sensitively inquire further at the time ("Do you want to say more about that?") or make a note to yourself to return to the topic in subsequent sessions. For example, you might ask whether a client has any spiritual or religious beliefs or practices and notice that she says no but gets wistful or her eyes tear up. Alternatively, she may respond with anger ("No way. I don't go in for that hogwash!") or say, "No, but I really want to." These are all signals that the client may benefit from further gentle inquiry.

Learning More

Once you discover what a client's SRBPs are, or that she doesn't have SRBPs, the next step is to learn more about that faith, tradition, or set of beliefs if these are unfamiliar to you. There are two levels at which you can approach this. One is taking time outside the therapy room to learn more about the SRBP, and the other is learning more about the client's lived experience of her religion or spirituality.

Learning Outside the Therapy Room

You don't need to become an expert in each client's spiritual or religious tradition, but it is valuable to learn about the essential tenets, values, and activities associated with a client's faith. The resources section at the back of the book lists several excellent books, films, and websites where you can learn more about various religious and spiritual traditions. Of course, a great deal of information is available on the Internet—just be sure to be careful of the source.

One of the most powerful things you can do when encountering a form of religion or spirituality that's new to you is to visit the place of worship or practice. You can gather a lot of information from just a brief visit. You might also choose to have a brief phone conversation or visit with a clergy member or committed practitioner of that faith. Reading a popular book or watching a movie that highlights a given tradition can be enjoyable and illuminating, if not always completely accurate. If you only have a bit of time to spare, you might focus on exploring aspects of the tradition that may be most relevant to your client's psychological well-being:

- Is there a deity, and is that deity viewed as benevolent, punishing, or both?

- What is the leadership hierarchy, if any, in this tradition?

- How do people access the divine in this tradition?

- What are the essential rituals, ceremonies, or activities in this tradition?

- What are the major tenets or beliefs that set this tradition apart from others?

- What norms, rules, and taboos exist in this tradition?

- How are men, women, and relationships viewed in this tradition?

Even a brief exploration of a client's SRBPs will enhance your understanding of who he is and what resources are available to him.

Learning from Clients' Lived Experience

In addition to learning about the formal aspects of a client's tradition, it's crucial to focus on the client's lived experience of it. In fact, scholars are paying increasing attention to what they call *lived religion*, in an approach that recognizes that the ways that people engage in their SRBPs are typically highly idiosyncratic and fluid, rather than conforming to one precise doctrine or set of activities or beliefs (Hathaway, 2013; McGuire, 2008; Sharpe, 2009). For example, just knowing that someone is a Catholic and understanding the basics of the Catholic faith may tell you very little about how that person engages with his religion in his everyday life.

In other words, learning about the general doctrines of a client's faith tradition isn't sufficient for understanding the client. Each denomination, church, or temple has its own traditions, and each individual within that system has unique experiences. There is considerable variability in the ways people express their beliefs, from daily meditation or attendance at mass to just the occasional celebration around certain holy days. Thus, listening to the client's lived experience of his religion or spirituality is critical.

If clients want to talk about their SRBPs, you might ask questions along the following lines to learn more about their lived experience (adapted with permission from Hodge, 2013):

- What sort of spiritual or religious experiences stood out for you when you were growing up?

- What do you hold sacred in your life?

- What religious or spiritual rituals or practices are particularly important to you?

- In what ways has your spirituality or religion helped you understand or cope with your problems?

- In what ways has it been a source of difficulties or problems?

- How does your spirituality or religion relate to your goals in life?

You may find that some clients are tempted to answer these questions using doctrine or teachings from their tradition, which may or may not reflect their lived experience. If you notice this, you can gently encourage them to share their own lived experience by simply asking, "And how is that for *you*, personally?"

A Note About Religion, Spirituality, and Culture

Don't assume that the religious or spiritual activities clients engage in always reflect their most deeply held beliefs. Sometimes these activities may have more to do with clients' cultural identity than their religious or spiritual beliefs. For example, many immigrant families or descendants of immigrants bond with their community around traditions from their country or culture of origin. In this way, attending Orthodox Easter services may be reflective of a connection with Eastern European roots, rather than representing a religious belief. To tease out these distinctions, you might simply ask, "What does attending that service mean to you?"

Conclusion

It's important for you to know that a vast diversity of religious and spiritual traditions exists and that your clients may be affiliated with any of them. Furthermore, this diversity is increasing, even in communities that have previously been relatively homogeneous. And even within one denomination or tradition, there can be an enormous amount of variability in the beliefs, practices, and lived experience of individual participants. Taking the time to learn more about religious and spiritual traditions that are important to your clients will increase your effectiveness as a therapist. In addition, your religious and spiritual clients will probably feel pleased that you've made the effort to learn more about this important part of their lives and how it connects with the issues they're presenting. You can learn more outside of your sessions, through books, films, visits to a place of worship, or consulting with clergy. You can also learn about your clients' lived experience by sensitively inquiring about their SRBPs in session.

As you may have discovered in your exploration of clients' various religious and spiritual beliefs and practices, both in general and as lived by each client, there's a difference between organized religion and the more general category of spirituality. In the next chapter, we explore how religion and spirituality are related yet also distinct from one another.

Chapter 5

UNDERSTANDING SPIRITUALITY AND RELIGION AS DIFFERENT BUT OVERLAPPING

Throughout this book, we discuss "spiritual and religious" competencies, an approach that tends to lump spirituality and religion together. While religion and spirituality are related for many people, they are different from one another. In order to effectively address the religious or spiritual domains of clients' lives, it's important to understand the difference between the two.

COMPETENCY 5: Psychologists can describe how spirituality and religion can be viewed as overlapping yet distinct constructs.

While the words "spirituality" and "religion" have historically often been used interchangeably, spirituality and religion are increasingly being viewed as distinct yet overlapping constructs (Kapuscinski & Masters, 2010; Piedmont et al., 2009; Schlehofer et al., 2008; Zinnbauer et al., 1997). As we mentioned in the introduction, we use the term "religion" to refer to affiliation with an organization guided by shared beliefs and practices, whose members adhere to a particular understanding of the divine and participate in sacred rituals. "Spirituality" is a bit trickier to define. We use it to refer to an individual's internal sense of connection to or search for the sacred.

As you may recall from the introduction, Pargament and Sweeney (2011) have defined "spirituality" as "the journey people take to discover and realize their essential selves and higher order aspirations" (p. 58–59), or a "search for the sacred" (Pargament, 2011, p. 52), whereas "religion" has been defined as "the search for significance that occurs within the context of established institutions that are designed to facilitate spirituality" (Pargament et al., 2013, p. 3). Recently, Mario Maj (2010), president of the World Psychiatric Association, offered this definition of spirituality: "Spirituality shares with religion the personal belief in ideas of religious significance such as God, the Soul, or Heaven, but rejects the administrative, often bureaucratic and hierarchical, structure and creeds of a particular organized religion" (p. xiii).

Of course, definitions change with the times. More than a century ago, William James (1902/1988) defined "religion" as "the feelings, acts and experiences of individual men in their solitude so far as they apprehend themselves to stand in relation to whatever they may consider the divine" (p. 32). This definition would perhaps be a better fit with our twenty-first-century understanding of spirituality, rather than religion.

The Changing Landscape of Religion and Spirituality

Why is the distinction between religion and spirituality important for therapists?

Your client may be among the 73% of Americans who are affiliated with Christianity, a specific religion you're probably familiar with. However, a rapidly growing number of people are unaffiliated—currently about 18% (Pew Forum on Religion and Public Life, 2012b). American sociologists Robert Putnam and David Campbell (2012) talk about "nones"—people who belong to no religion but still believe in God. Indeed, as mentioned in the introduction, today about 72% of Millennials (eighteen- to twenty-nine-year-olds) describe themselves as spiritual but not religious (Phillips, 2010).

One reason for this may lie in the observation social scientists have made that in modern times, organized religion has taken on somewhat negative connotations for some people because of perceptions of the following distinctions (Zinnbauer, Pargament, & Scott, 1999):

Religion	Spirituality
Institutional	Individual
External and objective	Internal and subjective
Old	New
Structural	Functional
Fixed and frozen	Flexible and dynamic
Bad	Good

Times are changing. In the current generation of teens, except for the minority of youth (20%) who are affiliated with a "one faith" church, there is little evidence of religious exclusivity or belief in the superiority of one's own faith (Pearce & Denton, 2011). Indeed, many young people who claim to be firmly committed to religion are strikingly unfamiliar with the teachings of their own faith, as well as those of other major religions (Ellison & McFarland, 2013). In fact, scholars interested in religious trends have found widespread disinterest in religious institutions and doctrines, which are increasingly perceived as irrelevant among younger people (Wuthnow, 2007).

Wuthnow, among others, claims that religious communities and other key social institutions are failing to provide the kind of guidance and support they once did to young adults for crucial decisions about major domains of life such as marriage, family, career, and finances (Ellison & McFarland, 2013; Wuthnow, 2007). Answers given by clergy and study groups are at times perceived as "canned" and not attuned to the spiritual and emotional needs of young adults.

On the other hand, this trend in drawing a distinction between religion and spirituality is confounding to some. Many scholars are concerned that the two constructs are being too starkly contrasted. Pargament and colleagues (2013) have said that the "growing polarization in the meaning of religion and spirituality is problematic for several reasons" (p. 12). In some of the current research and literature, religion is even described as excluding an individual's spirituality (Ammerman, 2010; Robinson, 2007; Schneiders, 2003).

For many, this notion is a false dichotomy that doesn't make sense, and an indication that secular scholars misunderstand religion. In an article published online, writer James Martin (2010) voices what many believe to be true, saying, "Spirituality without religion can become a self-centered complacency divorced from the wisdom of a community" (para. 16). Yet it remains the case that most people in the United States continue to have a mainstream Christian religious affiliation and find their spirituality within their religion (Marler & Hadaway, 2002).

Contradicting claims regarding the increasing irrelevance and obsolescence of organized religion, there is a groundswell of new and vibrant religious movements in the United States. One significant phenomenon has been the rise of the "seeker church" (Sargeant, 2000). In an approach based on analysis of congregational needs, seeker churches incorporate contemporary worship styles and dynamic preaching and allow members to choose from a menu of workshop options, activities, and services (Ellison & McFarland, 2013). Often these seeker churches are also megachurches, with an average weekly attendance in excess of two thousand (Thumma & Bird, 2009). Megachurches are typically theologically conservative, although in practice, doctrinal issues are often de-emphasized. They are most common in suburban areas near major cities and in the Sunbelt region. Although some megachurches are affiliated with evangelical denominations, many are independent congregations.

For the past two decades, large congregation sizes have become more the norm in virtually every Christian denomination except sectarian groups, such as Jehovah's Witnesses and Mormons. A critique of this is that larger gatherings may lessen the chance for social mechanisms that foster connection and accountability (Ellison, Krause, Shepherd, & Chaves, 2009). This may lead parishioners to prefer large congregations over smaller ones that require more from them, such as regular attendance, tithing, volunteering, and other activities that produce crucial congregational resources (Thomas & Olson, 2010). In response to this critique, Thumma and Bird (2009) note that megachurches are misunderstood, and that widespread and often repeated opinions about them tend to be inaccurate. They point out that megachurches have responded to the changing reality of American society in ways that religious Americans find appealing, that they share many beneficial characteristics with other churches, and that they have unique value.

On the spiritual but not religious side, there has also been a proliferation of nonreligious spiritual communities and practices in modern times. Of the nearly 20% of people who identify as unaffiliated, nearly 40% identify as spiritual but not religious (SBNR).

Who are these people and what kind of spirituality do they engage in? What Jeffrey Kripal (2007) calls the "religion of no religion" includes a subgroup of people who engage in a self-created blend of SRBPs that are no less important to them than traditional religions are to their adherents. Many of them find their spiritual home at an ashram, meditation center, or yoga or aikido studio, in transformational workshops and events, or a combination of these. For such people, the relatively modern option of engaging in a self-created set of spiritual practices, often comprised of components amalgamated from many different traditions (yoga, meditation, martial arts, and so on) and including elements of neuroscience and positive psychology, is immensely freeing. They often report that this approach supports a level of spiritual growth they felt they couldn't get in a traditional religious context.

A *Huffington Post* article by Diane Collins (2014) claims that there's a "new mainstream," which she calls the "consciousness crowd." A defining characteristic of many of these unaffiliated people is, as Sam Harris (2014) points out in his book *Waking Up*, that many are trying to understand how the worlds of science and their own spiritual experiences fit together. In truth, people who are spiritual but not religious are often critical of both religious and secular perspectives (Mercadante, 2014), and instead create personal theologies or explanatory meaning systems that are consistent with their own beliefs and experiences.

However, the spiritual but not religious movement is not without its critics. Daniel (2014) rather scathingly critiques such viewpoints as convenient, complacent, self-centered, and even hedonistic, lacking the character-building challenges that traditional religious communities and doctrine provide. Another potential drawback of these self-created spiritual paths is that they can at times be subject to decontextualization and even distortion of the practices, and this approach can also result in less structured, built-in support for practitioners (Smith, 2013). Interestingly, in the absence of formal religious explanatory narratives or clergy to provide guidance, this may lead clients to want more support from mental health professionals in understanding their experiences.

Religion and Spirituality in Clients

Clearly, there is an ever-increasing array of forms of religion, spirituality, or both (or neither) that you may encounter in your practice. Relevant to psychology, evidence shows that subjective spirituality and tradition-oriented religiousness are independent from one another and have distinctly different correlates in the domain of personality, suggesting that individuals with different dispositions tend toward different styles of religious or spiritual beliefs (Saucier & Skrzypinska, 2006).

How might this show up in clients? The Venn diagram below shows that for some people, religion and spirituality might be represented by two completely aligned circles (equally religious and spiritual). For others, religion and spirituality overlap (mostly religious but also spiritual, or mostly spiritual but also religious), while for still others, the two might be connected only peripherally, if at all (religious but not spiritual, or spiritual but not religious). And some clients may have no spiritual or religious beliefs or practices at all. None of these positions are better than another. They simply represent a spectrum of diversity to be aware of when attending to clients' SRBPs, or lack thereof, in clinical practice. To that end, let's take a closer look at each combination of religiosity or spirituality you may encounter in your clients.

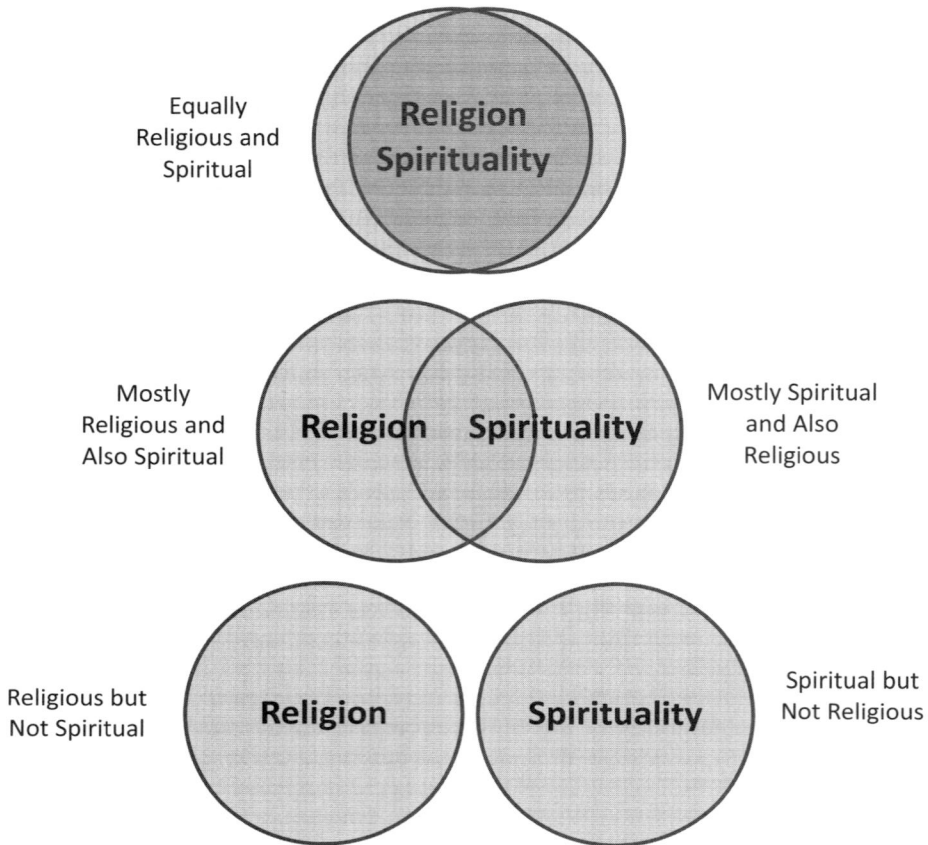

Equally
Religious and
Spiritual

**Religion
Spirituality**

Mostly
Religious and
Also Spiritual

Religion   **Spirituality**

Mostly Spiritual
and Also
Religious

Religious but
Not Spiritual

Religion

Spirituality

Spiritual but
Not Religious

Equally Religious and Spiritual

For some people, the words "spirituality" and "religion" are synonymous; their religious affiliation completely encompasses their spirituality. For example, Adam, who is Jewish, attends synagogue, celebrates Jewish holidays, and follows Jewish traditions. Adam feels that his Jewish faith and practice *are* his spirituality, and he doesn't have spiritual experiences or practices that lie outside his faith. Adam considers himself both religious and spiritual, in ways that overlap almost completely.

Mostly Religious but Also Spiritual

Other people have a religious affiliation that is important to them and overlaps with their spirituality, but have some aspects of their lives that are spiritual without necessarily being connected to their religion. For example, Veronica was raised Roman Catholic and goes to mass each week, uses the rosary for prayer, and has had her children baptized. She also has a very strong love of nature, engages in meditative practices, and feels a sense of the sacred in nature that she experiences as going beyond and being somewhat distinct from her Catholic affiliation.

Mostly Spiritual but Also Religious

Still other people have a strong set of spiritual beliefs, practices, and values, while also engaging in religious practices or communities that are important to them. For example, Shari does aikido as a form of both exercise and spiritual practice, and she also engages in contemplative practices. She feels that both of these spiritual practices strongly guide her life. She also attends Presbyterian church on Sunday mornings, as she has since she was a child. For her, this is less about serving her spiritual needs and more about keeping her connected with her neighbors and the religion of her childhood.

Religious but Not Spiritual

A minority of people identify with a religion, but don't find the term "spiritual" helpful in describing their experience of the sacred. For example, Richard is a devout member of a small, conservative Christian sect and considers himself religious, but he might object to using the word "spiritual" to describe himself.

Spiritual but Not Religious

As mentioned above, a growing number of people identify as spiritual but not at all religious. In other words, they have no religious affiliation, but they do think of themselves as anywhere from just a bit spiritual to deeply spiritual. They may simply experience their spirituality more generally, not in connection to any particular set of teachings or practices, or they may pursue it through more formal practices. For example, Bruce and Jane, a young married couple, each have strong spiritual practices and viewpoints. Bruce practices meditation at a community center regularly, and Jane has a strong yoga practice, but neither has an affiliation with a specific religion.

Not Religious or Spiritual at All

Finally, some people don't consider themselves either religious or spiritual. They may be agnostic—unsure where the truth lies in regard to religion or spirituality—or atheistic and decidedly not affiliated with any spiritual or religious belief system. Other people simply have no interest whatsoever in the topic.

Addressing Both Spirituality and Religion in Therapy

How can you incorporate your knowledge of the distinction between religion and spirituality in therapy? You can begin by inquiring about both religion *and* spirituality during your initial assessment. For many years, the phenomenon of increasing numbers of spiritual but not religious people was missed because the question simply didn't appear on censuses and General Social Surveys. People were asked to check a box to identify which religion they were affiliated with, choosing from a list that included "other" or "none." Therefore, those who were spiritual but not religious had no box to check.

As you complete your initial assessment, you might ask, "Are you affiliated with or do you practice any religion? Are you a member of a church or synagogue?" However, we recommend that you also ask, "Do you have a form of spirituality? Do you engage in any spiritual practices?" You might also consider less formal questions, along the following lines: "When do you feel most connected to a larger sense of meaning or purpose?" "What is most meaningful to you?" "What guides your life?" "What do you hold sacred?" By including these questions, you may learn about aspects of your clients' lives that are very important to their overall worldview and psychological well-being, but that you might have missed if you hadn't asked.

You might also examine your own assumptions about religion versus spirituality. Do you hold the view that religion is less dynamic than spirituality? Or do you think spiritual practice without religion carries less weight than a formal religious affiliation? Do you assume that one is more important or better than the other? Are you generally a secular person, not routinely thinking about either spirituality or religion or seeing them as having an impact on clients' cognitive or emotional functioning? Or do you believe that those who have no spiritual or religious beliefs are missing something important in life? Uncovering your own assumptions and biases in this regard can help you be more thoughtful about how you attend to these domains of clients' lives.

Conclusion

Being curious about both religious and spiritual dimensions of clients' history, beliefs, and practices will help you better understand how they see themselves, their lives, and the world around them. Your attention to these important aspects of clients' lived experience will increase your effectiveness as a therapist. Your inquiry may also help clients clarify what they believe. When we've pursued these topics, clients have sometimes responded with statements like "I never really thought about it; no one has asked me these questions before," followed by a rich and fruitful self-exploration. And through this process, you too may learn something new about your own beliefs and worldview.

Just as religion and spirituality are distinct from one another but can overlap quite a bit, there are times when religious or spiritual experiences can look similar to and overlap with psychopathological symptoms, even though they are distinct from one another. In the next chapter, we'll examine this phenomenon.

Chapter 6

KNOWING THE DIFFERENCE BETWEEN SPIRITUALITY AND PSYCHOPATHOLOGY

P art of your practice as a mental health professional may be helping people who have serious mental illness. According to the National Institute of Mental Health (2013), a serious mental illness is "a mental, behavioral or emotional disorder (excluding developmental and substance use disorders)…of sufficient duration to meet diagnostic criteria specified within the…*DSM-IV*…resulting in serious functional impairment, which substantially interferes with or limits one or more major life activities" (para. 2). The overall prevalence of serious mental illnesses among US adults in 2012 was 4.1% (National Institute of Mental Health, 2013; US Department of Health and Human Services, 2012), and lifetime prevalence of psychotic disorders exceeds 0.6% (Karg et al., 2014).

At times, psychiatric symptoms such as delusions or hallucinations have strong religious or spiritual content. Conversely, sometimes religious or spiritual experiences can look like psychiatric problems but actually be common and well-documented aspects of a religious or spiritual path. Not all visions are hallucinations, not all ecstatic bliss is mania, and not all existential distress is depression. At the same time, not all experiences with religious or spiritual content are genuinely religious or spiritual; they may indeed be psychiatric problems that require immediate intervention. It can be tricky to differentiate what is a religious or spiritual experience in clients and what is not.

COMPETENCY 6: Psychologists understand that clients may have experiences that are consistent with their spirituality or religion, yet may be difficult to differentiate from psychopathological symptoms.

If you've traveled to India or other parts of the world where religious behaviors are different from what's typical in the United States, or if you've been to religious services of certain sects in the United States, you may have seen behavior that the creators of the

DSM might find bizarre. For example, speaking in tongues, which is common in some Pentecostal churches, could look psychotic when viewed out of context. Routinely speaking with one's ancestors, the deceased, or benevolent spirits is not normative for many people in Western culture, but it is a matter of course for many Native American and First Nations people. Sitting still for a long period of time in meditation while in your mind's eye bathing your guru in ghee and honey is not typical for most people in the United States, but it is traditional for those following some Vedic scriptures. Sitting quietly with your eyes half open for five to ten hours a day for days at a time, as is common in the Zen Buddhist tradition, may seem isolating or depressive to those outside the tradition. Therefore, cultural context is key to understanding the beliefs and practices of individual clients.

As part of their spiritual and religious beliefs and practices, people can have experiences that cause cognitive or emotional agitation, unusual or bizarre ideation, or visual or auditory phenomena. When a client presents with unusual or extreme emotions or experiences associated with SRBPs, it can be difficult to ascertain whether the material the client is presenting is 1) unfamiliar to you but completely consistent with his spiritual or religious tradition; 2) is consistent with his spiritual or religious tradition but also causing unnecessary cognitive and emotional distress; or 3) contains religious or spiritual elements but is maladaptive or symptomatic of psychopathology.

Here, we need to reiterate that we are working toward competence, not proficiency. This is an important distinction. It may require a certain degree of proficiency to fully differentiate between spiritual or religious issues and psychiatric problems. For competence, you simply need to be aware of these phenomena and be able to assess when you can address them on your own. If not, you may need to make a referral, consult, or work with a clergy member or spiritual teacher. This chapter should help you make that call.

Mystical Experiences

Historically, psychological theory and diagnostic classification systems have tended to either ignore or pathologize intense religious and spiritual experiences. The mystical experience has been described as symptomatic of ego regression, borderline psychosis, psychosis, and temporal lobe dysfunction (Lukoff, Turner, & Lu, 1992). Freud (1930/1961) reduced the "oceanic experience" of mystics to a regressive return to "limitless narcissism" (p. 20) and saw religious engagement as "patently infantile" (p. 22). There are numerous published accounts of individuals in the midst of intense religious and spiritual experiences that were misunderstood by mental health professionals, and some have been hospitalized and medicated when less restrictive and more therapeutic interventions could have been utilized (Lukoff, 2007).

So, what is a mystical experience, and how is it different from a breakdown? Maslow (1970) described the mystical experience as an aspect of everyday psychological functioning, saying, "It is very likely, indeed almost certain, that these older reports [of mystical experiences], phrased in terms of supernatural revelation, were, in fact, perfectly natural, human peak experiences of the kind that can easily be examined today" (p. 20). Mystical experiences can be highly adaptive, spurring on psychological maturation. In fact, one study showed that those reporting mystical experiences scored lower on psychopathology scales and higher on measures of psychological well-being than control subjects (Wulff, 2000).

Spiritual Emergencies

Sometimes mystical experiences can reach such a high level of intensity and duration that they become cause for concern. During or following prayer, meditation, or other spiritual practices, or at times spontaneously, people may have profound childhood memories, visions or hallucinations (depending on your perspective), or insights into the nature of reality or their own nature that cause psychological disruption for a time. "Spiritual emergency," a term coined by Christina and Stanislav Grof (1986), refers to "a crisis involving religious, transpersonal, and/or spiritual issues that provides opportunities for growth" (Viggiano & Krippner, 2010, p. 118).

As an example of this, one of our colleagues has openly written about his own experience with a spiritual emergency. David Lukoff, who as mentioned earlier went on to coauthor the "religious or spiritual problem" category for the *DSM-IV*, had the following experience in his twenties, after engaging in spiritual practices and dropping out of Harvard:

> I stopped in front of the mirror and gazed at my reflection. Suddenly I noticed that my right hand was glowing, giving off a white light. My thumb was touching my forefinger in the ancient mudra position of the meditating Buddha. Immediately the meaning of this sign was clear to me: I had been Buddha in a previous life. Then another thought came: Buddha had been reincarnated as Jesus Christ. Therefore, I had also been Jesus Christ. Now, in this moment, the luminous image in the mirror was awakening me to my true purpose: to once again bring the human race out of its decline. My journal writing was actually the creation a "new Bible," a Holy Book which would unite all people around the common tenants of a single belief system. Instead of unifying just one social group, as Buddha and Christ had, my mission was to write a book that would create a new worldwide society free of conflict and full of loving relationships...

Over the next five days and nights, I worked with only short breaks for meals and naps. I found I could contact the "spirits" of eminent thinkers in the social sciences and humanities to help me with the task of writing the new "Bible." As I reflected on their relevance for my work, I would "become" these people of wisdom, and "think their thoughts with them.".…

Over the next five months of writing, I was so preoccupied with my mission that I didn't work to earn money. (Lukoff, 1990a)

While this experience could have been seen as a classic first psychotic break, over time, with the help of friends and psychotherapy, David's crisis resolved and he went on to become a pioneering scholar in the field of spiritual emergency and the intersection of psychology with religion and spirituality. As a therapist with religious and spiritual competency, you should know that these kinds of experiences do occur, and while they can significantly disrupt people's psychological and emotional functioning temporarily, they may not always be maladaptive. Some experiences related to SRBPs may seem to fit diagnostic criteria for psychopathology while actually being consistent with a client's spiritual or religious tradition.

Forms of Spiritual Emergency

After observing thousands of people who had mystical experiences in response to engaging in transformative workshops and spiritual practices, Stan and Christina Grof (1986) formulated categories for types of spiritual emergencies. Though these experiences are highly individual, with no two cases of spiritual emergency being exactly alike, the Grofs identified the following ten common themes:

- The shamanic crisis

- The awakening of kundalini

- Episodes of unitive consciousness (peak experiences)

- Psychological renewal through return to the center

- The crisis of psychic opening

- Past-life experiences

- Communications with spirit guides and channeling

- Near-death experiences and after-death experiences

- Experiences of close encounters with interdimensional domains

- Possession states

Describing each of these is far beyond the scope of this book, so our intention is to simply make sure you know that these experiences can happen. And while they may represent symptoms of psychosis, these experiences may also be what Grof & Grof called "manifestations of evolutionary crises" (1989, p. 19), in other words, normative, adaptive experiences that offer opportunities for clients to grow.

There are other forms of spiritual emergency that can mimic psychiatric symptoms as well. Consider the dark night of the soul (Borchard, 2014), a period of time in which a crisis of faith or profound spiritual concerns cause distress in people's lives. Though these periods of angst and disillusionment can be disruptive and distressing, when assigned religious meaning they can provide opportunities for people to deeply reflect on their lives. Rather than being pathological, these experiences can serve as agents for positive change (Dura-Vila & Dein, 2009). Michael O'Connor (2002) suggests how caregivers can effectively respond to dark night experiences, which can be misperceived as depression. He notes that while there are commonalities between depression and the spiritual dark night experience, there are key differences between the two as well. Whereas the dark night is experiencing a loss of one's connection to God, an individual experiencing depression is processing a loss in the secular realm, such as loss of a family member, job, finances, or health. Thus, while they may share the components of relational and cognitive disruptions, with dark night experiences, there is also a crisis around one's relationship to God. Similarly, Thalbourne (1991) points out that there is much in common between religious ecstasy and mania, such as feelings of profound joy, a sense of purpose and meaning, a perception of connectedness between previously unrelated events, a conviction that the experience is absolutely true and very valuable, transcending ego boundaries and having a sense of oneness and unity, and feeling immortal. However, psychotic mania more often includes aggressive outbursts, paranoia, and personalization.

Triggers for Spiritual Emergencies

The trigger for a spiritual emergency or religious crisis can be physical, such as an illness, disease, accident, operation, extreme physical exertion, or prolonged lack of sleep. At times, a spiritual emergency can follow a powerful emotional experience, such as the loss of an important relationship, for example, the death of a child, a divorce, or the end of a love affair. Similarly, being fired from a job, major property loss, or a series of failures can precede the onset. In women, a transformational crisis can be instigated by childbirth, miscarriage, or abortion. For some people, such an experience can be triggered by an experience of intense awe or wonder, an encounter with beauty in nature, meeting with a spiritual teacher, or even simply reading a profound book. It can also result from an experience with altered states of consciousness caused by psychoactive substances or other agents, or participation in experiential therapies. And for some people, it may result from spiritual practices, a phenomenon well described by the Grofs:

> One of the most important catalysts of spiritual emergency seems to be deep involvement in various forms of meditation and spiritual practice. These methods have been specifically designed to activate spiritual experiences. We have been repeatedly contacted by persons whose unusual experiences occurred during the pursuit of Zen, Vipassana Buddhist meditation, Kundalini yoga, Sufi exercises, or Christian prayer and monastic contemplation. As various Oriental and Western spiritual disciplines are rapidly gaining popularity, more and more people seem to be having transpersonal crises—yet another reason that correct understanding and treatment of spiritual emergencies is an issue of ever-increasing importance. (Grof & Grof, 1989, p. 8)

While these kinds of spiritual emergencies may seem extreme and unfamiliar to you, take a moment to look back over those times in your own life when you experienced awe or felt an elated state or, alternatively, a period of existential distress—sadness, anxiety, or even something approaching irrationality or madness. What were the circumstances? Did that experience stay with you a long time or shift your worldview or any of your normal daily behaviors? How did you respond to that experience over time? Did you share it with people? What did you notice about their reactions? Did you ever feel anxious about how people responded or might be judging you? Did you ever feel concerned that there might be something wrong with you during extreme experiences? If so, how did you respond to those feelings? While you may not have experienced anything quite as extreme as a spiritual emergency, as a clinician you may find it helpful to reflect on times when you had extreme experiences or were challenged to navigate rocky points in your life and to consider what would have helped you most during those times.

Differentiating Spiritual Emergency from Psychopathology

According to the *DSM-5*, symptoms of psychosis may include "positive symptoms" such as delusions, hallucinations, disorganized speech (for example, frequent derailment or incoherence), markedly illogical thinking, or behavior that is grossly disorganized or catatonic, as well as "negative symptoms" such as diminished emotional expression and avolition (American Psychiatric Association, 2013, pp. 94–117). Psychosis can appear as an element of a number of disorders, including schizophrenia, bipolar disorder, depression, substance abuse, and PTSD. Symptoms of psychosis often include religious and spiritual elements (Mohr et al., 2010; Siddle, Haddock, Tarrier, & Faragher, 2014).

Problematically, these same symptoms—or experiences mimicking them—can occur during a spiritual emergency or religious crisis. Yet because psychotic episodes often include religious or spiritual content, such as a client thinking he's Jesus, the devil, or a ghost or spirit, how can you differentiate these potentially long-term experiences from a temporary religious or spiritual experience?

First, recognize that commonly accepted diagnostic criteria are culturally determined. Ideas about everything from the names of disorders to their causes and expected course to optimal treatment are highly influenced by culture, and also vary within cultures (Weiss & Somma, 2010). Our current Western models for explaining mental illness are not universal (Luhrmann, 2001). In other words, the *DSM* is just one way of explaining seemingly dysfunctional behavior.

Depending on the cultural context, delusions or hallucinations can be explained in varying ways (Mohr, 2013). For example, the belief that malignant forces can cause psychiatric illness exists in nearly every culture, including some religious and spiritual groups in the United States (Mohr, 2013). Consequently, it should not be surprising that research (Loewenthal, 2010) found that up to 70% of patients attempt one or more spiritual healings before seeking professional help. The "positive symptoms" as defined by the *DSM-5* are similar, and identical in some cases, to spiritual experiences described in detail in sacred texts, such as hearing voices, having visions, or experiencing ecstatic states and trances (American Psychiatric Association, 2013, pp. 87–88, 94). How can you, as a mental health practitioner, determine which clients are experiencing something maladaptive, and which are experiencing something transformative that lies on the continuum of spiritual or religious ecstatic experiences?

A client who is experiencing spiritual and religious issues that are difficult to distinguish from manic, psychotic, or other clinical symptoms may need to be referred to a mental health professional who is proficient in the intersection of religion or spirituality with psychology. However, you can make a determination regarding what kind of intervention or referral is needed by asking screening questions that inquire into the following nine topics (inspired in part by Grof & Grof, 1990):

1. Could medical issues explain the client's symptoms?

2. Is the client functioning well physically, socially, and emotionally?

3. Is the client finding meaning in his experience?

4. Is the client coherent in his presentation?

5. Can the client reflect on his experience or demonstrate insight into it?

6.   Did the onset occur after an event or was it spontaneous?

7.   Is the experience acute, or has it been chronic?

8.   Does the client have language, context, or knowledge about his experience?

9.   Does the client have social support, or is he isolated?

Below, we offer specific guidance on inquiring into these areas, along with examples. These questions should help you determine whether the material your client is presenting is more likely to be a religious or spiritual issue, or more likely to be a psychiatric problem. Either may require some intervention, but the interventions for religious or spiritual problems may be different from those you might choose to address a psychiatric problem.

1. Potential Medical Issues

First of all, have you ruled out a physical disease, medication, or psychoactive substance that may be causing hallucinations or delusions with spiritual or religious content? All altered states of consciousness, including those with spiritual or religious content, can be caused by medical conditions such as a tumor or infection in the brain, diseases of other organs, or electrolyte imbalances. As in every case, be sure to rule this out before proceeding to assess whether the material a client is presenting is spiritual/religious, psychopathological, or a blend of the two. Physical examinations and laboratory tests can aid in detecting physical diseases that cause psychological symptoms, so insist upon them if you feel they're warranted. Also be aware that there are psychological correlates of organic impairments of the brain, such as problems with intellect and memory, clouded consciousness, difficulty with basic orientation (name, time, place), and poor coordination. In addition, confusion, disorganization, and impaired intellectual functioning can occur for any number of physiological reasons and, of course, can interfere with communication and cooperation.

2. Level of Functioning

First of all, look for level of functioning, currently and historically. Is the client capable of handling her daily life while continuing her religious or spiritual practices? Is she still paying her bills, getting to work, taking care of her children, handling friendships, and so on? Is she able to work a full-time or part-time job, either paid or as a volunteer? If the client is a student, is she able to attend school full-time, despite the intensity of the experience?

An important distinguishing quality of a psychotic episode is lacking the ability to handle the everyday stress of a forty-hour workweek or to meet societal or familial responsibilities. Someone in a manic episode with psychotic features may be forced to drop out of normal daily functions if visions or hallucinations occupy her mind persistently. On the other hand, Shelley has worked with a number of clients who had spiritual emergency experiences and were still able to function in school, handle their finances, and maintain friendships. Clients experiencing spiritual emergencies may have temporary setbacks, during which they drop out of normal functioning as they take time to integrate the experience, but they generally return to a full life.

Also, notice the quality of relationships the client has with her family of origin and friends. Does she have friendships that are sustained over time? Is she able to live independently? Can she manage her finances, school schedule, or work obligations? Does she have a partner or spouse, or children? If so, how would you rate the quality of her social, marital, and work life? If she's generally able to manage life and sustain relationships, this portends well for her ability to return to normalcy—if she's ultimately able to integrate her experience and make meaning of it within the context of her religious or spiritual beliefs.

Alternatively, does the client seem to be spiraling out of control? Is she withdrawing from others? Is she aggressive, controlling, or manipulative in her interactions? When a client presents with spiritual or religious material associated with distress, also be sure to note whether she has a history of serious difficulties in interpersonal relationships, an inability to make friends and have intimate relationships, or poor social adjustment—all signs of a history of psychiatric problems. This makes it more likely that the client's issues are psychiatric in nature.

Finally, whether or not there are religious or spiritual elements in the presentation, if there are symptoms that may be dangerous, such as extreme neglect of hygiene, refusal to eat or drink for extended periods of time, suicidal or homicidal ideation, immediate intervention is necessary.

3. Finding Meaning in the Experience

Is the client finding meaning in his experience? How does he currently perceive his experiences? Does he speak of an important, expansive experience he's working with to include in his understanding of himself? Does he have insights into the process that may be healing in nature, including change and development of personal life themes? Or is there a lack of meaning in his description, perhaps demonstrated by repetitive or circular thinking patterns or compulsions that don't seem to have a purpose? Religious or spiritual issues are more likely to present with some sense of meaning, whereas lack of insight, purpose, or meaning is a hallmark of psychiatric issues. Bragdon (1988) states that "flexibility to adapt and accommodate to new areas of experience is part and parcel of the spiritual emergence process—in contrast to inflexibility, which characterizes deeply entrenched psychosis" (pp. 74–75). Note that the term "spiritual emergence" in the preceding quotation refers to something now more commonly called spiritual or religious struggles or problems. These can be a normative part of ongoing developmental processes related to interest in and pursuit of spiritual or religious knowledge, practices, and beliefs. "Spiritual emergency," on the other hand, refers to a crisis point in which intervention or substantial support may be needed.

A notable difference is often the quality of the experience, vision, or voice. A healthier outcome can be expected if the vision is positive, loving, or at least non-threatening. For example, Jesus, Buddha, or a spirit in a tree speaking positively to a person typically won't have the same impact as a figure or voice that is demonic, threatening, scary, or negative. With experiences of a negative nature, the likelihood of a return to normal healthy functioning is lower. Although there are situations where negative forms of experience are positively integrated into people's life experience, this scenario seems to be more challenging and less likely (Betty, 2012; Mercer, 2013; Zuk & Zuk, 1998).

4. Coherence

Can the client talk about her spiritual or religious experience, and life more generally, in a coherent fashion that weaves together her values and lifestyle? Or does she seem disjointed when telling you her current situation or life story? Is her presentation poorly organized? Are there loose associations or incoherence, with no direction or development? Does her story make sense, first to her, and also to you? Religious, spiritual, or mystical experiences may be unfamiliar, distressing, or even frightening, but they tend to be more coherent than not, whereas psychotic or manic episodes are characterized by a lack of coherence.

Ultimately, a spiritual or religious experience will eventually be integrated, with the visions, voices, and trance states subsiding and being understood within the context of the person's life. Unfortunately, an organic psychosis, on the other hand, probably won't take that course. It may leave a person disabled for a lengthy period of time, maybe a lifetime, and typically disrupts a person's life in negative ways, rather than illuminating it.

5. Capacity for Self-Reflection

Can the client self-reflect on his condition? A client experiencing a religious or spiritual problem is more likely to able to report that he's having difficulty functioning, whereas those with psychiatric issues often lack insight or blame others or circumstances for their difficulties. If a client perceives the world and other people as hostile, such as having a deep mistrust of others, delusions of persecution, or acoustic hallucinations of enemies (voices) with a very unpleasant content, his experience is probably maladaptive and requires psychiatric intervention. When the process is more intrapsychic and contained, it is more likely to be a religious or spiritual issue.

6. Circumstances of Onset

Consider your client's premorbid functioning. Before the incident, was she generally high functioning at home and in school or at work? Did she mostly arrive to her appointments on time, pay her bills, and hold a job or attend classes? Was she generally responsible regarding her life and commitments? Did her family consider her relatively healthy and functional? There are special considerations around this issue for people with bipolar disorder or schizophrenia, who may have functioned well enough through their teens and into their early twenties, only falling prey to instability later. However, when their families look back on these clients' earlier behavior, they may in retrospect have seen early warning signs and often admit that their relative hadn't seemed "normal" for quite some time.

In the case of spiritual emergencies, the onset of the symptoms is likely to have been triggered by identifiable circumstances. If the client was holding down a full-time job or attending school full-time and had a sudden shift in consciousness after an event that could be considered a stressor (such as the loss of a loved one, a major shift of life circumstances, a serious illness or near-death experience, or a spiritual or religious event such as a shamanic journey, a silent retreat, work with a new religious or spiritual teacher, an intense yoga weekend, or ingestion of a mind-altering substance), you may want to hold off on assuming that she's psychotic. Instead, you might monitor closely over time to see what happens. Seemingly psychotic behavior could be temporary. And although the client may need help initially, and over time, to integrate the experience, if it arose after a specific event that could have triggered her difficulties, it might best be diagnosed as a religious or spiritual problem, as defined in *DSM-5*, code Z65.8 (American Psychiatric Association, 2013, p. 725).

7. Duration

Also consider how long these issues have been present. Are they acute, or have they been going on for months or years? Psychiatric issues can be either chronic or acute, and a spiritual or religious transformation may take weeks, months, or even years to fully comprehend and integrate into a new worldview. If the issues have been present for a short period of time, they may call for different interventions than if they're chronic. For example, if a young man suddenly begins to claim that he's a reincarnation of Jesus without prior symptoms, it could be either a facet of a spiritual emergency or a first break (the first time psychotic symptoms are detected). However, if a client reports this repeatedly over a number of years, your assessment might lean toward a psychiatric problem. Assess how the client is integrating his experiences into his current and future life plans. Is the process of integration within normal limits, or are his attempts to adjust negatively impacting his current life functioning or future plans?

8. *Knowledge About the Experience*

Does the client have any knowledge or context about her religious or spiritual experience? Sometimes clients may present with religious or spiritual issues that they've never heard of anyone else having, so they don't even have words for what they're experiencing, whether it be a "crisis of faith," a "dark night of the soul," or a "kundalini awakening." For such clients, learning more about others who have had such experiences and how they dealt with them can go a long way toward alleviating distress, fear, guilt, or embarrassment. So be sure to assess whether the client has any knowledge, context, or language for what's happening. Does she have contact with an expert in this realm, or access to books, websites, and other resources that describe or explain what may be occurring? Is she interested in investigating how others may have traveled similar paths? Some self-centeredness or feeling of being unique is natural in these processes, but focusing too much and for too long on oneself can be isolating and detrimental.

9. *Social Context*

Is your client's spiritual or religious experience in alignment with his family of origin or social circle? One thing that can be very important to assess when a client presents with spiritual or religious issues is whether he's isolated in his experiences, beliefs, and practices, or whether he has family support, social support, or both. Does he have a community with which he can share what's happening, or is he feeling alone? If he's isolated, is that something he describes as contributing to his journey or as hindering it? Does he desire greater community and connection? If so, is he making moves in that direction? Or does he have a history of poor interpersonal skills and withdrawal or self-isolation? Knowing whether the client is more isolated or has family or social support may influence your choice of intervention (Grof & Grof, 1990, pp. 254–255). In some cases, you might encourage clients to seek support and share what's going on with trusted others. However, some people prefer solitude in these situations because they feel overwhelmed or vulnerable in the presence of others. Being around others without needing to interact directly, such as working in the kitchen during a silent retreat, is another possibility. An intervention where a person may be more physically active but not necessarily interactive with others, such as gardening or painting, can be a wise choice at times. For the latter, other possibilities include bicycle riding or hiking with others while remaining mostly quiet, going to a coffee shop to be around others without talking, or studying in a library or other safe public space.

Choosing Interventions

The nine lines of inquiry outlined above can help you determine whether you should treat the issues a client presents as a religious or spiritual problem, a psychiatric problem, or a blend of the two. They will also help you understand the context and severity of the issues. If a client is facing a religious or spiritual problem, you might choose a combination of talk therapy, social support, and consultation with clergy or a spiritually oriented therapist. If it appears to be a problem in need of psychiatric intervention, you might consider a psychiatric evaluation, medication, hospitalization, or cognitive behavioral therapy. If it appears to be a blend of the two, you could opt for a blend of interventions.

Then, based on the length of time the client has been experiencing distress, whether she has a context for it, and whether she has social support, you can include other intervention components as appropriate. For example, you might recommend group therapy for someone who's isolated, a more intensive intervention for someone who's been distressed for a long time, or, if the situation isn't as severe, bibliotherapy—helping the client learn about her experiences through reading books on the subject.

Next we offer two case examples reflecting some of the clinical realities you could face when working with clients who report distressing or extreme experiences with religious or spiritual content. Consider the nine lines of inquiry we've discussed as you read on.

✳ Clinician's Diary

Over the past decade, Shelley has given presentations on differential diagnosis and religious and spiritual emergency to various graduate programs in the San Francisco Bay Area. After one presentation, Joan, a young graduate student, came to her asking for further information privately. They met soon thereafter in Shelley's office. After Shelley asked some basic questions about Joan's place of residence, occupation, previous therapies, psychotropic medications, hospitalizations, suicidal ideation, and so on, the interview proceeded as follows.

Shelley: Thanks for answering all those questions. So, what brought you here today?

Joan: I'm having a hard time concentrating during classes. In truth, I don't know how I'm making it through graduate school.

Shelley: What's going on?

Joan: Well, I've only told one friend about this, but I'm having strange experiences. I've been meditating for about a year now, and a few months after starting, I began to have strange experiences. I feel as if energy comes out of nowhere, and I get sucked into another place for a while, where I feel hostage to this energy, while visions come through my head. I can't concentrate at all, and am totally absorbed by this force.

Shelley: That sounds scary. Is it?

Joan: Yes, It is scary sometimes. The visions I get can go on for hours if I let them. It's not fun sometimes, and I can't control when they come. Sometimes I leave class and go sit in my car, waiting for it to pass. Other times I can sit still and listen to the lecture just fine.

Shelley: What do you make of these experiences?

Joan: I don't know. Recently, I've been reading a lot about kundalini energy. Is that real? I don't have a history of this previously; I'm not sure what's happening. I don't think it's usual, is it?

Shelley: Well, it's not common, but it happens sometimes when people start spiritual practices. These practices can seem benign, and often are, but also can sometimes open people up to a bigger energetic process.

Joan: Am I crazy?

Shelley: I don't think so. Are you able to work at your part-time job and take your courses in graduate school?

Joan Yes, I can always get to work and somehow finish my papers for school. It almost seems as if this energy knows when I need to function and stays away until I get my work done.

Shelley: And your sleep?

Joan: Occasionally I get awoken by the energy and can't sleep, but I'm not tired generally.

Shelley: And eating?

Joan: No problem.

Shelley: And how are your friendships? You mentioned a friend you've told about this.

Joan: Yes, I'm close to her and have a few other graduate school friends. I moved here for school last year, so I'm just making friends. My boyfriend thinks what I'm experiencing is somewhat strange, but he's understanding of it.

Shelley: So, he's pretty understanding?

Joan: Yes, he's mostly just curious about it all.

Shelley: And you're able to socialize a bit?

Joan: Yes, mostly with my boyfriend and sometimes school buddies. After my work and school, I don't have time for much else.

Shelley: Have you been reading much about kundalini?

Joan: Yes, when time permits. I've been trying to write my papers around my experiences when I can. That way I can learn about what's going on with me while I'm writing.

What are your initial thoughts about this case? Using some of the guidelines above, what elements of this case indicate a potentially adaptive or nonpathological spiritual experience, and what elements indicate maladaptive psychological functioning?

After this initial interview, Shelley investigated Joan's comment about feeling hostage to and totally absorbed by the experience a little more deeply to determine whether Joan was externalizing the experience. In other words, was Joan feeling that this was being done to her by an outside force, rather than arising internally? She found that Joan used this language to describe the intensity of the experience, rather than feeling persecuted in some way. After further investigation, Shelley was generally convinced that this was a religious or spiritual issue, not a psychologically maladaptive process, so she continued to help Joan process the experiences while also keeping a close eye on any changes in Joan's functioning.

✳ Clinician's Diary

After Shelley made a professional presentation on differential diagnosis in a spiritual context some years ago, she was approached by Alice, a well-dressed, attractive middle-aged woman who wondered if too much meditation could be harmful. Shelley answered that she wasn't a meditation teacher, so she wasn't qualified to answer that question, and then said she did imagine it could strain people at times. After Shelley told Alice that she specialized in working with clients in spiritual emergency, Alice asked for Shelley's card and ended up coming in for therapy the next week.

Alice arrived early to fill out the intake form. She was appropriately dressed, non-defensive in her style, and friendly in her presentation. From the intake form, Shelley learned that Alice was married, employed full-time, had children, and had a long-standing meditation practice. Initially, Shelley presumed that all of this showed stability in Alice's life.

Alice had brought the beginnings of a screenplay she'd created in a workshop. She seemed anxious to share it, so Shelley let her lead, as this was a valuable way to get some history. Within a few minutes, however, it became apparent that Alice's rapid speech wasn't just excitement; it bordered on mania. She was pleasant enough and seemed to be holding down a full-time job, so Shelley continued to assess what was happening.

She asked Alice about her sleep patterns, and she admitted to not always sleeping as much as she used to, maybe only five hours a night, but had no complaints about being tired. Alice said she didn't smoke or use illegal substances of any kind, and drank only a glass of wine once or twice a week with her husband. Alice said she felt very connected to her spiritual practices and was reluctant to change her meditation practice of at least one hour per day, but she admitted that it was becoming a struggle because she was having difficulty concentrating. Alice described most of her distress as an integral part of her spiritual path, and some of this had been reinforced by various mediation teachers who reassured Alice that the experiences she was having were a normal part of meditation practice.

Over the next few sessions, Shelley began inquiring about Alice's longer-term history with depression or mania. It turned out that about once a decade since age twenty, Alice had experienced crippling depression that left her unable to work for a few months to a year and then subsided. The most recent episode had occurred ten years previously. At that time, she was prescribed an antidepressant, which she took for nearly a year, and it seemed to help. Thereafter, however, Alice had refused to take medication, preferring meditation as an ongoing method to support her mood. When she didn't feel as well, she simply meditated more, which, until now, had sufficiently alleviated her symptoms.

Although Alice's initial question was about the effects of too much meditation, she presented in a very tangential way, and for the first few sessions it was unclear what her primary concern was. She seemed delighted with her life. She wanted Shelley to help her choose the best future career based on her many spiritual experiences, such as filming a documentary about them. Then, after a few sessions, she admitted that her job was being changed to part-time because of her inability to perform as usual.

Due to this change, Alice was willing to look at herself in a more serious way. While she spoke quite a bit about a potential book project to help the world and new ways to make a living, she began to admit that her daily life was falling apart. She was having a harder and harder time getting to work punctually—or at all—and her boss seemed to be annoyed with her. She noticed that her husband was getting concerned and advocating she get more help for her problems. She was dead set against taking medication again because she felt it "dulled her down," so she chose to go to acupuncture several times a week. However, this didn't seem to alleviate her agitation, and she exhibited an ever-greater tendency to speak tangentially, with only loose associations.

With Alice's permission, Shelley contacted Alice's alternative medicine practitioner, a naturopath, who admitted to having little success helping Alice. Together, they agreed to encourage Alice to see a psychiatrist—one who was aligned with Alice's views on holistic, natural approaches but who utilized psychotropic medications as well. Alice's naturopath was aware that she would have to shift her treatment plan if Alice started taking other medications, and she agreed to do so.

So, after a few sessions with Alice, Shelley was definitely considering bipolar disorder as a potential diagnosis. Many of Alice's symptoms and patterns fit the criteria for a manic episode: her ongoing inability to sleep more than five hours a night; her pressured speech; her inflated self-esteem about changing the world through her potential film project (a film Alice hadn't yet started shooting); clear distractibility, as evidenced by decreasing competence at work; and the fact that she'd started to take extremely long walks daily to calm herself (unsuccessfully). Finally Alice admitted that while walking to work, she sometimes walked back and forth between home and work, unable to decide which way to proceed because a voice kept telling her to turn back. This made the diagnosis clear, especially given Alice's history of previous episodes of depression and a family history of bipolar disorder.

Thankfully, because both Shelley and the naturopath recommended that Alice see a psychiatrist, she agreed to go. After Alice had seen the psychiatrist, Shelley spoke with him and found he had come to the same diagnosis independently. Over the next few months, they coordinated Alice's care. Because Alice hadn't had any suicidal ideation or serious problematic behavior (shopping sprees, running up credit cards, and so on), they were able to help her stabilize without terribly negative consequences. Alice was able to continue to work part-time, and she came to realize it actually suited her better than full-time work, reducing her stress and helping her sustain a positive lifestyle with her family.

On the other hand, Alice came to fear meditation. Before she began using the mood stabilizer, Alice admitted that she could no longer meditate for any length of time and said negative voices started entering her mind during meditation, as well as at other times in the day. Shelley recommended that Alice consider eating more protein to help her ground herself and that she stop trying to meditate for a while. Alice reluctantly agreed, and as she continued to take psychotropic medication, she began to stabilize.

Over a year later, Alice once again started to meditate in a group setting at a nearby temple, for short periods of time only. By then, her therapy sessions had been reduced to only two a month. Alice continued to work part-time, and used her free time to take classes that interested her and go for walks in the hills. She wasn't depressed or manic anymore and realized that changes in her spiritual practices and taking medication had been key to her progress. She no longer envisioned making a documentary about her spiritual experiences, but she did feel that she was working on integrating her various experiences within herself.

Customizing Your Approach

As you can see, the cases of Alice and Joan were quite different, though both initially reported having distressing experiences associated with their meditation practices. Joan seemed to be doing well as assessed by the nine lines of inquiry discussed in this chapter—functioning well physically, socially, and emotionally; finding meaning in her experience; being coherent in her presentation; and having the ability to self-reflect. With Alice, on the other hand, there was cause for concern in nearly all nine areas. For her, a combination of psychiatric care, psychotherapy, and lessening stressors was appropriate. Meanwhile, for Joan, a better approach was to help her understand and manage her spiritual issues while keeping a close eye on her functioning. However, a mental health professional who didn't possess the sixth competence might have recommended psychiatric medication to reduce Joan's symptoms of agitation, intermittently overwhelming energy, and occasional difficulties with sleep.

You also may encounter cases that have elements of both psychopathology and religion or spirituality; it's not an either-or proposition. And even when you utilize the nine lines of inquiry above, it can be difficult to disentangle spiritual and religious experiences from manic or psychotic symptoms. If you find yourself having difficulty determining whether a client is experiencing a spiritual emergency or a psychotic break, seek consultation or make a referral to a clinician who's proficient in working with spiritual or religious issues.

By learning more about the variety of experiences people can encounter due to their SRBPs and paying special attention to those that look similar to psychiatric symptoms, you can develop greater effectiveness as a diagnostician and a therapist. As evidenced in the examples above, when clients present with distress or agitation that includes spiritual or religious content, it's not always easy to distinguish between whether they're dealing with spiritual and religious issues or psychopathology. If you can't differentiate between the two, which can be challenging even for the most proficient clinician, it's important to avoid jumping to conclusions, even if a client presents experiences that are unfamiliar, intense, and perhaps frightening. It's tempting to allay clients' fears and your own by focusing on eradicating the distress in short order. This isn't always the best course of action.

If you have a client who's religious or spiritual and reports unusual experiences, you might consult with a clinician who is proficient in spiritual or religious issues, a transpersonal therapist, or a clergy member or spiritual teacher to investigate whether what the client is experiencing is consistent with the framework of her SRBPs. At times, religious and spiritual paths of development involve distressing experiences that are not pathological—in other words, they aren't symptoms of an underlying disorder. At the same time, any experiences that involve potential harm to your client or others, or that cause more than a temporary inability to attend to responsibilities or health and hygiene, should be targeted by interventions, regardless of spiritual or religious content.

Conclusion

There are multiple types of mystical and spiritual experiences, and the features of some of these experiences look very similar to symptoms of psychopathology. Spiritual emergence is a form of religious or spiritual realization, insight, or opening that causes a shift in perspective or worldview. A spiritual emergency is when that experience or shift in perspective throws a person into a crisis or temporarily interferes with functioning. Spiritual and religious struggles include loss of faith, doubting one's relationship with God, questioning one's spiritual or religious beliefs, or leaving or changing religious affiliations. All of these can include periods of intense sadness, grief, anxiety, or fear; experiences of unity, transcendence, or depersonalization; or perceptions of connections with entities such as angels, deities, demons, or the deceased.

In this chapter, we've given you tools for beginning to differentiate spiritual emergence, emergency, or struggle from forms of psychopathology such as depression, mania, or psychosis with religious or spiritual content. This can be tricky, and at times it will require consultation with someone who's highly proficient in the intersection of spirituality and psychology. However, all competent therapists should know that these experiences can occur, that they can overlap with psychopathology, and that they can require different interventions.

At different points in a client's life, or throughout the course of treatment, the role of religion and spirituality may change—sometimes becoming a source of support, and at other times becoming a source of difficulty; sometimes being very important, and at other times being less so. In the next chapter, we describe how SRBPs can drastically change over the life span, and how this knowledge can help you better attend to religious and spiritual issues in therapy.

Chapter 7

RECOGNIZING LIFE SPAN DEVELOPMENT

Like most other aspects of our clients' lives, their SRBPs will probably metamorphose over time. These days, about half of US adults change their religious affiliation at least once during their lifetime, usually in young adulthood, with most of those becoming unaffiliated with their childhood religion. Still, a full 47% of adults report that they haven't changed their religious faith since childhood (Pew Forum on Religion and Public Life, 2009/2011).

In addition to changing faith or becoming unaffiliated, over time people often experience changes in their religious or spiritual belief systems, level of involvement, internalization of values systems, frequency of attendance at services, and types of religious and spiritual coping. Knowing this will allow you to attend to clients' religious and spiritual development, just as you do their psychological, cognitive, emotional, relational, educational, and professional development.

COMPETENCY 7: Psychologists recognize that spiritual or religious beliefs, practices, and experiences develop and change over the life span.

The literature on religious affiliation over the life span describes several religious or spiritual shifts clients might experience. One is switching, moving from one denomination to another within a faith. Another is apostasy, meaning dropping out of one's religion never to return. There is conversion, or shifting to a new faith or belief system, and deconversion, meaning dropping out of a previously chosen group. Intensification involves a revitalized commitment to a religion; this may be a religion in which the person was raised or one he chose later in life. In fact, some denominations include procedures designed to induce experiences of intensification, such as being born again. Finally, there is cycling, in which people shift their religious affiliation or involvement repeatedly, dropping out of a religion and returning later, or periodically falling out of faith (Sandage & Moe, 2013; Sherkat, 2014).

Early definitions of "conversion" focused on highly emotional "lightning bolt" experiences, where people dramatically changed their religious beliefs (like the archetypal story of Paul on the road to Damascus). Perhaps more relevant in today's world is a conversion paradigm based on a more gradual process. Lewis Rambo (1993), professor of psychology and religion at San Francisco Theological Seminary, offers a seven-stage model of religious conversion (pp. 7–18, 165–170). It's a useful model for understanding the stages people may have gone through, or may go through, as their SRBPs change over their life span.

1. Context. The context refers to what brought a person to his current situation. It includes upbringing, educational background, work, social network, previous religious training and experience, mental health, social skills, and core values, along with current cultural trends. The challenge of this stage is moving beyond one's history toward a new, chosen life in a meaningful, healthy, nondestructive way (1993, pp. 20–22, 164–165).

2. Crisis. A crisis may occur that destabilizes a person's religious identity, such as a trauma, a sudden and painful discovery, illness, or the loss of a loved one. Sometimes mere dissatisfaction can lead to a hunger for something more or different and set off a quieter kind of religious crisis. The challenge of this stage is to move through the crisis using some aspect of it for growth, rather than stagnating in the crisis (1993, pp. 44–48).

3. Quest. As a result of this crisis, people may engage in a quest in which they search for helpful alternative approaches, whether within or beyond their original faith tradition. They may use any number of methods: reading from a wide array of sources, watching broadcast media, visiting houses of worship, talking with friends affiliated with different religions, or searching for alternative forms of spirituality. The challenge of this stage is to bridge from anger to hope. Healthy reaffiliation requires moving toward something good, not just moving away from something bad (1993, pp. 56, 63–64).

4. Encounter. At this point, a person might experience an encounter. This usually involves coming into contact with someone who exemplifies a healthy, active, devout stance in a chosen path. If she perceives this person as truly spiritual—honest, kind, wise, and grounded—she may choose to explore the same path. This person may answer her questions, loan her reading material, take her to services, or introduce her to a clergy member who can provide more information (1993, pp. 87, 167).

5. Interaction. People may engage in interactions with a new religious community that seems to suit them better. They may spend some time in a new religious or spiritual context as a guest or a participant observer, attending public services or rituals, learning the customs, and getting to know the community (1993, p. 102).

6. Commitment. Having explored the possibilities, people may then choose to make a commitment to a new path and formally, usually ritually, join the new faith community. In doing so, they take on all the ritual and moral obligations of membership (1993, p. 125).

7. Consequences. People participate fully in the new faith community while continuing to learn more about its ways. Their hopes may or may not be fulfilled. Some people cycle through the previous stages of this model several times before they find a religion that truly meets their needs (1993, p. 143).

Conversion to a new faith or denomination can take place at any age but more frequently occurs when people are in their teens or early twenties. If a client is in the midst of a change in her SRBPs you might inquire further about her experience. You might also recommend that she read about other people's changes in religious or spiritual beliefs to normalize her experience (Kahn & Greene, 2004; Rambo, 1993; Rambo & Farhadian, 1999).

Development of Faith

Various psychological models of how faith unfolds across the life span may be useful to you in understanding clients' spiritual and religious development. For example, several decades ago Fowler (1981) outlined six phases of religious or spiritual maturation across the life span. He suggests that from birth to two years of age, children have a "primal" or "undifferentiated" relationship to the divine (pp. 119–122), which precedes the first stage. Then in the "intuitive-projective" stage, they learn about religion mostly through stories, images, and relationships (pp. 117–134). During school age, in the "mythical-literal" stage, children tend to have literal interpretations of deities and symbols and be focused on justice and reciprocity (pp. 135–150).

Fowler posits that in the teen years, during the "synthetic-conventional" stage, many people conform to religious authority until they reach the "individuation-reflective" stage, in which they may experience some angst (pp. 151–174). In this stage, there can be a greater openness to gray areas, awareness of inconsistencies, and complexity of faith (pp. 174–183). In midlife, in the "conjunctive" stage, people have an increased capacity to acknowledge paradox and tolerate complexity (pp. 184–199). Finally, in later life, people may move to a "universalizing" faith that transcends any particular affiliation or tradition (pp. 199–210).

Just as in other psychological models, this one does not assume that all people reach the final stage, or that the stages always happen in exactly this order. In addition, the model, which was developed before the recent increases in nonaffiliation among the general public, is probably more relevant to those who hold a continuing faith throughout their life span.

Yet even with these considerations, it's a useful model, offering an essential reminder to pay attention not only to clients' SRBPs right now, but also to where they are in their spiritual and religious development over time. If a client is in a stage in which he's being highly literal regarding his religious or spiritual beliefs, you may find that this interacts with his mental and emotional well-being in ways that are different from the effects experienced by a client who's questioning or struggling with his beliefs. There isn't enough research on this topic to date to be able to say how different stages affect psychological well-being, but as a clinician, knowing whether your client is in a phase of rigid belief, questioning, or contentment with his SRBPs may help you better understand him.

A Contemporary Model of Spiritual Transformation

More recently, Cassandra and her colleagues (Schlitz et al., 2008; Vieten, Amorok, & Schlitz, 2005; Vieten, Schlitz, & Amorok, 2009) conducted research on how people transform spiritually over the life span across a variety of different Western, Eastern, and indigenous religions and spiritual traditions (Christianity, Judaism, Hinduism, Buddhism, Native American religions, paganism, and so on), as well as other, less well-known spiritual paths (Religious Science, Unitarianism, nondual meditation, neo-shamanism, aikido, Course in Miracles, and so on). For over a decade, they engaged in a series of studies that included analysis of individual narratives of personal transformations; focus groups with teachers of transformative processes; in-depth interviews with sixty representatives of ancient and modern wisdom traditions; surveys of over two thousand people who had experienced spiritual transformations; and longitudinal studies of people engaged in transformative practices. They found that while there is an enormous amount of variability in individuals and traditions, there appear some common milestones along the path, as documented in the following figure.

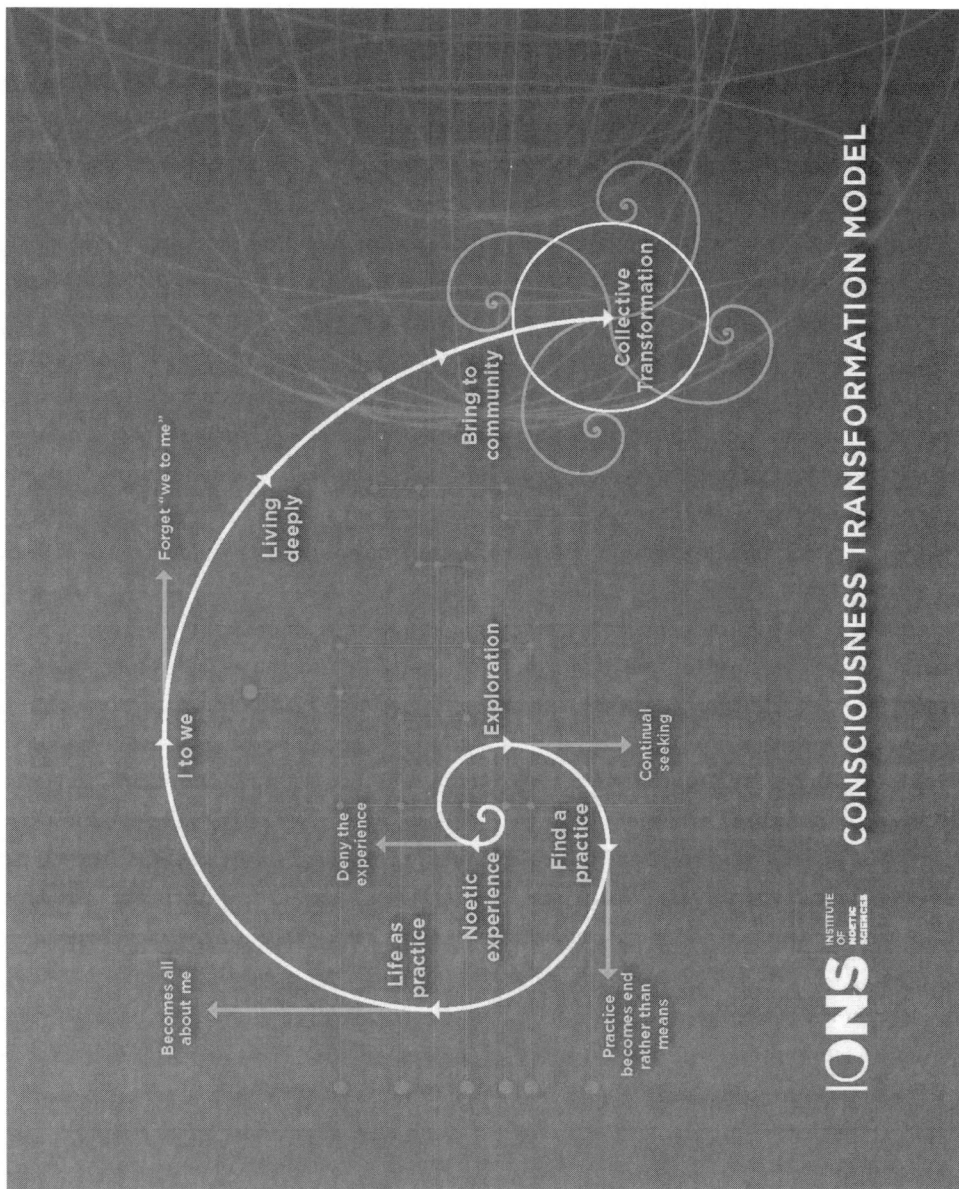

The Institute of Noetic Sciences Consciousness Transformation Model (© 2011) by Cassandra Vieten, Tina Amorok, and Marilyn Schlitz. Used with permission from the copyright holder.

The center of the spiral (not labeled) encompasses changes in clients' spirituality that may have begun long before they were aware that change was occurring. Genetics, environment, peak experiences, numinous or mystical moments, life transitions—all of these lay the groundwork for what is to come. Even when clients can point to a pivotal moment in their spiritual journey, they can also identify, in retrospect, a combination of factors that set the stage.

The noetic experience. Then, there can be a specific episode, period of life, or series of experiences that culminate in an aha! moment. Whether an encounter characterized by awe and beauty or one of deep pain or loss, this experience arrives with insights that can challenge people's previous assumptions, leading them to change the way they see the world. Attempts to fit the new experiences or realizations into their old perspective may fail, often inspiring (or compelling) people to seek a new way of understanding the world to help them integrate their new insights.

Exploration. At this point, some people turn to religion or develop newfound interest in their religion, others convert to a different religion, and yet others reject religion altogether. Some may move toward spiritual or philosophical inquiry, find a teacher who's familiar with this kind of experience, or join a community of like-minded people with whom it's safe to talk about their noetic experience. Some get obsessed with continually chasing after new epiphanies. Driven by a desire to repeat the original experience, they can get caught up in always looking yet seldom finding.

Finding a practice. Through this seeking, people are often led to discover a set of beliefs and practices that help them integrate new insights as their transformative path unfolds. These practices can take many forms, such as prayer, rituals, attending services, meditation, or martial arts. In general, transformative practices involve four essential elements: attention toward greater self-awareness; intention toward personal growth and benefit for the community; repetition of new behaviors; and guidance from trusted others who are experienced in the practice.

Life as practice. At this point in the journey, people often become increasingly involved in their practices and, over time, face the challenge of finding ways to integrate these practices into everyday life. During this period, people are often tempted to isolate their practice from the rest of their life, but doing so can inadvertently stall the process of spiritual growth by not allowing new patterns of thinking and behavior to suffuse each moment of each day. Eventually, people typically do find ways to integrate their spiritual and religious beliefs and practices into their everyday lives, including in the ways they cope with stress, how they make decisions, their attitude toward life in general, and how they treat others.

"I" to "we." The next common challenge is that even when these practices are integrated into everyday life, the process can remain a somewhat narcissistic quest—all about oneself or about achieving some outcome for personal benefit. Given our goal-oriented culture, this is completely natural, but for true spiritual growth and development, it appears that the process must move from "I" to "we." Generally, as people's practices infuse their lives, they increasingly cannot help but wish for and actively work toward the transformation of their community. Altruism and compassion born of shared destiny rather than duty or obligation often emerge here (Vieten, Amorok, & Schlitz, 2006). At the same time, people can become so immersed in a sense of oneness and shared responsibility that they lose sight of the complementary movement from "we" to "me." The results of this can range from a cult mentality to becoming so fatigued by helping others that one forgets to care for oneself. Equally important as serving the community is discovering how best to channel one's own unique combination of talents, resources, experiences, and skills in ways that serve one's own well-being.

Living deeply. Once the tensions between self-actualization and self-transcendence, formal and informal practice, and receiving and giving begin to resolve, people report increased equanimity in the face of life's challenges. They experience an almost daily sense of wonder and meaning in which even the most mundane aspects of life become sacred in their own way.

Service to community. Finally, once people have seamlessly integrated spirituality and/or religion into their lives, they often feel inspired to orient their lives toward enhancing quality of life for others or assisting others in advancing their spiritual development. They report a strong and embodied sense of kindness and compassion that serves as their moral compass. The more people this happens to, the more there is a collective transformation—in organizations, communities, and society.

Attending to Religious and Spiritual Development in Therapy

The "stage" types of models exemplified above, addressing religious conversion, development of faith, and spiritual transformation over the life span, may be useful overall maps to hold in your awareness when considering clients' religious or spiritual development. Even if a client has no SRBPs, it's likely that at some point in her life, she encountered religion or spirituality in ways that had some influence on her current worldview. It's helpful to know whether someone is in a seeking phase, has a very concrete and inflexible view of her religion or spirituality, is in the process of integrating her SRBPs into her everyday life, and so on.

An important distinction to make here is that changes in SRBPs over a person's lifetime may not be the same as psychological growth. For example, some people may find profound contentment and a sense of meaning and purpose in religious or spiritual development while still facing unresolved psychological symptoms, such as anxiety, depression, or addiction. Conversely, people may experience psychological development over time with relatively little spiritual or religious growth. Although it isn't your job to become a spiritual guide, you can attend to clients' religious and spiritual processes as a part of their overall psychological development. Until now, most mental health professionals haven't been trained to routinely ask about these aspects of clients' lives. So you may wonder why it might be important to include assessment of religious and spiritual development in both initial and ongoing assessments of your clients.

First, just as you might track growth in clients' cognitive processing, emotional reactivity, capacity for healthy relationships, professional development, and so on, it makes sense to stay cognizant of where clients stand on issues related to religion and spirituality. For many people, current and past religious and spiritual experiences are key to how they view themselves, make meaning of events in their lives, deal with illness and death, make moral decisions, and deal with their own failings. For example, someone who was raised in or now engages in a form of religion that promotes the idea of a compassionate and forgiving God may be more likely to view his own mistakes as learning opportunities, whereas someone who was exposed to a punishing God might experience more guilt and shame about his shortcomings.

Second, being aware of clients' changing levels of involvement in religious or spiritual communities over time will give you a sense of what resources are available to them outside the therapy room in terms of social support and guidance. For example, a client experiencing depression may benefit from increasing his involvement in a service activity at his church, so this can become part of his treatment plan. As another example, a gay man who's left a conservative church and moved to a new city may feel liberated and more in alignment with his true identity but have much less social support than he had access to before. So you may need to help him set up new social structures to support his psychological well-being.

Ways to Cultivate This Competency

In chapter 12 we'll provide you with tools to inquire about clients' SRBPs as a standard part of taking a history. As you do this, pay special attention to ways clients have changed in their religion or spirituality over time. For example, a client may mention changes in her SRBPs, such as being raised as a Catholic but no longer practicing, converting to a new religion when she got married, or taking up meditation with a local group. You might consider taking a moment to reflect the change back to her with a gentle probe: "So, you said you are no longer a practicing Catholic. Do you have any form of religious or spiritual involvement at this time?" or "What year did you start meditating? How has that influenced your life?" Brief inquiries along these lines will probably reveal important information about who your client is, what her coping resources are, and how she sees the world. You may be surprised to learn that such changes often represent milestone events for the client.

It also can be useful to ask explicitly, "Is there any way I can be supportive of your religious or spiritual development?" This conveys your care for and attention to this aspect of clients' lives and opens the door for them to ask for help. They might say, for example, "Yes, now that you mention it, I really want to sing in the church choir, but I feel too anxious. Singing with the group is when I feel closest to God, but I'm scared of being up in front of people." Based on what you learn, you can be a positive force in the client's spiritual development, as part of her psychological development over time.

Since SRBPs can change over time, if the topic doesn't come up be sure to check back in with clients every several months about how their involvement in religion or spirituality, if any, is going. You might say, "By the way, how is everything going at church?" or "Has your involvement in your meditation practice changed since last time we talked about it? How has it changed? What have you learned?" You will probably find that clients are pleased to be asked about this aspect of their lives. Questions like these can also uncover useful information about clients' relationship functioning, coping skills, and whether they feel like they're struggling, growing, stagnant, or content overall. And if you sometimes find yourself addressing repetitive content (depressive rumination or complaints about others, for example) in sessions with a given client, such questions can also inspire the client to consider larger, existential issues—or to take a larger view of his life.

Also track whether any changes in your client's involvement in SRBPs are causing problems and address those. Keep in mind that when addressing religious or spiritual issues, it's best to avoid interpretation or evaluations and instead reflect and support positive aspects of their development (for example, "It sounds like you're coming up with ways to incorporate the sacred in your everyday life" or "I'm hearing that prayer really helps you cope when you're feeling down"). You can also sensitively express concern by asking exploratory questions (for example, "You've expressed some dissatisfaction with your experience at the meditation center [church, synagogue, and so on] lately. What's causing you to feel that way?").

Conclusion

For many clients, religious and spiritual development over the life span is just as important as their professional, educational, relational, and socioeconomic development. How clients' SRBPs change over time is worth exploring in therapy and continuing to monitor as therapy progresses. Using sensitive inquiry into changes in SRBPs, you can find out quite a lot about clients.

Ideally, therapy involves supporting increased health and well-being in all aspects of clients' inner world. So in the next chapter, we'll delve more deeply into the relationship between SRBPs and psychological well-being, providing guidance on how you can help clients access both internal and external religious and spiritual resources that, when appropriate, can aid in their treatment.

Chapter 8

Learning About Clients' Spiritual and Religious Resources

A robust body of empirical evidence has demonstrated beneficial relationships between various dimensions of SRBPs and psychological health (for example, Green & Elliott, 2010; Koenig et al., 2012; L. Miller & Kelley, 2005; W. R. Miller & Thoresen, 2003; Oman & Thoresen, 2005; Wong, Rew, & Slaikeu, 2006). To be a competent therapist, you need to know that clients may have SRBPs that can serve as valuable resources for their psychological and emotional well-being, as suggested by the research.

COMPETENCY 8: Psychologists are aware of clients' internal and external spiritual or religious resources and practices that research indicates may support psychological well-being and recovery from psychological disorders.

Longitudinal studies demonstrate a strong correlation between engaging in SRBPs and better mental health (L. Miller, Wickramaratne, Tenke, & Weissman, 2012). In a systematic review of the literature, Bonelli and Koenig (2013) found that 72% of studies reviewed demonstrated a positive relationship between level of religious or spiritual involvement and fewer mental disorders, 19% found mixed results (positive and negative), and 5% reported more mental disorders in those who engaged in SRBPs. Religious involvement was strongly related to better mental health in terms of depression, substance abuse, and suicide, and somewhat related to better outcomes in stress-related disorders and dementia. There was insufficient evidence in relation to bipolar disorder and schizophrenia, and for many other disorders the relationship remained unknown.

Other research shows that SRBPs can provide meaning and support in times of stress (Oman & Thoresen, 2005; Park, 2005), and positive religious coping has been shown to contribute to successful stress management (for example, Ano & Vasconcelles, 2005; Cornah, 2006; Pargament et al., 2005; Pargament, Koenig, Tarakeshwar, & Hahn, 2004).

SRBPs are important in the psychological functioning of most adolescents and adults (Hathaway et al., 2004), contributing to their identity development (Fukuyama & Sevig, 2002; Magaldi-Dopman & Park-Taylor, 2010), worldview (Arredondo et al., 1996; Leong et al., 1995), avoidance of risky scenarios (McNamara et al., 2010), and ability to cope with difficulties (Arredondo et al., 1996).

Spirituality and religion substantially color the way people understand themselves and the world around them, including how they interpret the meaning of events and situations, their values and morals, their behaviors, their stance or orientation toward other people, their feelings of happiness and safety, their capacities for forgiveness and gratitude, their level of social support and engagement, and how they approach illness and death in themselves and others (Emmons & Paloutzian, 2003; Norenzayan, Dar-Nimrod, Hansen, & Proulx, 2009; Park, 2013; Schultz, Tallman, & Altmaier, 2010; Tay, Li, Myers, & Diener, 2014; Vallurupalli et al., 2012).

Over 80% of severely mentally ill patients report using religion to cope (S. A. Rogers et al., 2002; Tepper et al., 2001), and spirituality has long been recognized as a core component of recovery from substance use disorders (Delaney et al., 2009). Spirituality has also been linked to an increased sense of meaning, purpose, resilience, satisfaction, and happiness (Fredrickson, 2002; Fry, 2000; Pargament, 2011; Pargament et al., 2013).

Since this competency is focused on being aware of clients' internal and external spiritual or religious resources and practices that may support psychological well-being and recovery from psychological disorders, as evidenced by research, the keys to developing it are to explore the literature to learn more about how elements of clients' existing SRBPs may serve as resources for them, and to become aware of other resources you might harness to more effectively treat a given client.

Exploring the Literature

Developing the eighth competency begins with knowing that there are research-supported relationships between SRBPs and psychological health, as highlighted above. For the most part, SRBPs are associated with better mental and emotional health, though some SRBPs have been linked to negative psychological outcomes (the topic of chapter 9).

In addition to the studies we reviewed above, several excellent resources exist for learning more about the relationship between SRBPs and psychological well-being. Koenig, King, and Carson's *Handbook of Religion and Health* (2012) is a great place to start. The American Psychological Association's journals *Psychology of Religion and Spirituality* and *Spirituality in Clinical Practice* are also good sources, filled with the latest research in this arena. Kenneth Pargament's 1997 book *The Psychology of*

Religion and Coping: Theory, Research, and Practice and his latest book, *Spiritually Integrated Psychotherapy: Understanding and Addressing the Sacred* (2007), are also excellent resources. The Duke University Center for Spirituality, Theology, and Health (http://www.spiritualityandhealth.duke.edu) is focused on conducting research, training others to conduct research, and promoting scholarly activities to expand understanding of the relationship between spirituality/religion and health. In addition, you can use PsychINFO, Medline Plus, and Google Scholar to search for specific topics, like "prayer and depression" or "religiosity and obsessive-compulsive disorder." Please see chapter 15 for more suggestions on how to keep up with the research literature.

Inner and Outer Resources

Clearly, SRBPs in general can be helpful in supporting psychological well-being. But what specific aspects of SRBPs can be helpful to clients? What resources provided by SRBPs are linked to psychological well-being?

When considering how religion or spirituality might be helpful to your clients and support their treatment and recovery, be aware that SRBPs can offer both outer and inner resources to support psychological health. For example, in analyzing results of a large population-based survey, the relationship between church attendance and lower depression was mediated through church-based social support, an outer resource (Nooney & Woodrum, 2002). In the same study, the effects of prayer on depression were mediated through religious coping (an inner resource).

On this note, some people are thought to have a more extrinsic religious orientation, whereas others have a more intrinsic orientation (Allport & Ross, 1967; Whitley & Kite, 2010). Those who have an extrinsic religious orientation tend to use religion in a utilitarian manner: to provide security and safety, social interactions, status and identity, and, at times, distraction. Those with an intrinsic religious orientation, on the other hand, have internalized the teachings of their religion. They truly believe in the tenets of their faith, religion is very important in their lives, and they use it as an active directing force (Batson & Ventis, 1982).

A third orientation has been dubbed the "quest orientation." For people with a quest orientation, religion is a search for truth rather than a doctrine (extrinsic) or guiding principles (intrinsic). They see religion or spirituality as a set of important questions and believe that through deep inquiry into these questions people find humility, love, compassion, and higher meaning in life (Batson & Ventis, 1982; Whitley & Kite, 2010).

For clinicians, it can be helpful to know how clients use religion or spirituality in their lives. Those who have an extrinsic orientation may primarily use external resources, and those with an intrinsic orientation may primarily turn to internal resources. However, in most cases, people use a blend of the two.

External Resources

External resources that might be offered by clients' SRBPs include social support, such as shared meals, engaging in positive activities with others, or opportunities to be of service to others. Clients may also be able to access services through their congregation or spiritual community, such as counseling, spiritual guidance, or inclusion in a prayer or healing circle. The schedule of activities provided by clients' SRBPs may provide a source of structure and motivation to get out of the house and into a more positive environment than the one they may find themselves in. Even activities such as church-sponsored bingo or quilting, while perhaps not immediately psychologically relevant, can be valuable antidotes to loneliness and rumination. In some cases, clients' religious or spiritual community may provide more functional support as well, such as meals, clothing, or housing.

Internal Resources

One primary way that people use religion or spirituality as an inner resource is for coping with difficulties in their lives. Internal resources include such things as the use of prayer or meditation to seek guidance for making decisions, or cultivating a sense of closeness with God that reduces loneliness. And religious coping is a method of dealing with stress or difficult situations. Imagine two people, each of whom gets a flat tire on the way to an important job interview. One experiences a great deal of anger and distress and views the situation as just more proof that he has bad luck and life is working against him. He changes the tire in a rage and then, feeling defeated, decides to scrap the interview and go to a bar for a drink. The other uses positive religious coping, taking a moment to pray and bolster his internal fortitude by sensing a connection with a benevolent God who is there to help, and then changes the tire and makes it to the job interview, albeit fifteen minutes late.

Positive and Negative Religious Coping

Positive forms of religious coping include working collaboratively with God to solve a problem, seeking God's love and care, seeking spiritual support from others, or reappraising a situation in a benevolent way. Negative forms of religious coping include such things as spiritual discontentment; feeling angry with God or questioning God's existence, benevolence, or power (after having believed strongly in it); or appraising difficult situations as a manifestation of having been abandoned or punished by God.

Imagine a religious or spiritual client with a terminally ill loved one. Positive religious coping would entail seeking support from prayer, meditation, clergy, or a spiritual community—relying on religious or spiritual beliefs as a source of strength and support. Negative religious coping, on the other hand, would include thoughts of the illness being a punishment from God, taking the illness as proof that God doesn't care or doesn't exist, or feeling abandoned by or angry at God or the spiritual community. Such responses can be understandable, but when repeated in many situations over time, they may reinforce a worldview that's distressing rather than helpful to the individual (Pargament et al., 2004; Pargament & Saunders, 2007).

Many studies have shown that using positive religious coping predicts psychological well-being more strongly than other measures of religious beliefs and practices (e.g., Loewenthal, MacLeod, Goldblatt, Lubitsh, & Valentine, 2000; Nooney & Woodrum, 2002; Roesch & Ano, 2003). As you might imagine, positive religious coping is associated with better mental health outcomes, whereas negative religious coping is associated with worse psychological health.

Though the relationship between religious attendance and well-being was once thought to be primarily explained by social support and other external elements of spirituality and religion, there is some evidence that the internal aspects of SRBPs may be more important than the external aspects. For example, Cruz and colleagues (2009) examined depression and hopelessness in older adults as a function of their public and private religious involvement. By "public," they meant church attendance, and by "private," they implied prayer and the strength of a person's spiritual beliefs. Interestingly, they found that the frequency of prayer and meditation, but not church attendance, predicted lower hopelessness and depression severity scores in older adults being treated for depression. That is, prayer and meditation helped, while the social dimension of church attendance—repeatedly cited in studies as potentially responsible for people's sense of connection, leading to less of a sense of isolation and therefore depression—wasn't as important a factor.

Similarly, a unique longitudinal study (L. Miller, Wickramaratne, Gameroff, et al., 2012) examined children of depressed and nondepressed parents, assessing them over ten to twenty years. Those who reported that religion or spirituality was highly important to them at the ten-year time point had only one-fourth the risk of experiencing major depression between years ten and twenty than other participants. In fact, those who were at highest risk because of having a depressed parent but who also reported that religion and spirituality were highly important to them had only one-tenth the risk of major depression between years ten and twenty. Interestingly, religious attendance and denomination were unrelated to the outcome: the self-reported importance of spirituality and religion in their lives was the key protective factor. So while external resources such as social support and positive activities are linked to psychological health and well-being, be sure to pay attention to cultivating your clients' inner resources as well.

Other Spiritual Practices

An ever-growing body of research indicates that various practices drawn from religious and spiritual traditions, such as mindfulness meditation, can improve psychological well-being. Mindfulness involves the cultivation of moment-to-moment, nonjudgmental awareness of one's present-moment experience. The goal of mindfulness is to cultivate an awake and aware way of being—a stance from which people can make choices that are in alignment with both short-term and long-term goals, rather than reacting "mindlessly" or habitually to life's events.

Mindfulness-based stress reduction (MBSR: Kabat-Zinn, 1991) is often taught in the form of an eight- to ten-week, group-based educational program focused on the development of mindfulness. The weekly sessions include teaching mindfulness meditation practices, along with instruction and group discussion on the practical applications of mindful awareness, particularly in terms of managing stressful life events and difficult mental or emotional states. Mindfulness principles and practices have also been incorporated as a central component of two other therapeutic approaches: dialectical behavior therapy and acceptance and commitment therapy.

Studies show that mindfulness training can improve mood, reduce anxiety, increase a sense of control, and reduce symptoms of illness (Astin, 1997; Rosenzweig, Reibel, Greeson, Brainard, & Hojat, 2003; S. L. Shapiro, Schwartz, & Bonner, 1998). It has been shown to decrease stress and fatigue and improve mood, sleep, and overall quality of life in cancer patients, even six months after participating in mindfulness training (Carlson & Garland, 2005; Carlson, Speca, Patel, & Goodey, 2003). In addition, MBSR training has been shown to reduce stress and improve mood among caregivers of chronically ill children (Minor, Carlson, Mackenzie, Zernicke, & Jones, 2006).

Mindfulness has also been combined with cognitive therapy to prevent relapse in depression (Fjorback & Walach, 2012). In a randomized, controlled trial, researchers reported that for patients who'd had three or more previous episodes of depression, participation in mindfulness-based cognitive therapy (MBCT; Segal, Williams, & Teasdale, 2002) reduced the rate of relapse to approximately one-half that of patients receiving standard treatment (Ma & Teasdale, 2004; Teasdale et al., 2000). Other studies have shown that mindfulness-based therapy can be effective in reducing depression in treatment-resistant patients (Kenny & Williams, 2007) and fibromyalgia patients (Sephton et al., 2007). Both theory and empirical research indicate that mindfulness training positively affects the aspects of therapy that account for successful treatment. On the part of the client, this includes improved emotion regulation and response flexibility and decreased reactivity. On the part of the therapist, benefits include increased empathy, compassion, attention, and counseling skills; decreased stress and anxiety; and ethical behavior in clinical practice (D. M. Davis & Hayes, 2011; Germer, Siegel, & Fulton, 2013).

Other forms of meditation interventions seem to be promising as well. For example, passage meditation (Easwaran, 2008), which in part involves repetition of self-chosen passages from scriptures underpinning a variety of the world's religious and spiritual traditions, has shown beneficial effects on a number of psychological health outcomes, including reduced stress, improved mental health, and greater capacity for forgiveness (Oman, Hedberg, & Thoresen, 2006; Oman, Shapiro, Thoresen, Plante, & Flinders, 2008). You can also find links to many published articles on the benefits of Transcendental Meditation (TM) at http://www.tm.org/research-on-meditation.

A complete review of meditative practices is beyond the scope of this chapter, but in general, meditation training appears to have positive effects on psychological well-being in both youth (Black, Milam, & Sussman, 2009) and adults (Sedlmeier et al., 2012). It is well worth exploring how these and other complementary approaches drawn from religious and spiritual traditions might enhance the efficacy of your treatments.

Conclusion

To be competent as a therapist, you must be aware of religious and spiritual resources that may support clients' psychological well-being. These resources can be ones clients already have or have had access to in the past, such as being a member of a congregation, having a meditation practice, or using prayer as a coping mechanism. They could also be new to your client, and perhaps new to you, such as learning a new form of meditation, taking a class being offered at the synagogue or mosque, or participating in a form of shamanic journeying or energy healing with a practitioner.

These resources may be external, such as social support from one's spiritual community, opportunities to participate in activities, or symbolic practices such as using a rosary, lighting a candle, or observing the Sabbath. They may also be internal, such as contemplative prayer or meditation to deal with anxiety or depression, repeating passages from spiritual texts to oneself internally, or drawing upon an inner sense of being part of a larger whole.

During intake and assessment, it is always worthwhile to inquire about clients' existing spiritual or religious resources, if any, or ones they may be interested in accessing. At times, it may be appropriate to suggest a new spiritual or religious resource to a client, especially those that have empirical support. However, be careful not to act as a spiritual or religious guide for clients unless you're trained to do so and a given client is explicitly seeking spiritually oriented therapy.

In addition to being aware of positive spiritual and religious resources available to clients to aid in their psychological well-being, you must also be on the alert for religious or spiritual problems that may arise. The next chapter shifts the focus from the positive to potentially negative aspects of spirituality and religion for clients.

Chapter 9

RECOGNIZING HARMFUL
INVOLVEMENT

As reviewed in the introduction to this book and chapter 8, most of the research literature indicates that, in general, SRBPs appear to be linked to improved psychological well-being. However, there are forms of SRBPs that can be maladaptive or harmful for clients—emotionally, psychologically, and even physically. This chapter is dedicated to helping you recognize when this may be the case.

COMPETENCY 9: Psychologists can identify spiritual and religious experiences, practices, and beliefs that may have the potential to negatively impact psychological health.

Throughout this book we've encouraged you to be open-minded regarding clients' SRBPs, even if they're unfamiliar to you. If they are unfamiliar to you, we've recommended that you learn more about them. In chapter 1, however, we cautioned against going overboard in efforts to be respectful and appreciative of clients' SRBPs. If, in the course of your exploration, you learn that a client's SRBPs may pose a risk to his health or well-being, you may need to intervene. When a client engages in *any* activity that causes or exacerbates mental, emotional, or physical symptoms, it's appropriate to inquire further and potentially take action, and this applies equally to SRBPs.

In this chapter, we'll discuss some of the more common types of harmful SRBPs you may encounter when taking a religious and spiritual history or in the course of treatment with clients, including:

- Negative religious coping

- Religious scrupulosity

- Overinvolvement with SRBPs

- Belonging to a cult or cultlike group

- Unresolved religious and spiritual struggles

- Difficulty integrating spiritual or religious experiences

Negative Religious Coping

While positive religious and spiritual coping can be very useful for people, there are forms of religious coping that appear to be unhelpful (Pargament, Koenig, & Perez, 2000), as alluded to in chapter 8. Rather than using religion and spirituality to reframe situations in a positive way, people sometimes use negative religious coping instead. For instance, they may use the concept of a punishing God to understand their situation (such as seeing a child's illness as a punishment from God). Or they may abandon their faith due to an unexpected traumatic event, such as a divorce or loss of a job. It may seem odd to refer to this as coping, but for those who engage in this, there seems to be a paradoxical relief in feeling punished for their sins or being angry at God for abandoning them, rather than facing the reality of the traumatic issue at hand. Often, people are taught negative religious coping via their family of origin or their perceptions of the teachings of their religion (whether accurate or not). In adults, greater endorsement of negative religious coping has been associated with higher symptoms of PTSD after a trauma (Feder et al., 2013), greater frequency and intensity of suicidal ideation, depression, and anxiety in psychotic patients (Rosmarin, Bigda-Peyton, Ongur, Pargament, & Bjorgvinsson, 2013), and poorer mental health outcomes in general (Weber & Pargament, 2014).

When you encounter negative religious coping in clients, it may serve you to read the literature on this phenomenon more closely and to gently examine clients' use of those coping methods. You might ask a client whether those thoughts are helpful for her in dealing with stress or difficult situations, or if they actually make her feel worse. It may be that negative religious coping springs from deeply ingrained world-views about God and religion; it may also be inherited or the result of habitual ways of thinking—outdated schemas from childhood, for example. Helping clients shift from negative to positive religious coping, or from negative religious coping to other forms of coping, could be helpful for their psychological well-being.

Religious Scrupulosity

Scrupulosity, which is a feature of certain kinds of obsessive-compulsive disorder (OCD), involves obsessive religious doubts and fears, unwanted thoughts and images perceived as blasphemous, and compulsive religious rituals, reassurance seeking, and avoidance (Abramowitz & Jacoby, 2014). In these cases, fears of punishment from God or fears of having committed a sin dominate the obsessions and drive the compulsive behaviors (Abramowitz, Huppert, Cohen, Tolin, & Shawn, 2002; Greenberg & Huppert, 2010). Some have suggested that scrupulosity is a disorder separate from OCD, and that it's "characterized by pathological guilt or obsession associated with moral or religious issues that is often accompanied by compulsive moral or religious observance" (C. H. Miller & Hedges, 2008, p. 1042).

It is important to note that some scholars think that religiosity itself influences this form of OCD (Himle, Chatters, Taylor, & Nguyen, 2011), while others believe that scrupulosity isn't caused by religion but is a symptom of OCD that assumes a religious form (Greenberg, 2013). Often clients with scrupulosity have symptoms that express themselves in nonreligious obsessions and compulsions as well.

However such symptoms arise, they can cause a great deal of suffering and have a substantial negative impact on functioning. Current treatments are similar to those for other forms of OCD, including medication and cognitive behavioral therapies such as exposure and response prevention. If you encounter the scrupulosity form of OCD in a client, you'll benefit from the growing body of research literature on the topic, and you may also find it useful to consult with an expert in this arena.

Overinvolvement with SRBPs

While SRBPs are generally linked to better psychological health, too much of any one practice can be maladaptive. One client with whom Shelley worked—Alice, from chapter 6—had meditated daily for half an hour for many years. While going through a stressful time, however, Alice increased her sitting time to four to five hours a day, apparently in an attempt to deal with her stress and achieve a breakthrough. After only a few weeks, she developed mild symptoms of psychosis. Psychotropic medications helped return her to a balanced state. While it's unlikely that the meditation alone instigated her breakdown, the increased time she spent alone may have been counterproductive, even though it was in service of spiritual growth. After another year of therapy, responsibly taking her medications, downshifting her work schedule, and resting more, Alice was able to return to meditating—in a group setting for twenty to thirty minutes at a time with a teacher present—and benefit from it.

One sign of overinvolvement with spiritual or religious practices is when clients perform them with a compulsive quality. Listen for words that indicate a lack of conscious choice, such as "I feel like I have to pray more" or "I can't help it." This may indicate that a client's SRBPs have become obsessional, rather than supportive and adaptive.

In itself, spending a lot of time engaged in religious or spiritual practices isn't maladaptive, particularly if someone makes religious or spiritual work their profession or avocation. But if time spent in SRBPs appears to interfere with functioning, causing disruption of relationships, avoidance of important responsibilities, too much isolation, increased symptoms, or physical pain or harm, these are all signs that while perhaps well-intentioned, the intensity of involvement isn't adaptive. You may need to work with a clergy member, spiritual advisor, or teacher in the client's spiritual tradition (if a formal tradition exists) to help guide the client to a more balanced quantity and frequency of spiritual engagement.

Belonging to a Cult or Cultlike Group

Another form of SRBP that can be risky to clients' psychological well-being is becoming involved with a cult or a religious or spiritual group with cultlike characteristics. According to Galanter (2013), a charismatic group or new religious movement can be "characterized by intense cohesiveness with an ideological commitment associated with a view of transcendence… Cults, on the other hand, can be considered a subgroup of this latter phenomenon, defined by the common culture as alien and deviant on the basis of values within that culture" (p. 729).

One defining feature of a cult is that members hold a shared belief system that can go so far as to deny reality in order to sustain the social cohesiveness of the group—often to the point that a distorted consensus emerges (Galanter, 2013). In essence, reality becomes less important to members than maintaining their ties to the group. The group works to preserve cohesiveness and interdependency and to maintain stability in the face of internal or external threat (Galanter & Forest, 2006). Cult members often regard those who aren't members negatively and may respond with a characteristic blank stare when encountering them. Members are strongly influenced by the group's behavioral norms and feel compelled to conform to them (Galanter & Forest, 2006). The group might employ manipulative techniques like powerful group pressure, special methods to increase suggestibility and obedience, managing information, and suspension of individuality or critical judgment (Langone, 2005). This can be problematic, as the following story illustrates.

Shelley once worked with Janet, a client who had been a member of a cult for nearly ten years when she was in her late teens and early twenties. Although Janet never told Shelley the name of the group, she did share that she'd contributed most of her inheritance to them. Even so, as she lived with the group for nearly a decade, she had to build her own living space and perform menial labor to earn her keep. Janet was isolated from most of the other members of the group, and she eventually admitted to engaging in sex with the married leader, which made her unpopular with other women in the group. Paradoxically, as Janet increasingly gave up her personal rights, she gained more acceptance from the group. Janet told Shelley that living with this group was extremely challenging, but she believed that learning the teachings of the group's "spiritual" tradition was worth the price.

Why would someone join such a group? According to Galanter (2013), risk factors include social isolation, a high level of life dissatisfaction, lack of self-confidence, lack of assertiveness, gullibility, the desire to belong to a group, low tolerance for ambiguity, cultural disillusionment, frustrated spiritual seeking, susceptibility to trancelike states, and naive idealism. There can also be positive elements to the attraction to a cult, such as a desire to be of service, a spiritual passion, a wish for self-improvement, and a trusting, generous nature. As in other abusive relationships, those leading cults are often highly skilled in twisting those positive impulses into dependency and self-doubt.

In this age of social alienation, cults can provide a way to satisfy people's evolutionary longing to be part of a cohesive in-group (Wenegrat, 1989). The social system of a cult is designed to reward members who accept the group norms and to instill fear or a sense of threat among those who consider leaving—sometimes doing so implicitly, and sometimes quite explicitly. Like operant conditioning, this can serve as a very strong reinforcer of behavior. Over time, coercion is no longer necessary to enforce even highly ego-dystonic behaviors. In a sense, members feel they have no choice but to unconsciously make peace with the group's agenda and yield to its expectations in order to achieve emotional relief (Galanter & Forest, 2006).

Keep in mind that even people with few or no risk factors or past psychiatric issues can fall prey to a cult. Then, with time, conforming to the group and fulfilling its demands can cause considerable guilt and lead to psychiatric disorders and eventually post-traumatic stress symptoms (Aronoff, Lynn, & Malinoski, 2000).

In Janet's case, when she took on this group's identity, she behaved in ways that would have been unthinkable before she joined the group. This is not uncommon. It took a lot of courage for Janet to leave the group. Shelley and Janet worked together for well over a year to deal with her symptoms of post-traumatic stress and feelings of embarrassment, guilt, and shame associated with that experience. In time, Janet was able to forgive herself and understand how she could have allowed herself to be treated in such a way. Eventually, she developed a new sense of self-confidence and wisdom that allowed her to marry and have children. Janet was even able to retain some of the positive teachings from her decade of experiences with the group and felt these elements were worthwhile to bring with her into her new future.

According to Galanter (2013), when a therapist is working with someone who is leaving or has left a cult or a charismatic group, the following clinical issues should be considered:

- These clients should not be directly confronted in a negative way.

- A nonjudgmental exploration of the client's views may help the clinician understand how and why that client became involved in the group.

- Cult members typically aren't pathologically disturbed, even though some of their ideas may be highly deviant or even delusional.

- Some groups of a spiritual nature that have highly stylized rituals, tightly knit communities, and activities that are unfamiliar may seem like cults but in fact not be cults.

That final point is important. There is now unprecedented diversity in the forms of SRBPs, and clients may have SRBPs that are quite unfamiliar to you. Just because a practice is rare or unfamiliar doesn't make it harmful or cultlike. Groups that aren't cults engage in ritualized use of substances, fasting, sweat lodges, asceticism, or other activities that may seem extreme. The key to determining whether involvement in these activities is harmful is not so much the content of the practice but how it is impacting a client's psyche and life. To differentiate cults from other spiritual or religious groups, look for these signs:

- The group has a charismatic leader who is controlling and is considered unimpeachable—and sometimes even divine or omnipotent.

- The group requires excessive devotion or dedication to a person or idea.

- The group requires its members to recruit others.

- The group engages in manipulative exploitation of its members through methods such as actively isolating its members from family and friends.

- The group requires large financial contributions or takes control of members' financial decisions.

- Members are closely monitored by other members of the group and are reported and sometimes punished for stepping out of line.

- Individual autonomy is suppressed, and asking questions is discouraged or seen as disloyal.

- Members are threatened psychologically or physically (either implicitly or explicitly) if they leave or consider leaving, and in some rare instances, they and their family members are followed and harassed.

- Often, groups that function as cults discourage members from seeking or continuing in therapy.

If you suspect that a client may be a member of a cult or was in the past, you might consider obtaining supervision or consultation with a clinician who specializes in this area (Langone, 2005). You might also consider having the client do individual or group work with an expert as an adjunct to therapy. This is a unique set of circumstances that may require proficiency in this domain.

Unresolved Religious and Spiritual Struggles

According to Pargament and Saunders (2007), "spiritual struggles" can be defined as tension and conflict over matters of the sacred and can occur in three primary domains:

- A divine struggle, such as feeling angry with God

- An intrapersonal struggle, such as being unable to forgive oneself for a transgression

- An interpersonal struggle, such as feeling betrayed by a leader or member of one's religious or spiritual group

Divine Struggle

A divine struggle is one in which an individual feels a sense of conflict with or betrayal by God or another important divine figure, such as Jesus or Allah. The quintessential divine struggle is Jesus on the cross asking, "God, why hast though forsaken me?" or Gautama sitting under the Bodhi Tree being tempted by Maya before awakening to become Buddha. While addressing such a struggle may seem out of the scope of practice for a mental health professional, these struggles can cause a great deal of psychological and emotional suffering and can be acknowledged with empathy and compassion in therapy.

Take, for example, a religious client who loses a child or sibling to cancer. You may feel equipped to deal with the psychological effects of grief, but in addition to grief and sadness this client may be overwhelmed by feeling angry at and betrayed by God. In a way, such clients are processing both the loss of their loved one and the loss of an important divine figure they previously relied on as a part of their life schema to feel safe and cared for, and to cope.

What is your role as a mental health professional in this kind of situation? For one thing, you can help by witnessing and processing the grief surrounding loss of a loved one while also explicitly addressing loss of the previous belief system or divine figure. You can do this by including the divine struggle in the conversation, just as you address the loneliness and sadness associated with losing a loved one. Rather than ignoring or excluding the spiritual struggle, note it as it arises by reflecting the client's experience and gently inquiring to learn more about it. Ideally, over time you can help the client contain his grief and diminish the associated suffering. This may be an instance when you choose to collaborate with a clergy member or spiritual leader. Some clients may leave religion due to this kind of crisis of faith, whereas others may reach a more mature and nuanced understanding of the role of God or religion in their lives.

It's important to tread lightly here, no matter what your own belief system is. If you're an atheist, internally you may support a client's movement away from religion, yet for that client, reconciling with God and his religion may be the best pathway forward psychologically. Alternatively, if you're a devout believer in God or follower of your religion or spirituality, you might implicitly encourage going further into a tradition when what the client actually wants and needs is to move away from his reliance on religious beliefs and God. Allow for the autonomy of the client and his process, bearing in mind that if you are to be effective, the therapeutic atmosphere should be noncoercive and value clients' desires (Richards & Bergin, 2005). What has worked for you personally may not work for others; we all need to navigate these issues in our own way.

Intrapersonal Struggle

In a similar way, a religious or spiritual intrapersonal struggle can involve a crisis of faith or doubting of one's SRBPs. The classic example would be the "dark night of the soul" as experienced by Saint John of the Cross or, more recently, the spiritual struggles of Mother Teresa (2009), as reflected in a letter she wrote: "I am told God loves me—and yet the reality of darkness and coldness and emptiness is so great that nothing touches my soul... Did I make [a] mistake in surrendering blindly to the call of the Sacred Heart?" (p. 187). When clients experience these intense periods of doubt or struggle, you can be just as present and empathic as you would be for any other extremely difficult moment in their lives, such as divorce, loss of a job, death of a loved one, or a severe medical illness.

On a more mundane level, many clients may struggle with incorporating religion or spirituality into their lives. They may hold the intention to pray, meditate, or practice yoga every day or to uphold spiritual values, such as honesty or compassion, but fall short of their intentions. This can lead to depression and even despair. Again, your role as a mental health professional is not to exclude such issues from the clinical encounter, but to include them as an integral part of whatever your client is working with, just as you'd address intrapersonal struggles around career or life path or client doubts about choices made in other arenas of life. Here, you might find it particularly useful to collaborate with clergy from the client's church or the client's spiritual advisor (if there is one), or to consult with a spiritually oriented therapist who may be able to shed light on how to help your client resolve or hold and cope with these inner struggles.

Interpersonal Struggle

Finally, being part of a spiritual or religious community can lead to interpersonal struggles. Just as in any social group, there can be gossip, judgment, or hypocrisy on the part of leaders or other members of the community. In addition, conflicts with family members may revolve around differences in religious or spiritual beliefs. Clients may also encounter interpersonal struggles in their social life or workplace due to their SRBPs. Helping clients work through these challenging experiences can be beneficial and is an appropriate task for therapy.

Difficulty Integrating Spiritual or Religious Experiences

As mentioned in chapter 6, some of the experiences people have while engaged in long contemplative prayer, meditation, or other methods of spiritual development can be so powerful that people leave these practices with psychological or emotional difficulty or suffering. As discussed in chapter 6, these events can trigger a spiritual emergency and elicit experiences and behaviors that mimic psychiatric symptoms.

However, religious and spiritual practices can also trigger very real psychological distress or disorders that don't necessarily fall into the more adaptive category of spiritual emergency and are not easily resolved. Recently, one of our colleagues at Brown University, researcher and psychologist Willoughby Britton, has become interested in potentially negative effects of meditation and other contemplative practices. While most of the recent research on mindfulness and other contemplative practices has focused on their benefits (as reviewed in chapter 8), Britton has asked "[W]hat about when meditation plays a role in creating an experience that then leads to a breakup, a psychotic break, or an inability to focus at work?" (Rocha, 2014, p. 3).

Empirical investigation of this phenomenon is being conducted under the name "The Dark Night Project," and preliminary results show that a small proportion of those who engage in intensive contemplative practice can experience impairments for anywhere from six months to many years afterward. Meditation teacher Shinzen Young (2011) addresses this in his blog:

Almost everyone who gets anywhere with meditation will pass through periods of negative emotion, confusion, [and] disorientation… The same thing can happen in psychotherapy and other growth modalities… I would *not* refer to these types of experiences as "Dark Night." I would reserve the term for a somewhat rarer phenomenon. This phenomenon, within the Buddhist tradition, is sometimes referred to as "falling into the Pit of the Void." It entails an authentic and irreversible insight into Emptiness and No Self… Instead of being empowering and fulfilling…it turns into the opposite. In a sense, it's Enlightenment's Evil Twin. This is serious but still manageable through intensive…guidance under a competent teacher. In some cases, it takes months or even years to fully metabolize, but in my experience the results are almost always highly positive.

Sometimes, as the therapist, you'll be the only person to hear about these types of experiences, which may range from mild to extreme. Shelley has had well over one hundred people come to her with such experiences, most of whom had tried to talk about their experience with other therapists and sometimes their spiritual teachers, yet had often been dismissed or had their experiences minimized. With so many people practicing yoga and meditation without the background knowledge and context of the full tradition and accompanying guidance, it is no wonder unusual experiences arise. Although these types of states have been well documented in Asian cultures, only relatively recently has Western science begun to try to understand them. These experiences can be frightening and, without special expertise on the part of the therapist, may be mistreated as psychosis.

Sometimes difficulties in integrating spiritual or religious experiences can come from participation in intensive workshops or retreats. Michael Murphy, founder of the Esalen Institute, shared in a personal conversation with Cassandra that when he and George Leonard developed Integral Transformative Practice (a combination of physical, relational, mental, emotional, and spiritual practices that could be done at home, described in Leonard and Murphy's book *The Life We Are Given*), it was partly in response to people who'd had a life-changing experience at Esalen and then went home wanting to immediately quit their jobs, leave their families, or make other drastic changes in their lives to match their perceptions of their newly liberated inner selves. Murphy and Leonard advised against making such radical decisions, at least in the short term, and instead promoted integration of the new insights to improve people's current lives.

Here are some techniques you can recommend to clients to help them integrate profound religious or spiritual experiences into their lives: journaling, spending time in nature daily, engaging in regular exercise or physical movement, getting good nutrition and sleep, meeting with others who have had similar experiences, or putting objects that remind them of their experience in their house or workplace or carrying them on their person (such as jewelry or a stone carried in a pocket). As always, consult with an expert in this arena if you reach the limit of your competence.

Conclusion

In this chapter, we've discussed just a few ways that SRBPs can be harmful or maladaptive in clients' lives. Many others exist, such as hanging on to religious and spiritual beliefs that no longer serve the purpose of connecting with the divine but instead are sources of stress, or holding resentment toward specific (or all) religious and spiritual beliefs and practices based on a previous trauma, impairing the client's ability to connect or respectfully interact with people who hold those beliefs. Your role as a therapist is not only to support clients' SRBPs in the ways we've encouraged throughout this book, but also to identify and address potentially harmful involvement with SRBPs.

Sometimes this can require a bit more delicacy than confronting other aspects of clients' lives that may be dysfunctional, just as addressing other elements of diversity often requires extra sensitivity. We highly recommend consulting with a clergy member or spiritual leader from the tradition your client is struggling with or a spiritually oriented therapist to help frame your concern. At times, issues involving clients' SRBPs, whether rooted in how clients participate in them or in how clients are treated because of them, can reach the level of a legal or ethical concern. Therefore, in the next chapter we examine legal and ethical issues than can arise when dealing with SRBPs in therapy.

Chapter 10

BEING AWARE OF LEGAL
AND ETHICAL ISSUES

I n every facet of psychological work, we have to consider not only the content of what clients present, but also the frame. A critical aspect of any therapeutic frame is legal and ethical considerations. Therefore, this competency addresses some of the possible challenges that may arise when working with clients in regard to their spiritual or religious orientation.

COMPETENCY 10: Psychologists can identify legal and ethical issues related to spirituality and religion that may surface when working with clients.

There are several ethical considerations to remember working with religious or spiritual issues in therapy. As a mental health practitioner, you (and the organization you work for, if applicable) must treat the religious or spiritual background and affiliation of your clients the same way you do other types of cultural diversity, such as gender and race. For example, the American Psychological Association's *Ethical Principles for Psychologists and Code of Conduct* states, "Psychologists are aware of and respect cultural, individual, and role differences, including those based on age, gender, gender identity, race, ethnicity, culture, national origin, religion, sexual orientation, disability, language, and socioeconomic status, and consider these factors when working with members of such groups" (2010, Principle E, p. 4).

Such competence is required in other branches of mental health care as well. As mentioned in the introduction to this book, as early as 2002, the American Psychiatric Association (Campbell et al., 2012) began to require training in spiritual competencies during residency, and religious and spiritual competencies for psychiatrists have been partially established (Josephson et al., 2009; Verhagen & Cox, 2010). There have also been efforts to create guidelines for social workers (Hodge, 2007) and professional counselors (Council for Accreditation of Counseling and Related Educational Programs, 2009; G. Miller, 1999; Robertson, 2010; J. S. Young et al., 2002).

Avoiding Discrimination and Bias

Ethically and legally, all mental health professionals and health care workers must treat religion and spirituality as a form of multicultural diversity and refrain from discrimination based on religious or spiritual affiliation or lack thereof. Beyond avoiding outright discrimination, ethical guidelines state that psychologists must actively apply themselves to eliminating the effects of biases based on religious or spiritual (or other multicultural) factors on their work, and must "not knowingly participate in or condone activities of others based upon such prejudices" (American Psychological Association, 2010, Principle E, p. 4). We suggest that you take this to heart, both on an explicit level (the ways you know you might hold biases toward those with certain SRBPs) and through an ongoing process of recognizing and managing your implicit biases, as discussed in chapter 3. It is also incumbent upon you to recognize and intervene if you become aware of discrimination against clients based on their SRBPs perpetrated by your own agency or another organization providing mental health services.

If for any reason you are unable to work in a professional manner with a client, referral may be necessary. The American Psychological Association ethics code mandates that "psychologists consult with, refer to, or cooperate with other professionals and institutions to the extent needed to serve the best interests of those with whom they work" (2010, Principle B, p. 3). For example, if you're working with a Mormon client whose religious worldview is at odds with your own and you are unable to resolve that conflict within yourself, it is your duty to refer that client to a more appropriate clinician. Another alternative is to closely collaborate with a religious professional or a team of professionals on the case so your focus remains on the clinical issue only, rather than the religious content.

Working Within Your Scope of Expertise

Another ethical consideration is to work only within the bounds of your scope of expertise. In much the same way as therapists without a medical degree might work with a psychiatrist or physician when medical issues are present or medication is necessary, or work with a teacher, school system, or attorney in the case of a custody or abuse issue, you can make it a routine practice to actively work with clergy members and spiritual teachers when called for. Even if you have the same religious affiliation or community as your client, if you aren't a trained clergy member or spiritual advisor, you must operate within your professional boundaries. Collaboration with religious or spiritual leaders can yield very positive outcomes.

On that note, only utilize interventions in which you have adequate training. Standard 2.01a of the American Psychological Association ethics code states:

"Psychologists provide services, teach, and conduct research with populations and in areas only within the boundaries of their competence, based on their education, training, supervised experience, consultation, study, or professional experience" (2010, p. 4). You may help clients access their religious or spiritual resources, or recommend they explore new ones. In general, however, we recommend avoiding prescribing religious or spiritual practices or employing religious or spiritual interventions in session if you lack specialized training in doing so. Even simple forms of SRBPs can be tricky to handle in the therapeutic context, as Hathaway (2011) points out: "A psychologist who is not trained to appropriately use spiritually oriented interventions would be wise in avoiding their use until he or she takes steps in ensure competency and avoidance of client harm. Until such training is received, it would be appropriate to make a referral for a client who requests explicit use of spiritually oriented interventions or who presents with prominent religious and spiritual issues" (p. 71).

The primary point here is that you can recommend that a client consider religious or spiritual interventions that research indicates may be helpful for her symptoms (something we'll discuss further at the end of the chapter). But if you don't have specialized training with such interventions, you should avoid implementing them on your own. And unless you are specifically trained and openly advertise your services as a religiously or spiritually oriented therapist, you are required to remain clear about your role as a therapist, and not a spiritual advisor, when working with clients. As stated in the 2008 American Psychological Association policy, "Psychologists are encouraged to recognize that it is outside the role and expertise of psychologists as psychologists to adjudicate religious or spiritual tenets" (p. 433). You must remain within the scope of your license and training.

Navigating Dual Relationships

Another factor in working with clients, especially in a small-town setting, is the possibility of blurred boundaries or dual relationships. If a religious or spiritual leader in your faith community refers clients within your church community to you, you could easily run into the client outside of the therapy room in your community of worship. If you decide to take the case, it's critical to keep your boundaries clear and hold strict confidentiality—even the fact that the person is seeing you at all, and even if they share that fact publicly. You are the guardian of the confidentiality of your clients, and you must take that very seriously, especially in a tight-knit community.

As Principle B of the American Psychological Association ethics code (2010) states, "Psychologists establish relationships of trust with those with whom they work. They are aware of their professional and scientific responsibilities to society and to the specific communities in which they work. Psychologists uphold professional standards of conduct [and] clarify their professional roles and obligations."

In the case of such referrals, take care. It may be that your best choice is to refer to a colleague across town or in the next town over if at all possible.

Recommending Religious or Spiritual Practices

The field of psychology is based on its "scientific responsibilities to society" (American Psychological Association, 2010, Principle B, p. 3) and tends to elevate scientific knowledge above religious or spiritual wisdom. On the other hand, many of the SRBPs you'll encounter in your practice have been used for hundreds if not thousands of years. They were developed through different means than our current scientific paradigm would deem valid. The separation of church and state that is a foundational tenet of our society is, with some exceptions, generally adhered to in both health care and mental health care. In our society, it's typically unethical to force or strongly recommend religious or spiritual practices in a hospital, clinic, or health care setting.

However, methods drawn from religious and spiritual traditions are now being studied scientifically. These days, if people are in chronic pain or have stress-related heart disease, it isn't uncommon for them to be referred to a mindfulness-based stress reduction program, another contemplative program, or a yoga class. Although these programs and classes are largely secularized, it wouldn't be unusual for them to include the ringing of bells, a prayer of compassion, or other elements with quasi-spiritual undertones. The boundaries between conventional, science-based health care and spiritual practices are becoming thinner—to the elation of many and to the horror of others.

Our suggestion is that when recommending interventions drawn from religious or spiritual practices, you rely on your own clinical expertise—to be clear, not your religious or spiritual beliefs, but your clinical experience—along with leading theories and, above all, evidence. Meditation, mindfulness, Christian prayer, and yoga, among many other practices, have been the focus of scientific inquiry for several decades, and some can validly be used with clients by those who have been properly trained (Bingaman, 2011; Cahn, Delorme, & Polich, 2013; Cahn & Polich, 2006; Lake, 2012; Luhrmann, 2013; McQuaid & Carmona, 2004; Segal et al., 2002; S. L. Shapiro & Carlson, 2009; Williams, Teasdale, Segal, & Kabat-Zinn, 2007).

As stated in the 2008 American Psychological Association policy, "Psychologists can appropriately speak to the psychological implications of religious/spiritual beliefs or practices when relevant psychological findings about those implications exist" (2008, p. 433). Practices that have been studied and validated scientifically may, at times—with training and supervision—be appropriate for use in certain cases.

Ethically, you cannot recommend the use of any practices that have not been studied scientifically or that lack data supporting their efficacy. You can, however, facilitate clients' independent exploration of such practices, listening carefully for what has worked well and what hasn't and reflecting that back to clients.

You can also explore well-researched religious or spiritual practices with clients, but be sure to hold your own personal values and beliefs lightly when advising them. Proselytizing or presenting your own spiritual or religious worldview in the context of therapy, even when done with the best of intentions, is never appropriate. If you feel yourself becoming unclear on these boundaries, seek consultation or supervision.

What if you do have sufficient training, background, and supervision in a given practice? Then, if relevant, you may recommend a practice that you decide would suit a client well. The American Psychological Association's Standard 2.01b addresses this issue: "Where scientific or professional knowledge in the discipline of psychology establishes that an understanding of factors associated with…religion…is essential for effective implementation of their services or research, psychologists have or obtain the training, experience, consultation, or supervision necessary to ensure the competence of their services, or they make appropriate referrals" (2010, p. 5).

This doesn't mean that you can never facilitate clients in accessing experimental treatments. If you decide to work with a treatment that isn't fully researched and accepted by the larger psychological community, please follow this advice from the American Psychological Association's ethical standards: "When obtaining informed consent for treatment for which generally recognized techniques and procedures have not been established, psychologists inform their clients/patients of the developing nature of the treatment, the potential risks involved, alternative treatments that may be available, and the voluntary nature of their participation" (2010, 10.01b, p. 13).

Also, we agree with Division 36's 2005 Preliminary Practice Guidelines for Working with Religious and Spiritual Issues I-6, if you have concerns about a client's capacity for any intervention: "Psychologists are mindful of contraindications for the use of spiritually/religiously oriented treatment approaches. (a) Generally, psychologists are discouraged from using explicit religious/spiritual treatment approaches with clients presenting with psychotic disorders, substantial personality pathology, or bizarre and idiosyncratic expressions of religion/spirituality; (b) Psychologists should discontinue such approaches if iatrogenic effects become evident" (Hathaway & Ripley, 2009, p. 47).

Self-Disclosure

You may wonder whether you should self-disclose your own beliefs or preferences to your clients. In general, our attitude is "preferably not." This is a complicated arena, however, and we bow to the 2005 guidelines presented by Division 36, which have not yet been formally adopted: "Psychologists are mindful of factors that influence the appropriateness of their own religious/spiritual self-disclosure to a client. These include but are not limited to disclosures that are (a) congruent with the treatment orientation or approach used, (b) consistent with other general background self-disclosures offered to a client at the outset of treatment, (c) facilitative of the treatment, and (d) necessary to address a potential value conflict that might impede treatment" (Hathaway & Ripley, 2009, p. 47).

Conclusion

As mental health practitioners, we are trained to work with the diagnoses presented in the most current version of the *DSM*. Most of us are more practiced at treating one or more specialized populations with which we have worked extensively. This is wise, as developing a niche or specialty in a field implies you have spent many supervised hours learning your trade. That said, no matter what your area of specialty, being culturally competent in the domains of spirituality and religion will, in itself, increase the ethicality of your practice of therapy. In this chapter, we've reminded you to pay attention to avoiding discrimination and bias based on SRBPs, as well as countering any that might arise at your place of employment, to pay attention to dual relationships particularly in tight-knit communities or small towns, and to practice within the scope of your expertise.

In part 2 of this book, we have reviewed the knowledge-based competencies that we believe to be essential for spiritual and religious competence. In part 3, the final part of this book, we'll describe six skill-based spiritual and religious competencies that must be cultivated through training, and that should be demonstrated upon licensure. The most fundamental aspect of spiritual and religious competence is simply to have the skills to work empathically and effectively with people from a diverse array of SRBPs. So to that end, the next chapter focuses on development of these skills.

Part 3

SKILLS

Chapter 11

WORKING WITH RELIGIOUS AND SPIRITUAL DIVERSITY

Among the 7 billion or so humans on the planet, there is remarkable spiritual diversity. Nearly 4 billion follow religions with Abrahamic (Middle Eastern) origins. According to the Pew Forum on Religion and Public Life (2012a), the world religious population breaks down as follows: Christians make up 32%, Muslims 23%, Hindus 15%, Buddhists 7%, Folk Religionists 6%, Other Religions 1%, and Jews 0.2%.

Among the 2.2 billion Christians, Catholics account for over 1 billion; approximately 37% of Christians are Protestants, including nondenominational and independent churches and Anglicans; about 12% are members of the Greek and Russian Orthodox churches; and 1% adhere to various other Christian traditions, such as Christian Science, Mormonism, and Jehovah's Witnesses.

About 1.5 billion people follow Eastern religions, and among the global population, Buddhists are about 7% and Hindus 15% (Pew Forum on Religion and Public Life, 2012a).

Finally, there are over 1 billion, or 16%, who regard themselves as unaffiliated, a category that includes secular, irreligious, agnostic, and atheists. Among the unaffiliated, there are many who believe in God or a universal spirit but who may not attend services (Pew Forum on Religion and Public Life, 2012b).

In our survey of psychologists (Vieten et al., 2014), of the sixteen competencies presented in this book, two were rated as most important: competency 1 (demonstrating empathy, respect, and appreciation for clients with diverse SRBPs) and competency 11 (the subject of this chapter). This is fitting because all aspects of religious and spiritual competence comes down to respecting and working with clients' religious and spiritual diversity.

COMPETENCY 11: Psychologists are able to conduct empathic and effective therapy with clients from diverse spiritual or religious backgrounds, affiliations, and levels of involvement.

There is considerable variability in the type, intensity, frequency, and content of people's beliefs and practices, even among those who are affiliated with the same majority religion, such as Christianity. For example, in the United States where 78% of people identify as Christian, 24% are Catholic, 27% are evangelical, 18% are mainline Protestants, and 7% belong to historically black Christian churches. In addition, Mormons constitute 1.7%, Orthodox Christians are 0.6%, Jehovah's Witnesses are 0.7%, and other Christians are 0.3% (Pew Forum on Religion and Public Life, 2008). And although some of the main tenets of Christianity are the same across denominations, there is an enormous degree of variability in degree of adherence to the literal word of the Bible, frequency of attendance, and views on proselytization among Catholics, as well as within other Christian denominations.

Because of this incredible diversity, religious and spiritual competence doesn't require that you know everything about each of the SRBPs you might encounter on a daily basis. That would be impossible. Instead you must know that an enormous amount of diversity exists, even within religious denominations and spiritual traditions, and cultivate skills that allow you to navigate religious and spiritual diversity sensitively, without avoiding or ignoring it, and also without placing too much emphasis on it.

You may be familiar with the term "color blindness," which has been used to teach professionals and others to treat people from different racial backgrounds exactly the same, no matter what their ethnicity. This approach was well-intentioned and rooted firmly in an ideal of equality, but it came with two problems. First, research on implicit conditioning has shown that while it is possible, through training, to suppress or change perceptions based on deeply ingrained biases (Devine, Forscher, Austin, & Cox, 2012), implicit biases contrary to one's conscious beliefs and values tend to remain (Wittenbrink & Schwarz, 2007). Knowing this, a good approach is to bring these biases into the light of day, be aware of them, and then consciously choose behaviors that are in alignment with your values rather than your conditioning. Second, ignoring someone's racial or ethnic background isn't at all effective in therapy. A more skilled approach is recognizing, acknowledging, and appreciating the unique differentiating characteristics clients bring to the table because of their race or ethnicity, and including them in therapy.

The same is true for religious and spiritual diversity. Clients' SRBPs are highly relevant to their psychological, emotional, and mental health. Their religious and spiritual beliefs are often an important part of their overall worldview and can be both sources of distress or stress and resources for psychological health and well-being. SRBPs also have wide effects in clients' lives, influencing how they dress, eat, behave toward others, make sense of their difficulties, date, have sex, marry, and parent. It's up to you as a competent therapist to be aware that clients' background with SRBPs can influence all of these things.

With diversity continuing to increase in the United States, it's very likely that you'll encounter some clients who have SRBPs that are unfamiliar to you, others who are unaffiliated and have a self-created form of spirituality, or yet others who aren't religious or spiritual at all. There are countless numbers of variations in religious and spiritual beliefs and practices you may encounter in the course of your work. Your main task in this regard is to explore your conscious and unconscious biases toward SRBPs that differ from your own and to take care to assess your own perceptions and responses in the course of your clinical practice.

✳ Clinician's Diary

Here are just a few examples demonstrating the wide variability in religious or spiritual content you might encounter as a clinician. Reflect on each example and consider what skills might be needed to effectively conduct therapy for that client.

Case A. A client comes in who is deeply religious in a tradition you know nothing about. Her religion is very important in her life and significantly influences the way she views herself and the world. She makes many life decisions based on her religious beliefs and values. She is coming in to discuss marital difficulties and depression.

Case B. You are a devout Christian but have taken care to avoid wearing a cross or otherwise revealing this to your clients in order to maintain your own privacy and be discreet. You have a new client is a passionate atheist and frequently talks about the "idiots" who are Christian and destroying the fabric of our society, sometimes mentioning that he'd like to "get rid of them all."

Case C. A client is affiliated with a conservative evangelical sect of Christianity and, in no uncertain terms, tells you that his beliefs are "the one and only truth." With great concern, he asks whether or not you've been saved.

Case D. Your best friend growing up was Jewish, and her grandparents survived the Holocaust. You spent many hours in childhood learning about that history. Now a client tells you about his discomfort working with the "greedy Jews" in his line of business.

Case E. A client comes in telling you that she "saw Buddha" during a ten-day meditation retreat and that now she understands everything. She seems euphoric, but you notice that her hair is disheveled and she doesn't seem to have bathed in a few days.

Case F. Due to an abortion in her late teens, a client struggles with religious guilt she can't seem to resolve. You yourself went through the abortion process in your early twenties, and you also have some unresolved emotions about it, especially because you and your spouse are now having trouble conceiving.

Case G. You are a practicing Sufi, and a psychotic client's delusions center around the evils of Islam and being "watched by Muslims."

Case H. A client's daughter is sick, yet the client refuses to get medical help, despite her daughter having a fever of 104 degrees for several days. She's been praying with members of her church nonstop and comes in agitated and full of fear for her daughter.

Case I. A client comes in one day and asks if you could please remove the "graven image" of the Buddha in your office because it makes her uncomfortable. Your partner, who studies acupuncture, gave it to you as a gift. You're not even sure what all of the symbolism of the Buddha is, but you enjoy the beautiful statue.

Case J. A client's mother lives in an area where Santería is still practiced. His mother invested in a property upon the advice of a woman that practices Santería, but the property lost all its value. In the end, his mother lost hundreds of thousands of dollars. Your client fears that his mother is still under the control of this "witch" and could lose his whole inheritance.

Case K. A new client comes in, having recently moved to your town. She asks that you meditate with her, as her previous therapist did. She feels that meditating with her therapist helped her tremendously, including with her family issues.

Case L. A new client calls about starting therapy and asks if she can work with you around her spiritual experiences. She tells you that her previous therapist wasn't interested in her spiritual experiences, which are very important to her, so she felt shut down. Despite learning a lot from her previous therapist, she couldn't hold her shifting beliefs out of therapy any longer and is seeking another type of therapist.

Skills for Working with Diversity

You may wonder what skills you'll need to conduct effective and empathic therapy with people from all walks of religious and spiritual life. For each of the cases above, multiple possible responses exist, rather than one right approach. However, there are several skills, outlined below, that will help you conduct empathic and effective therapy in any of the cases above, and with all of the diverse clients you'll surely encounter in your practice.

Inquire

Throughout this book we've suggested that therapists inquire about clients' SRBPs as part of taking an initial history, and on an ongoing basis. Here are some tips for making your inquiries as sensitive and fruitful as possible.

Ask open-ended questions that don't have yes or no answers. For example, rather than asking, "Is your religion or spirituality important to you?" ask, "In what ways does your religion or spirituality influence your life?"

While reflecting and summarizing can be useful tools, when initially inquiring about a client's SRBPs, avoid asking questions that contain a conclusion, such as "So it sounds like you're very involved in your congregation." Instead, make the slight shift to "How involved are you in your congregation?"

Make sure to inquire about both positive and difficult aspects of religion or spirituality, without assuming that either will be present. For example, you might say, "I have two questions for you. First, how does your meditation practice help you or serve as a resource for you, if at all, and second, what aspects of your meditation practice or community, if any, do you find difficult or a struggle? Let's start with the first question." This opens the door for clients to feel comfortable talking openly about all aspects of their SRBPs and gives you much more information about the role of SRBPs in their lives.

Make your inquiry curious, gentle, sensitive, and compassionate. If a client makes a joke about his religion, avoid laughing too hard or agreeing too enthusiastically, as he may be testing the waters to see how safe it really is to talk about this topic with you. He may have been put down or teased for his religious or spiritual beliefs in the past.

Explore, Listen, and Probe

Above all, don't be afraid to ask questions. Let clients know when you need more information in order to help them. If a client shares an SRBP that's unfamiliar to you, explore with genuine interest and curiosity. "I'm not familiar with that, tell me more" is a useful phrase. However, rather than spending valuable therapy time asking clients to educate you on a general level, bring the conversation back, as quickly as you can, to how their SRBPs interact with their thinking, their emotions, and, especially, the presenting problem. An example might be "I understand that you can't come in next week because of Ramadan. Tell me more about what Ramadan means to you—not so much the rules or doctrine, but what it means to you personally." Then really listen for clues about how that practice may help or hinder, or how it might provide more information relevant to his psychological well-being: "It sounds like Ramadan brings you to a place of clarity and peace. I wonder if there's any way we could take a little piece of that and bring it into your life daily or weekly, in some small way."

As we've mentioned before, a helpful practice is to find out more about clients' SRBPs by reading about them, watching films, visiting a place of worship, or talking with a clergyperson or spiritual advisor. You can also use this approach to learn more about nonreligious perspectives, such as atheism. To do this skillfully, it may be wise to ask clients about it directly: "Would you mind if I learn a little more about your tradition? What would you recommend I do to learn more? Is there something I can watch, read, or listen to?" Just be sure to not promise things you can't do; your client may come in the next week and ask if you've read the book he suggested yet. It's fine to simply learn more at an introductory level, rather than trying to become an expert overnight. Also note that it's often best to keep what you learn to yourself, rather than sharing it with clients. Allow clients to be the experts in their own SRBPs, even if you know quite a bit about them. After all, they're sharing an important part of *their* internal world with you.

This may seem obvious, but as you inquire, be sure to listen carefully to what clients say about their SRBPs, and don't form premature conclusions. Pay attention to their facial expressions and body language as they speak. For example, say you have a client who shares that he's Presbyterian and has gone to the same church every Sunday since he was a child, and then shrugs, smiles sadly, and says, "It's okay." Your temptation might be to assume an uncomplicated mainline church attendance and move on to the next question, but you might also stop and say, "Tell me a little more about your church. What is it like for you?" Doing so could yield an answer like "Oh, it's fine—no problem," but you could get a quite different response, such as "I used to go with my grandmother, who died a couple of years ago. She was one of the best parts of my life, and since she's been gone I haven't really felt any presence of God. I sometimes wonder why I still go." In this way, the act of listening and gently probing based on a small nonverbal cue can open the door to a wealth of information about some of the deepest aspects of clients' psychological well-being.

One risk when working with diversity is to stereotype and overgeneralize on the basis of very little information. Listening and probing can help you avoid making quick assumptions about clients. You need not belabor the spiritual and religious elements of clients' lives, since they are probably in therapy to discuss their depression, anxiety, trouble at work, or a host of other issues. So we aren't suggesting that you digress too far into religion or spirituality. But do take the time to inquire, listen, and ask one or two probing questions. This will establish your openness and interest in clients' religious or spiritual lives and may yield very helpful information relevant to their presenting problem.

Conduct Therapy Mindfully

An excellent tool for cultivating this competency is learning how to be mindful as a therapist. Mindfulness classes are now available in almost every major city in the world, and you can also access training online. (See the resources for chapter 8, in the resources section at the back of the book, to learn more.) Another excellent resource is *The Art and Science of Mindfulness: Integrating Mindfulness into Psychology and the Helping Professions* (S. L. Shapiro & Carlson, 2009).

Briefly, mindfulness is paying attention to your experiences on a moment-to-moment basis without making any effort to change them, instead allowing them to be just as they are. Mindfulness involves witnessing your own breathing, body sensations, feelings, emotions, and thoughts with an attitude of openness, curiosity, and compassion. Rather than judging any experiences you have as right or wrong or evaluating them as good or bad, just notice them. A good metaphor for taking this stance toward private, internal experiences is watching leaves floating down a stream. Our inner experiences are always changing; they are a constant flow of thoughts, feelings, and physical sensations. When you're mindful, you can watch as these experiences move through you. You might pick up a leaf from time to time to examine it more closely, and then put it back into the stream. The key here is that you are not your experiences; you are the one who is *aware* of your experiences.

Mindfulness is about being aware of, rather than not being conscious of, your ever-changing experiences and meeting them with acceptance. Mindful awareness encourages us to let go of our resistance to experiences we don't like and to stop chasing after or trying to maintain experiences we do like. This allows us to see things as they actually are more clearly. It also frees up an enormous amount of energy to make choices about how to respond to whatever is happening in ways that are in alignment with our values and goals.

Mindfulness is about keeping your attention on what's happening in the present moment, to the extent possible, rather than drifting to the past or the future (such as ruminating on a tense interaction or thinking about what you're going to say next or what you'll make for dinner). It involves being fully present and available to engage with whatever is happening right here, right now. In fact, a mindful stance is sometimes called beginner's mind, a reference to approaching each moment as though it has never happened before—and in truth, it hasn't. So even if you've been meeting with a client weekly for five years, the current session has never happened before. When conducting therapy, the idea is to approach each client and each session with a sense of possibility and openness, rather than being dominated by preconceived notions, which can be limiting, even though they may be based on previous experience.

This is easier said than done. Right now, take ten full breaths while keeping your attention on your breathing. Actually stop reading and try it.

What happened? Were you able to maintain your attention on your breathing for just ten breaths? Or did your mind have thoughts or begin to wander in different directions? This simple exercise often shows how tricky it can be to stay present, awake, and aware with curiosity, openness, and compassion.

Learning mindfulness typically requires training and practice, but you can apply some of the principles of mindfulness immediately when working with spiritual and religious issues in therapy. Here are some ways to do so:

- Before you begin each session, take the time to pay attention to your breathing or body sensations for three full minutes. You can pay attention to only your breathing and, whenever your mind wanders, gently return it to paying attention to the breath moving in and out of your body. Or you can scan your body from the bottom of your feet to the top of your head and notice any sensations you have without judging them as good or bad, whether a feeling of tension in your belly or sensations of being warm and relaxed. This practice will bring you into your body, into the present moment, and into the room.

- When clients bring up spiritual or religious material or respond to your inquiries into these matters (or any others), pay attention to their words, body language, tone of voice, and facial expression. And with mindful awareness, also pay attention to your own breathing, body sensations, emotions, and thoughts. You don't have to do anything about your experiences; just notice them with curiosity and compassion. This will allow you to be more attentive and genuinely interested in what clients are saying and how you're responding. In mindful therapy, you remain aware of both your client and yourself, in each moment.

- If you notice a reaction within yourself to religious or spiritual material a client presents, whether that reaction is negative or positive, just sit with it for a moment rather than taking action and speaking right away. When you pause for a moment with that kind of awareness, you can make a conscious choice about how to respond, rather than reacting automatically in a way that might be colored by your conditioning or biases.

- Notice if you have any tendency to reject parts of your own experience or your clients' experience. With a mindful stance, you welcome all experiences into the room and engage with them in a gentle and friendly manner.

- When you choose a response or intervention, carefully notice any attachment to or investment in what you're offering. Notice whether you're trying to make something happen, either for you or for your client. When you take a mindful stance, you'll be open to whatever might emerge, rather than trying to control the outcome. This approach will help your clients feel safe in openly exploring their SRBPs and discovering for themselves what role their beliefs and practices might play in their psychological well-being.

We highly recommend that you engage in some sort of mindfulness training. When you're present, awake, and aware and can take an open, curious, and compassionate stance, you can choose the clinical response that fits best. In this way, cultivating a mindful stance as a therapist will increase your ability to conduct effective therapy with all of your clients, including those with diverse religious and spiritual backgrounds and beliefs. As a bonus, it's also likely to enhance your own well-being.

Respond

When clients share information about their SRBPs, you can use the OARS approach (W. R. Miller & Rollnick, 1991; W. R. Miller, Zweben, DiClemente, & Rychtarik, 1992), initially developed for motivational interviewing, to respond in a sensitive and interested manner. Here's what OARS stands for:

O = Open-ended questions

A = Affirmations

R = Reflective listening

S = Summaries

Open-ended questions. When clients respond to your inquiries about their SRBPs or spiritual or religious background with minimal information or one-word answers, pose an open-ended question (which may be phrased as a statement), such as "Tell me a little more about when and how you pray" or "What do you notice about your symptoms of depression or anxiety after going to services?" Open-ended questions generally can't be answered with a single word or short phrase; therefore, they're more useful than asking questions like "Do you go to church?" "Do you enjoy it?" or "Does it seem to be helpful?" Open-ended questions encourage clients to reflect and elaborate.

Affirmations. By using affirmative statements, you can communicate that you appreciate and have empathy for clients' spiritual or religious experiences. Such statements are positive and focused on something the person has done or stated. Examples would be "It sounds like, for you, meditation can be a helpful way to deal with negative thinking, and it seems you were able to use it a few times this week" or "Instead of falling into drinking too much, it seems like you took the healthier route of praying and talking to your pastor. That took some courage."

Reflective listening. This technique is a way of asking, "Is this what you mean?" to determine whether you've accurately understood what clients are communicating. You can also use reflective listening as a way of encouraging clients to expand upon what they're saying. Simple reflections involve repeating what the person said using the same words or rephrasing with similar words: "You said that, in some ways, going to synagogue makes you feel safe and connected to your family and God, and that in other ways it's stressful because the teachings are more orthodox than you want to be. Is that right?" Sometimes, you can simply query the salient word in the client's statement. For example, if a client says, "I'm not sure why, but I felt really uncomfortable with the sermon at church," you can simply say, "Uncomfortable?" This often encourages clients to say more. Complex reflections involve slightly rephrasing the client's words to make guesses about unstated thoughts, feelings, or sensations. For example, say a client tells you, "When I overheard my coworker saying I was going to hell for being gay, I got this feeling in the pit of my stomach and couldn't move." You might respond by saying, "It sounds like you were stopped in your tracks, like a deer in the headlights. Is that right? Tell me more." Be careful to check with the client to see if you got it right, rather than assuming you've understood.

Summaries. Reflect what the client has said throughout a session or over the course of several sessions: "When you first started coming to therapy, I remember that you weren't really engaged in your meditation class. Even though you'd found it helpful in the past, you felt like you didn't have the time for it, yet you didn't want to disappoint yourself by dropping out. It seems like, over time, you've prioritized your well-being, and your meditation practice and community have become real resources for helping you with your anxiety. Is that right?"

By using the OARS approach when responding to spiritual and religious material clients present, you show your respect, empathy, and appreciation for their SRBPs. This approach allows you to display genuine interest without making religious or spiritual interpretations or recommendations that may be beyond your expertise or the scope of your practice.

Dealing with Strong Negative Reactions

It's likely that at some point in your career as a clinician, you'll notice within yourself a negative reaction to some form of religious or spiritual material a client brings to session. The phenomenon that has been called countertransference in psychoanalytic schools of thought can easily come up in the religious or spiritual arena. In chapter 3, we encouraged you to explore your own spiritual and religious background using approaches similar to taking a client's history of SRBPs. To the extent possible, become aware of your biases and know that you may also have implicit conditioning that you aren't aware of in relation to religious or spiritual issues.

When you initially notice a strong negative reaction arising in you during your clinical work, perhaps in cases similar to some of those in the preceding Clinician's Diary, employ the mindfulness skills described above, noticing your thoughts, emotions, and physical sensations and paying attention to your breathing. You may need to hold off on responding until a future session if you require some time to process what you're experiencing and possibly seek consultation. If, on the other hand, you do feel capable of making a conscious response in the session, here are some possible approaches.

Compartmentalize your feelings and inquire. Let's say a client is expressing an aggressive critique of Islam and is unaware that you practice Sufism. Perhaps she's even cursing and saying things that you find blasphemous or rude. If your reaction isn't too strong, you might consider simply setting it aside and using reflection or gentle, curious probing to broaden your perspective on what your client is sharing: "It sounds as though you're really frustrated with the Islamic perspective. I'm curious. Tell me more."

Appropriately self-disclose. With higher-functioning clients, forthright self-disclosure might be a viable option: "When you talk about Jews as greedy, I feel uncomfortable. It's hard for me to hear because I have so many good friends who are Jewish, and my experience is so different from yours. Don't take this as a rebuke or a judgment; I'm just being very honest with you. But what I get from what you're saying is that you feel you aren't treated fairly by some people in your business. Let's focus on that."

Redirect to the presenting problem. With many clients, addressing controversial religious or spiritual content or comments head-on is a recipe for disaster. It may not be wise or beneficial to treatment to encourage further discussion about what they're sharing. In fact, this material could be a proverbial red herring, offered to distract you from the larger issues at hand. It could also simply reflect a low level of social functioning on the client's part. If you're facing vitriol that's hard for you to listen to, you can simply redirect the conversation to the primary presenting problem and the goal of treatment: "I'm wondering how this affects the depression you were talking about last week." Or, "Do you feel this way more often when you're depressed?"

Address the content as a clinical issue. Sometimes it can be clinically useful to directly address clients' provocative words and behaviors. A client may have learned that the shock value of certain religious comments garners attention from others, either positive or negative, or baits them into an argumentative interaction. For some people, particularly those who were neglected in childhood, receiving any attention from others is better than eliciting no response at all. With these clients, you might want to address this pattern by reflecting upon what they're saying while also noting their apparent desire to create a reaction. For example, a client who's left a church and feels alienated might refer to her former congregation as "ignorant Jesus freaks." You could respond by saying something like "It sounds as though you're understandably upset with how your church and congregation treated you. And I bet your views on Christians probably raise a reaction in some of the people you share them with."

Use your reaction as information. Remember the psychoanalytic concept of projective identification: the idea that sometimes clients are unconsciously trying to make you feel inside the way they feel inside as a form of unconscious communication with you. So your own reaction may be a source of information for you about a client's experience. For example, if you feel angry, upset, or agitated about how a client is describing his Catholic upbringing and Catholics in general because you yourself are Catholic, you might notice this reaction within yourself and wonder whether the client felt angry, upset, or agitated by some of his experiences due to being involved with that faith.

Sidestep. Sometimes the best course of action is to use a form of relationship aikido—aikido being a martial art that skillfully sidesteps an attacker's aggression or uses it to throw the attacker off balance with minimal harm. If you can breathe through your own reactions, explore them in your own therapy or supervision, and stay focused on increasing the psychological well-being of the client while not ignoring her SRBPs as an important aspect of her life, you can remain effective as a therapist.

If you notice a pattern within yourself in which you frequently experience red flags or strong negative reactions to religious or spiritual content, you may need to do some personal work to build your skills for effectively dealing with this domain. All therapists have a few things with which they have more trouble dealing. If religion or spirituality tends to be a repeated trigger for you, here are a few tips:

- Engage in self-awareness practices, such as exploring your own religious and spiritual history using the methods in chapter 12, through autobiographical writing, or by journaling, to recognize your own point of view or religious or spiritual struggles. Increasing your self-knowledge can help reduce defensiveness and increase objectivity in the face of reactions to clients' spiritual or religious content (Wiggins-Frame, 2009).

- Focus on clients' spiritual or religious issues only to the extent that those issues are relevant to their psychological well-being. Encourage them to seek support for their spiritual or religious growth from experts in that realm (clergy, priests, ministers, rabbis, shamans, spiritual leaders, and so on). Keep your boundaries clear.

- In your work with clients, self-reflect on whether you're becoming either too involved with the spiritual or religious realm or avoiding it altogether.

- Recognize that clients' spiritual or religious development may not reflect yours, even if you share the same religious affiliation. Every person has a unique path. Avoid assumptions, stereotypes, and overgeneralizations.

- Know that if you hold strong religious or spiritual opinions, including opinions that are antireligious or antispiritual, you may be vulnerable to imposing those ideas on your clients, either explicitly or implicitly, perhaps with the best of intentions. Pay attention to clients' religious and spiritual lives and leave yours at home.

- Stay focused on the purpose of the therapy. Keep the needs and goals of clients above your own personal agenda.

- Seek continuing education, supervision, or personal counseling if you aren't clear about any aspect of this realm, either within yourself or in regard to clients.

Conclusion

Many skills for working with religious and spiritual diversity are the same skills you've already learned to conduct empathic and effective therapy with any client. The task here is to pay attention to explicitly applying those skills to the religious or spiritual realm. Sensitively and compassionately inquire about religion and spirituality as they relate to clients' psychological well-being. Explore, listen carefully, and probe for more information when you sense that it may be important to address something that's present psychologically or emotionally. Also examine your own responses and deal with any negative reactivity within yourself. When you encounter religious or spiritual traditions that are familiar to you, don't make assumptions about what they mean to the client. And when you encounter traditions that are unfamiliar to you, learn more about them, ideally from the client but also from outside investigation. As always, it is crucial to avoid overgeneralization. By being sensitive to clients' religious and spiritual worldviews, you'll increase the effectiveness of your therapy.

Exploring clients' spiritual and religious backgrounds, beliefs, and practices as a routine part of your intake and assessment will help put you in a good position to address these aspects of their lives later in therapy, and also aid you in understanding what religious and spiritual resources and struggles a given client may encounter. The next chapter provides specific skills for taking a religious and spiritual history and learning more about this realm of life, which is likely to be important to many of your clients.

Chapter 12

Taking a Religious and Spiritual History

Just like upbringing, social interactions, family relationships, education, socioeconomic status, race, ethnicity, and myriad other forces, religion and spirituality are cultural influences that dramatically impact people's worldviews (D. W. Sue & Sue, 2008). Indeed, religion and spirituality are primary interpretative frameworks through which many people understand who they are and how to live (Maslow, 1970). Clients often assume that mental health professionals are secular and scientifically trained and therefore may avoid discussing spirituality and religion (Hodge, 2013; Richards & Bergin, 2000). By including a spiritual or religious assessment in your intake, you give clients the message that you value this aspect of their life and will include it in your work together.

COMPETENCY 12: Psychologists inquire about spiritual and religious background, experience, practices, attitudes, and beliefs as a standard part of understanding a client's history.

As Hodge (2004) points out, there are many good reasons to do a religious or spiritual assessment. It "provides insight into clients' worldviews, serves as a vehicle to identify strengths, and demonstrates respect for client autonomy. In addition, the profession's ethics implicitly recommend the administration of a spiritual assessment and, for a growing number of accrediting organizations and agencies, it is explicitly recommended" (p. 183).

Hodge's first point is crucial: A spiritual and religious assessment can provide extremely useful information about how a client views the world and her place in it (Richards & Bergin, 2005). And the better you understand a client's values and point of view, the more wisely you can choose interventions that are a good match for her worldview. As Hodge (2013) notes, "by suggesting interventions that are congruent with, and even resonate with clients' spiritual worldview, clients' sense of ownership is enhanced, resulting in greater likelihood of client implementation and follow-through" with treatment recommendations and processes (p. 185).

For example, if such assessment indicates that prayer has been a valuable source of solace and comfort for a client throughout her life, you might facilitate her working with a clergy member to find specific prayers or contemplative practices, such as centering prayer, that she can use for coping with depression. On the other hand, if you're working with someone for whom yoga has been important, you might encourage him to consult his yoga teachers for practices that may help with his presenting problem.

In this way, doing a religious and spiritual assessment can be immensely beneficial, providing a mechanism for identifying important resources that might otherwise lie dormant. In this chapter, we'll present several specific assessment tools, beginning by framing religious and spiritual assessment as a two-stage process: first, a brief preliminary assessment, and then, if indicated, a more extensive comprehensive assessment (Shafranske & Sperry, 2005).

Brief Initial Religious and Spiritual Assessment

To initially explore how important religion or spirituality is in a client's life, you can use four key lines of inquiry:

- Discovering how important spirituality or religion is to the client, with follow-up questions regarding past significance if that seems to be relevant

- Finding out whether the client attends services or is part of a formal religious or spiritual community

- Exploring how religion or spirituality helps the client, and revealing any religious or spiritual problems

- Determining whether religion or spirituality has a bearing on the presenting problem and if so, the nature of the effects (Hodge, 2005, 2013)

You might begin by saying something like "Now let's talk about your experience with spirituality or religion. How important is spirituality or religion to you, if at all?" If a client says these domains aren't important, you might ask, "Has religion or spirituality been important to you in the past? If so, in what way?" If a client reports that religion and spirituality have no real significance for him, either now or in the past, you can simply end the assessment at this point, perhaps saying, "Okay, here's one more question. Has *not* being religious or spiritual been important to you, in terms of how you see the world or who you are?" Then listen carefully. The lack of SRBPs can be an important part of a client's identity and worldview, in ways that may be positive ("I consider myself a strong, intellectual person, and not being religious or superstitious is important to me") or negative ("After I left the Catholic Church, I never found a path that worked for me, and I think I've felt kind of lost because of that").

If spirituality or religion has been at all important for the client, follow up with the second line of inquiry, asking something like "Do you happen to attend a church, temple, mosque, or some other type of spiritual or religious community or place of worship, or have you in the past?" This will give you information about the client's current and past religious or spiritual affiliations. You don't need to go into a great deal of detail at this stage, because the domain of religion and spirituality is just one part of the overall history you're taking, but do note the basic affiliations the client has now or had in the past.

Next, pursue the third line of inquiry, investigating strengths or struggles the client finds in spirituality or religion. You might ask, "Are there any spiritual or religious beliefs and practices that you find especially helpful in dealing with difficulties?" This can give you valuable insight into how the client uses or has used religious or spiritual resources for coping or comfort. You can follow up with "Are you experiencing any struggles or difficulties with your religious or spiritual community, or with your beliefs?"

If you have time, and religion and spirituality appear to be very important to a particular client, you could end with a fourth question seeking information about whether the presenting problem has had an impact on the client spiritually or religiously, and vice versa, whether his SRBPs have influenced his view of the presenting problem. For example, you might find that someone who has felt depressed has curtailed his religious or spiritual activities, even though this was a source of strength for him in the past. This is important to note for future treatment planning.

According to Hodge (2005, 2013), these questions can be asked as a set, or the first two may be asked as part of the initial intake regarding a client's roles and identity, along with occupation, family status, and so on. The third question can help you explore spiritual and religious resources available to the client, and the fourth can be used to determine the extent of impact on the presenting problem. Again, these can be relatively quick questions during the initial assessment, since you'll have many things to cover in the first few sessions. But simply by including them, you'll convey to clients that this arena of their life is important to you. Be sure to note what you learn, and then return to your notes when planning treatment or after the client's primary symptoms have stabilized.

Comprehensive Religious and Spiritual Assessments

Your initial assessment may quickly determine that a given client isn't operating from a religious or spiritual worldview, as is the case for 16% of the global population (Pew Forum on Religion and Public Life, 2012a), or that religion and spirituality aren't very important to the client. At other times though, clients' answers may indicate that a more comprehensive religious or spiritual assessment is warranted (Shafranske & Sperry, 2005). If religion or spirituality is an organizing principle in a client's life, or if significant religious or spiritual conflicts are present, you and the client may find that a more comprehensive assessment is useful (Hodge, 2005, 2013). You can conduct such an assessment verbally, or by using visual assessment tools. Both approaches are outlined below.

Verbal Comprehensive Assessment

Taking a more comprehensive history verbally in session may be advantageous for a variety of reasons: for people who enjoy face-to-face interaction, it allows the therapist to be flexible in interviewing; it helps develop the therapeutic alliance; it's easy to conduct and integrate into a broader assessment; and it's appreciated by people from cultures that value oral storytelling (Hodge, 2005; Hodge & Limb, 2010). Below, we offer a list of questions (reprinted with permission from Hodge, 2013, pp. 102–103) that you can pull from to conduct a more thorough religious and spiritual assessment.

Past Spirituality

Describe the spiritual/religious tradition you grew up in. How did your family express its spirituality?

When did you first personally discover or learn about the sacred?

How did you conceptualize spirituality when you were younger?

How did you express your spirituality?

What sort of spiritual experiences stood out for you when you were growing up?

What spiritual milestones have you experienced during your journey?

Present Spirituality

Conceptualizations of the Sacred

What do you hold sacred in your life?

How has your understanding or experience of the sacred changed since you were a child?

Why are you involved in spirituality?

What do you feel God wants from you?

What do you imagine God feels when he sees you going through this difficult time?

Have there been times when you felt the sacred was absent in your life?

Do you ever experience a different side of the sacred than you are experiencing now? What is that like?

Do you ever have mixed thoughts and feelings about the sacred? What are they like?

Expression and Experience of Spirituality

How would you describe your current spiritual orientation?

How do you experience the sacred in your life?

What has helped nurture your spirituality?

What has damaged or hindered your spirituality?

When/where do you feel most connected to the sacred?

When/where do you feel the sacred is not present?

What spiritual beliefs do you find especially meaningful?

What spiritual rituals or practices are particularly important to you?

What aspects of your spirituality are particularly uplifting?

When/where do you feel closest to God?

How have your present challenges affected your relationship with God?

Spiritual Efficacy

How has your spirituality changed your life for the better?

How has your spirituality changed your life for the worse?

To what degree has your spirituality been a source of strength? Pleasure? Meaning? Joy? Intimacy? Connectedness to others? Closeness with God? Hope for the future? Confidence in yourself? Compassion to others?

To what degree has your spirituality been a source of pain? Frustration? Guilt? Anger? Confusion and doubt? Anxiety? Fear? Feelings of personal insignificance? Feelings of alienation from others?

In what ways has your spirituality helped you understand or cope with your problems?

In what ways has your spirituality hindered your ability to understand or cope with problems?

Spiritual Environment

Who supports you spiritually? How so?

Who does not support you spiritually? How so?

In what ways has your religious (or spiritual) community been a source of assistance and encouragement?

In what ways has your religious (or spiritual) community been a source of difficulties and problems?

Future Spirituality

How do you see yourself changing spiritually in the future?

In what ways do you want to grow spiritually?

How does your spirituality relate to your goals in life?

How does your relationship to God affect your future life plans?

For the majority of cases, the entire assessment would be too extensive and detailed. However, you may select questions you think are particularly relevant to a given client. You might also consider suggesting that clients respond to these questions in writing as a homework assignment, especially those who are interested in exploring their religious and spiritual history in detail.

Visual Assessment Tools

Visual assessment may be more appropriate for certain clients. Having a client spend time—either in session or, ideally, outside session—creating one of the following two diagrams may be useful if the client is less verbally oriented, is reserved, or comes from a less directly verbal culture.

Lifemap

The lifemap (Hodge, 2005) is an approach to assessment that allows clients to create a comprehensive overview of their religious and spiritual history. A lifemap is created and controlled entirely by the client. The act of creating it will be revealing and may be cathartic. The visual presentation makes the activity engaging in a different way than talk therapy and puts the client's history into a format that's highly accessible for both client and practitioner. The lifemap can also be completed as homework and then shared with you, the clinician. Reassure clients that they need not be artists to create a lifemap, and that they need not worry about capturing every single thing that's important. Rather, they're creating a guided pictorial tour of their religious and spiritual life, so stick figures and cartoons are fine. If a client feels uncomfortable drawing, it may not be the best choice. But those who are comfortable with the process may find that it helps them see the shape of their life and identify which coping mechanisms have helped them get through challenging situations in the past.

To use this approach, ask the client to sketch or represent significant spiritual or religious life events on a large sheet of paper, placing them along a pathway, road, or single line that represents the client's journey. Typically, the path proceeds chronologically, from birth to the present and even beyond. Clients can draw symbols, cut out pictures, or use other media to represent the events. Encourage clients to include difficulties, perhaps representing them as hills, bumps, or potholes, along with any spiritual or religious resources they used to overcome those trials. These past coping strategies may be helpful in developing strategies for the current problem or future issues.

Spiritual Lifemap

✳ Clinician's Diary

The figure presented shows an example of a religious lifemap created by Shelley's client Martha, a sixty-two-year-old woman. She described her childhood as happy and said that she'd attended a traditional church as she was growing up. Her family, which included two older brothers, lived in the country in a house built by her father. At eighteen, Martha left for college, but she returned home after two years because she was unhappy about being so far from her family. She started working and then, when she was twenty-one, was in a terrible car accident that was the other driver's fault. Her best friend died, and Martha's physical recovery took nearly a year. She also suffered an existential crisis: How could God allow such a thing to happen?

Over the next few years, Martha met her husband, got married, and became a stepmother to his nine-year-old daughter. Her father built them a small home, which they loved. A few years later her own son was born, creating within Martha a desire to return to church. But she found that her childhood church didn't suit her any longer, so she started looking for a better fit. Ultimately, she and her family attended a more progressive Christian church for many years. During that time, Martha returned to college and got her master's degree, and her career took off. Martha's son, who was a good student, left home at eighteen to pursue a career as a health care professional. Her husband retired a few years later and wanted to fulfill his dream of living on a farm in New England. Martha was at the height of her career, and for the next six years she commuted between her husband's sheep farm in the country and her job near New York City. She finally gave up and retired to the farm, but she felt resentful about leaving her job and moving away from her family of origin.

Within a few years, her mother and father both died, and Martha sold her parents' home and her own home, which she deeply regretted because her father had built both of them. Depression set in, and Martha found herself seeking a new level of spiritual understanding and community. She had done yoga for years and now sought other alternative approaches, including Buddhist teachings and online courses. Eventually, due to Martha's profound loneliness in the country, she and her husband moved back to their hometown, relocating to be closer to family, their son, and golf.

By now Martha's belief system had shifted, including concepts of karma and reincarnation, as well as the possibility of angels and spirits. She found another liberal Christian church community and began to do charity work and attend worship services each week. She also continued to pursue online alternative spirituality courses, which helped her explore the mystery of life more fully.

Creating this religious and spiritual lifemap was useful to Martha, helping her recognize the role yoga had played in her life. Although she'd been connected to Christianity throughout most of her life, her belief system and practices shifted as she changed her life course in reaction to circumstances. Hers is an example of a belief system that increasingly incorporated spirituality and alternative practices over her life span while remaining within the Christian framework she'd been brought up in. Shelley benefited from the lifemap too, as it gave her a better sense of how Martha's way of making meaning had evolved over the course of her life. Shelley also gained a better understanding of the religious and spiritual resources available to Martha to support her progress in therapy.

Spiritual and Religious Ecomap

Another visual assessment tool is a spiritual and religious ecomap (Hodge, 2005, 2013). In contrast to the lifemap, an ecomap focuses on the here and now, not the client's familial or personal history. This is an easier map to draw, as it simply places the client in the middle of the map, with spokes going toward each of the spiritual or religious resources in his environment. These can include people, communities, practices, teachings, books, deities, or any aspect of the client's religious or spiritual life that he connects with.

Various types of lines can be used to indicate the quality of the current relationship to each person or resource. For example, a tenuous relationship might be a dotted line, a closer relationship that's fragile might be a dashed line, a typical relationship might be a plain line, and a strong relationship might be a thicker line. Relationships fraught with conflict might be represented with a line of Xs. And if there's a flow of energy, whether toward the client, from the client, or in both directions, this can be indicated with arrows. This allows the client to consider the level of support he's actually deriving from each relationship at the moment, and allows both of you to see this visually. For example, although a client may go to a church study group regularly, that may or may not represent a strong support. The lines will help clarify which sources of support are strong, and which may need work—or may need to be de-emphasized or even abandoned.

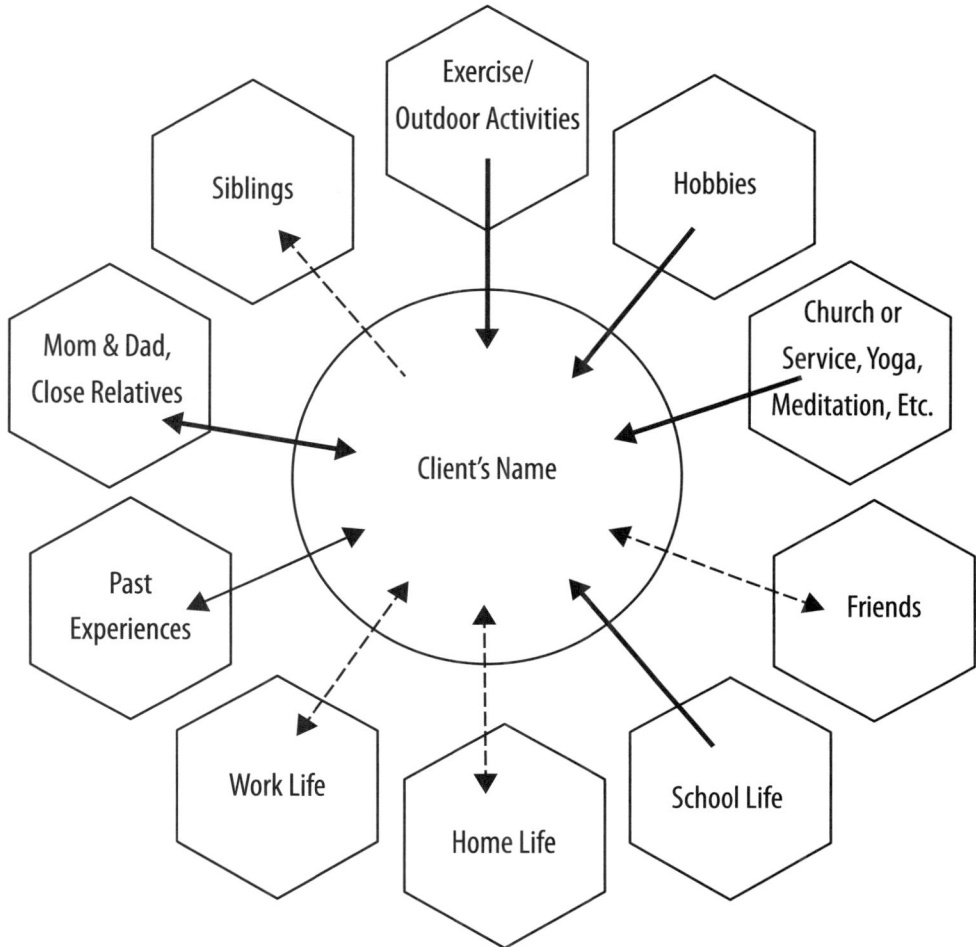

The advantage of ecomaps is that they're easy to construct and provide a reference point for discussing the spiritual and religious connections in clients' lives—both problematic and helpful connections. Once you understand a client's broader psychosocial environment, you can help him utilize the strengths indicated and support him in navigating the problematic people or organizations in his life.

Choosing an Assessment Method

You may wonder which assessment method you should use. There are no rules for this. It often depends on the client and what will work best for that individual or in the context of the presenting problem or the client's cultural background. Or, after some experimentation with various methods, you may find one that you prefer to work with due to your theoretical orientation or training or the time generally available for this kind of work in your sessions.

On that note, any of these assessments can be done in session; or you may wish to assign them as homework, asking clients to answer the questions or create the diagram at home and then bring it to the next session to share with you. However, do keep in mind that creating and using these maps or responding to all of the questions in the verbal assessment, whether given as homework or conducted in session, takes time. Before asking a client to complete any of these tasks, think through your purpose in taking that particular client through the process. Then, if such an approach seems called for, choose whichever form fits the client and situation best. If you assign one of these assessments as homework, be sure to allow enough time in session for exploration of the results.

Despite the time challenges, doing this work can lead to surprising discoveries. Clients may also appreciate having a pictorial reminder of your work together to use at home.

Also, be aware that numerous validated self-report questionnaires and surveys are available for assessing religious and spiritual issues. Although reviewing them is beyond the scope of this book, you can find a comprehensive list of them in the *APA Handbook of Psychology, Religion, and Spirituality: Vol. 2. An Applied Psychology of Religion and Spirituality* (Pargament, 2013). Although these measures are most often used for research, at times you may find them useful tools for assessment, or even for client self-assessment as part of an intervention. An example would be helping a client see how prevalent her negative religious coping is in relation to positive religious coping using the RCOPE (Pargament et al., 2000) or Brief RCOPE (Pargament, Feuille, & Burdzy, 2011).

Conclusion

In this chapter, we discussed several ways to learn about how clients may have engaged in SRBPs over the course of their lives. How in-depth such an assessment should be depends on the client, the extent to which religion or spirituality has been an important part of his life, and the role, if any, of SRBPs in his presenting problems. There are four key questions you can routinely ask clients to get a sense of this, and if their responses indicate that further exploration is merited, you can use one of the comprehensive assessments presented in this chapter, or others you may be aware of or devise on your own.

Inquiring about clients' religious and spiritual history should be a routine part of your intake assessment, just as you would learn about their work, education, and relationship history or be sensitive to their race and ethnicity, sexual orientation, or other aspects of human diversity. The information you receive will help you understand clients' worldviews and perspectives on life. It will also provide valuable insight into whether clients are experiencing religious or spiritual problems or struggles and indicate what religious or spiritual resources might be available to them. Skills for helping clients access those resources are discussed in the next chapter.

Chapter 13

HELPING CLIENTS ACCESS THEIR RELIGIOUS AND SPIRITUAL RESOURCES

I n chapter 8, we pointed out that an important element of religious and spiritual competence is the *knowledge* that clients may have internal and external spiritual or religious resources and practices that could support psychological well-being and recovery from psychological disorders. In this chapter, we discuss the skills you can employ to help clients access these religious and spiritual resources and draw upon those strengths.

COMPETENCY 13: Psychologists help clients explore and access their spiritual and religious strengths and resources.

In order to include any spiritual or religious resources clients may have as you plan their treatment, you must first assess what those strengths and resources might be. In the previous chapter we offered several methods for taking a religious and spiritual history and recommended a two-step approach, with the first step being characterized by brief inquiry. This can give you an idea, upon initial assessment, of the role and importance of religion and spirituality in a client's life. If religion and spirituality don't play a role in a client's life, you can focus on providing cognitive, emotional, relational, and behavioral resources. But when working with clients for whom religion and spirituality do play a role, you can help them harness their spiritual and religious strengths and resources to promote psychological well-being.

To get a sense of the extent to which a client's past or current SRBPs have served as strengths or resources, you might start by asking questions along these lines: "Is there anything about how you currently practice your religion or spirituality that helps you feel better mentally or emotionally? Is there anything that has helped you in the past? Are there parts of your spiritual or religious engagement that help you cope or make good decisions? Is there anything that helps you feel stronger or less lonely, depressed, or anxious?" The client's answers may well illuminate resources that could be valuable to utilize in treatment.

Helping Clients Access Outer Resources

In chapter 8, we reviewed research showing that both inner and outer aspects of people's religion and spirituality can support their psychological well-being. Outer religious and spiritual resources can include clergy members, leaders, or teachers in clients' place of worship or spiritual community, as well as places, objects, holidays, or gatherings that hold sacred meaning for them.

When inquiring about clients' potential spiritual and religious resources, be sure to ask whether and how often they attend spiritual or religious services or events. Sometimes when people are in a challenging time, they isolate themselves. This is a natural tendency of humans, as well as other animals. While spending some time alone can be useful for rest, recharging one's batteries, and reflecting on one's life, too much isolation can be harmful. Many studies have shown that regularly attending religious or spiritual services is associated with better mental health (Koenig, 1997; Levin & Chatters, 1998; Strawbridge, Shema, Cohen, & Kaplan, 2001). Whether the cause for that positive association is social support, listening to words of wisdom from clergy, simply getting out of the house, or something greater, it has clearly been shown that attending services is beneficial for mental, emotional, and spiritual health (Luhrmann, 2012; Schwadel & Falci, 2012).

If a client is already a member of a religious or spiritual community, find out what kinds of additional activities or services are available to him as a part of his participation in that community, such as counseling, spiritual direction, positive activities, shared meals, classes, or opportunities to be of service. If appropriate, ask if there are opportunities for functional assistance, such as meals, clothing, or housing. Often these services are available even to people who don't attend services regularly.

Sometimes you may also want to help clients revive a former spiritual or religious resource or practice that they've abandoned. For example, perhaps a client used to have a strong meditation or yoga practice that waned with the birth of a child, and reinstituting the practice might help her touch a quiet or transcendent spot in herself on a daily basis. Or perhaps a client valued attending church at one point, then moved and, due to the stress of the move, hasn't gotten around to finding a new church to attend. In the latter case, you could encourage him to prioritize finding a congregation that suits his current needs. Your encouragement may rekindle a source of meaning and purpose that has been dampened by psychological symptoms, grief, trauma, or stress.

Clients who aren't currently members of a religious or spiritual community may be able to access ongoing support, including more tangible forms of support, by joining or rejoining a community that reflects their personal beliefs, whether a church, syna-gogue, mosque, or sangha. Your role as a therapist is not to recommend any specific religion or spiritual community. But, with gentle inquiry, you may find that a client has been curious about a church down the street or one that a coworker attends, or a meditation center she'd always meant to check out but never got around to it; encour-age clients to follow through on such interests. Of course, if they aren't interested in a religious or spiritual form of support, there are many other sources of support.

When talking with clients, you might also inquire about religious and spiritual resources such as books, magazines, music, audio or video recordings, websites, and even smartphone apps related to their SRBPs that they have found useful or that they're interested in exploring. Take note of these as possible outer resources that you might encourage them to access. However, when encouraging clients to access outer resources, be sure to explore whether any of them cause additional stress or negative experiences, such as fear, control, guilt, or judgment. After all, involvement with SRBPs isn't always helpful, as discussed in chapter 9.

Informal religious or spiritual activities can also be useful. Visiting a sacred space, whether constructed (such as a church, chapel, or meditation garden) or a place in nature (such as a mountain, meadow, beach, or special tree), can be enormously healing, even when done on a one-time basis. You might ask, "Where do you feel most at peace? Are there any places near you that hold meaning for you, feel sacred, or are helpful to visit?" If so, you can include visits to this place as a part of your treat-ment plan. And if it is allowed, clients might take something from the area, such as a stone, feather, shell, or other object, to serve as a reminder of that sacred place, whether at their home, at work, in their purse or wallet, or in a hospital room.

Helping Clients Access Inner Resources

As mentioned in chapter 8, although a robust body of evidence links external factors such as attendance at religious services to greater psychological well-being, some research indicates that inner, or intrinsic, aspects of religion and spirituality may have a larger influence on psychological resilience and well-being. Actively inquire about the inner dimensions of clients' SRBPs. How frequently do they engage in mediation, prayer, or other religious or spiritual practices, and what is their percep-tion of how this influences their mental and emotional state? To what extent do they rely on their spiritual or religious beliefs to help get them through rough times? Many people routinely access an internal relationship with a manifestation of the divine—such as God, Jesus, a figure from scripture, angels, goddesses, power animals, or an inner guide—for help in times of need, especially when they don't have access to a therapist. Some people work with their dreams, journaling, or other avenues that help them access inner resources, and some use divination tools such as pendulums, tarot, or astrology to guide them. Keep an open mind about religious or spiritual inner resources that may be less familiar to you but very important to a given client.

Clients can also ground themselves in a higher meaning and purpose, even when they are in distress, by engaging in simple rituals that remind them of their outer or inner spiritual resources, such as reflecting on a sacred image, starting the day by praying, chanting out loud or quietly, or playing or listening to music, drums, or bells. Your best tool for illuminating these resources is delicate inquiry. Ask clients what is meaningful to them, and then encourage them to utilize those resources. When clients share inner resources that appear to be helpful, even if they're unfamiliar to you, your treatment plan might encourage them to access those resources when they experience symptoms or at a set time each day. If clients are willing, ask them to share their experiences with you as therapy progresses so that you can gain insight into the resources they're utilizing.

Bibliotherapy

Another resource for clients—one that's both inner and outer—is bibliotherapy. Shelley often recommends books or other written materials with religious, spiritual, or philosophical topics as a way for clients to reflect on a subject related to their presenting problem or life situation. She has lent books from her own library, recommended books easily obtainable in bookstores, and worked with clients to find further information on various topics on the Internet.

While reading relevant material on their own, clients invariably think of new ideas or discover elements related to their circumstances. They can then bring their new insights back into therapy. Discussing these insights can be illuminating and may shed light on factors that hadn't arisen during previous sessions.

In addition, clients can keep a book or magazine on their bedside table to be referenced again and again. Some of the books we most often recommend include Eckhart Tolle's *The Power of Now* (2004), Michael Singer's *The Untethered Soul* (2007), Rick Hanson and Richard Mendius's *Buddha's Brain* (2009), and Marilyn Schlitz, Cassandra Vieten, and Tina Amorok's *Living Deeply* (2008). At times, original sacred texts such as the Bible, Quran, Sutras, or others may be helpful.

Religious and Spiritual Coping Methods

In addition to providing clients with coping skills such as cognitive reframing, stress management, relaxation training, or physical exercise, you can also explicitly help them access and utilize spiritual and religious coping methods that are positive for them. This may help them face challenges when you or other mental health practitioners can't be present, such as in the middle of the night or on weekends, when people's own personal "demons" may come to roost.

When appropriate, meaning when clients already engage in or show an interest in exploring SRBPs, religious or spiritual coping mechanisms can become part of the coping tool kit you offer them. As mentioned in chapter 8, positive religious coping has been shown to help people feel a greater sense of control or comfort or to derive meaning in difficult situations (Pargament, 1997). Increased attendance at religious or spiritual services, greater contact with clergy or spiritual leaders, and various forms of prayer have all been used as positive coping mechanisms to help individuals and families get the support they need during difficult times (Pargament, 1997; Pargament & Raiya, 2007).

In addition to religious and spiritual coping methods, numerous techniques from the world's spiritual traditions may be useful for clients, particularly those in the growing group of people who identify as spiritual but not religious. Training in any number of meditation practices, such as guided visualization, mindfulness, mantra repetition, contemplative prayer, concentration, and compassion for self and others is now easily accessible in most urban areas and online, often at no charge. In addition, movement-based spiritual practices, such as tai chi and yoga, are available in nearly every city in the United States. Ways of being that find their roots in these spiritual practices can help as well, such as cultivating mindfulness, nonjudgmentally observing one's irrational thought patterns, or developing a "witness" stance toward one's fears and worries. As discussed in chapter 8, there is substantial evidence that such ways of being—often supported by practices such as meditation, yoga, or contemplative prayer—can be helpful in fostering psychological and emotional well-being, particularly for clients who are under stress, who are dealing with addictive behaviors, who are treatment-resistant to depression or prone to relapse, or who tend to ruminate. For them, contemplative practices that encourage metacognition can be especially useful.

When exploring new practices, clients may choose techniques that come easily to them or that might simply be conveniently located, such as a yoga studio on the corner. Over time, and on an ongoing basis, explore how beneficial these practices or resources actually are for clients. If they aren't especially helpful, alternative practices may be more effective. Using trial and error, help clients experiment with various methods to discover what works well for them.

If you and your client aren't sure where to start, a useful set of spiritual and religious tools has been outlined by Plante (2009, pp. 33–46), who crystallized them from a variety of traditions. Any of his thirteen tools may help clients cope with difficult thought patterns or distressing emotions:

- Meditating

- Praying

- Having a vocation, meaning, purpose, or calling in life

- Accepting oneself and others, even with faults

- Maintaining ethical values and behaviors

- Being part of something larger and greater than oneself

- Emphasizing forgiveness, gratitude, love, kindness, and compassion

- Practicing volunteerism and charity

- Participating in rituals and community service

- Emphasizing social justice

- Having spiritual role models

- Using bibliotherapy

- Emphasizing the sacredness of life

If clients are interested in using any of these tools, you may want to help them try the approach in session or in a real-world setting between sessions to see if it is in fact helpful. Over time, those that do help can be included in a client's menu of coping options.

At times, you may choose to utilize concepts that are foundational aspects of many religious and spiritual traditions, such as compassion or forgiveness, and not refer to religion or spirituality explicitly. For example, Shelley once conducted therapy with a woman who, many years before, had become pregnant. She was in graduate school and unmarried at the time and chose to have an abortion. Having been raised Catholic and still being a practicing Catholic, she found it difficult to fully accept her choice. Years later, in therapy, she was still consumed by guilt, doubt, and regret. Shelley introduced concepts around forgiveness and self-compassion, and together they worked out a way for this client to make amends for her act, which she felt to be an egregious sin. In the end, while the client continued to believe her choice was essentially mistaken, she was able to build new beliefs around self-forgiveness and self-compassion that served as antidotes to that belief.

Don't Overdo It

A caution is necessary here. It can be tempting to give clients several options when they're suffering. Be careful not to overwhelm them with too many new options or ideas at once. Try one at a time, and go with your instincts as a clinician. Your role may be to simply witness a client's process of discovery. Encourage clients to explore new things slowly and not get in too deep right away.

We can speak to this from our own experience. The first time Shelley chose to attend an intensive meditation retreat, she selected a thirty-day silent retreat. Although she had meditated about forty minutes each day for nearly eight years, this was jumping into the deep end. It turned out that the schedule was grueling: daily wake-up time was 4 a.m. and bedtime was at 10 p.m., only breakfast and lunch were provided, and the rest of the day was devoted to walking or sitting meditation and one work shift. Remarkably, she stuck with it for sixteen days before leaving, and even returned to the center a year later for several ten-day silent retreats. In truth, it would have been wiser for her to begin her retreat experiences with a daylong retreat, then a weekend retreat, and after that perhaps a one-week or ten-day retreat. Jumping in too far and too fast can be counterproductive.

Religious or Spiritual Interventions

So far, we've mainly discussed how you can help clients access their currently existing spiritual or religious resources. At times, with caution, it may be helpful to recommend that clients investigate spiritual or religious resources they haven't practiced or encountered before.

As alluded to in chapter 8, an ethical and safe way to do this is to rely on evidence-based interventions that have their roots in spiritual traditions. If you think this is warranted, it can be useful to simply share evidence indicating the benefits of these practices, such as a summary or abstract of an article, and tell the client why you think it might be useful for her particular set of symptoms or circumstances. Various forms of spiritually informed therapy have demonstrated success, particularly with clients for whom religion is important (Waller et al., 2010). Mindfulness-based interventions such as mindfulness-based stress reduction (MBSR) and mindfulness-based cognitive therapy (MBCT), each of which includes Buddhist concepts and practices, have demonstrated effectiveness for improving chronic pain, anxiety, and mood symptoms (Hofmann et al., 2010; Toneatto & Nguyen, 2007).

Dialectical behavior therapy (DBT) and adaptations of it, which include some elements of Zen Buddhism, have shown promise and efficacy for conditions that are notoriously difficult to treat, such as borderline personality disorder, self-harm, substance abuse, and eating disorders (Robins & Chapman, 2004). Acceptance and commitment therapy (ACT), which also includes some Buddhist elements, has demonstrated robust effect sizes compared to control groups across a number of client populations and psychological symptoms (Powers et al., 2009).

Richard Miller's Integrative Restoration (iRest) combines meditative techniques from Hindu yogic traditions with cognitive behavioral approaches. It has shown promise in treating symptoms of post-traumatic stress disorder in veterans (Nassif, 2013), and has also demonstrated positive results with depression, anxiety, insomnia, chronic pain, and chemical dependency (Eastman-Mueller, Wilson, Jung, Kimura, & Tarrant, 2013). The iRest program (Integrative Restorative Institute, 2013) is now being used in thirty veterans' clinics and hospitals across the United States and is an officially recommended treatment.

✳ Clinician's Diary

A colleague of ours, Daniel, works with veterans using techniques informed by meditation and mindfulness. One of his clients was Manuel, an inpatient air force veteran with post-traumatic stress disorder, mild traumatic brain injury, suicidality, and substance abuse issues. Daniel had been using traditional cognitive behavior approaches for treating PTSD and addressing the brain injury. Then Manuel heard that Daniel was a Buddhist psychologist and asked for meditation training to "help me get a grip on my demons." Daniel chose to use Richard Miller's iRest program to help Manuel access a deeper resource that might address his moral injury issues related to his deployment.

In the first session, Daniel used the iRest protocol to help Manuel reflect on his current mental state, first by identifying various sensations, which Manuel described as "a tense black ball of nothingness in my belly that wants to swallow me whole." He identified fear and shame as the emotions contained within this "tense black ball" and then reported seeing himself as a small child in his body, as if he was "sitting in a corner, alive and tense with fear." He broke out of his reflective state, stared at Daniel, and asked, "What just happened? I've never seen myself that way before, and it's scary."

The second session proceeded as the first, with Manuel again describing a tense black ball in his belly, but in this session he was able to tolerate the fear and watch the ball shift. He then reported feeling another sensation: warmth and softness in his chest, which spread to his back and neck. At that point, he said he felt a sense of total comfort and peace. Daniel asked Manuel if he could still observe the tense black ball, and he reported that it had become small and was now distant from his body—still there, but not consuming his entire attention. He reported being able to sit with the feeling of warmth and softness, and that black ball was only a small speck in the "bigger space of my comfort." During the course of treatment using iRest as an adjunct therapy, Manuel was gradually able to repeatedly access inner resources that offered safety and grounding. He reported that this state of "soft warm comfort" became increasingly available to him even between sessions.

This is an example of how a meditative technique, coupled with somatic and psychological processing, can help someone with PTSD. As a clinician, you may not choose to be trained in delivering such interventions, but you should know that they exist and can supplement the therapy you provide. For example, you may suggest to a client that, in addition to the therapy the two of you are engaged in, the client might also attend a MBSR program or work with a clinician who is skilled in dialectical behavior therapy, mindfulness-based cognitive therapy, or other interventions with elements that have spiritual or religious roots.

Conclusion

The suggestion to encourage clients to explore and access their religious or spiritual resources is actually quite a new idea for most psychologists and mental health professionals. As a group, we've tended to shy away from addressing the religious and spiritual domains of clients' lives, and most clinicians lack the knowledge or training necessary to recommend spiritual or religious practices such as meditation or prayer. It's true that you must tread lightly here, yet as a competent clinician, you can and should encourage any aspects of clients' lives that are positive and meaningful, or that have been in the past and could be helpful in the present. This includes everything from hobbies, activities, and relationships to religious or spiritual aspects of their lives.

As new research continues to emerge on the benefits of interventions drawn from religious and spiritual practices, the options for working with clients will expand, with research now indicating that incorporating SRBPs into treatment planning may sometimes be warranted. Our recommendation is that, in general, therapists not recommend religious or spiritual practices that clients don't already engage in or show a strong interest in. Instead, capitalize on the spiritual and religious strengths and resources they already utilize and encourage those that may be familiar to them. We hold that, with a few exceptions, most people can find a place of peace and acceptance within, given the right circumstances. So explore each client's moments of bliss or transcendence and build on those.

Just as important as building your clinical skills to help clients access their religious or spiritual resources is developing skills to deal with religious or spiritual problems should they arise. This is the topic of the next chapter.

Chapter 14

IDENTIFYING SPIRITUAL AND RELIGIOUS PROBLEMS

In chapter 6, we pointed out that clients may face religious and spiritual issues that are consistent with their religious or spiritual tradition but can be difficult to distinguish from various forms of psychopathology, such as depression, mania, or psychosis. And in chapter 9, we reviewed forms of SRBPs that have the potential to be harmful to clients' psychological well-being. To be a competent therapist, you must be able to recognize when spiritual or religious problems arise in the course of conducting therapy, have the skills to sensitively and effectively address them, and, as always, seek consultation or make a referral if addressing the problem is outside of your expertise.

COMPETENCY 14: Psychologists can identify and address spiritual and religious problems in clinical practice and make referrals when necessary.

The simplest way to find out if a client is facing a religious or spiritual problem is to ask, with openness and curiosity. When taking client histories, be sure to inquire about past and current SRBPs as a matter of routine. Remember to ask not only about formal affiliation with a religious or spiritual tradition, but also any spiritual but not necessarily religious practices clients may engage in. As discussed in chapter 4, it's also important to ask about clients' lived experience of their religious or spiritual practices—in other words, how they personally engage with their SRBPs on a day-to-day basis. Just as you've asked clients to let you know whether and how their SRBPs are sources of support for them (as discussed in chapter 13), you can identify religious or spiritual problems by simply asking, "Do you have any concerns about your religious or spiritual practice? Have you had any problems or conflicts, either within yourself or with others, with respect to your religion or spirituality?"

Be sure to listen and reflect back what clients tell you, just to make sure you've understood: "So, it sounds like your religious or spiritual beliefs and practices are going okay." "It sounds like your participation at church is helpful in some ways, but you don't see eye to eye with the pastor." "So, it sounds like you've got some real concerns that you've let God down or committed an unforgivable sin. Can you tell me more about that?"

If during the course of your assessment you find symptoms that have religious or spiritual content, this can be another doorway into identifying and addressing clients' potential religious or spiritual problems. Again, initially your role is to simply inquire and acknowledge whatever is happening for a client. Suspend judgment until you have the information you need to make an educated guess about whether she may be having a religious or spiritual problem or emergency, whether she's experiencing symptoms of a mental disorder with religious or spiritual content, or whether some blend of the two is occurring (see chapter 6 for some guidance on making this decision).

Diagnosing a Religious or Spiritual Problem

Over two decades ago, in 1991, our collaborator David Lukoff and his colleagues submitted a proposal for a new diagnostic code entitled "Psychoreligious or Psychospiritual Problem" to the Task Force on *DSM-IV* (Lukoff, Lu, et al., 1992). In their proposal, they argued that adoption of this new category would have four key benefits:

- Increased accuracy of diagnostic assessments when religious and spiritual issues are involved

- Reduced occurrence of iatrogenic harm from misdiagnosis of religious and spiritual problems

- Improved treatment of such problems by stimulating clinical research

- Improved treatment of such problems by encouraging training centers to address religious and spiritual issues in their programs

The American Psychiatric Association Committee on Religion and Psychiatry and the National Institute of Mental Health Workgroup on Culture and Diagnosis supported the proposal.

In 1993, the Task Force on *DSM-IV* accepted the proposal, changing the title to "Religious or Spiritual Problem" and including it in the *DSM-IV* as V code 62.89 (American Psychiatric Association, 1994, p. 685); in the tenth revision of the International Statistical Classification of Diseases and Related Health Problems (*ICD-10*), it appears as code Z65.8. This was a major step forward in recognizing spiritual and religious issues as important for psychological well-being, and as an area in which cultural competency is necessary. Articles on the new diagnosis appeared in the *New York Times*, the *San Francisco Chronicle*, and the American Psychological Association's journal *Monitor on Psychology* (Lukoff, 1998). The *DSM-5* retained this category virtually unchanged from the *DSM-IV*, stating, "This category can be used when the focus of clinical attention is a religious or spiritual problem. Examples include distressing experiences that involve loss or questioning of faith, problems associated with conversion to a new faith, or questioning of other spiritual values which may not necessarily be related to an organized church or religious institution" (American Psychiatric Association, 2013, p. 725).

Z (formerly V) codes are not psychiatric diagnoses per se; they are used to refer to conditions other than a disease or injury, or to report significant factors that may influence present or future care. Using this code may in some circumstances allow you to bill insurance companies for your services, or to complete required diagnostic aspects of a client's medical chart. It can also prevent you from prematurely assigning a more severe diagnosis that may stay in a client's records permanently, as you make a decision about the appropriate final diagnosis and treatment plan.

Examples of religious or spiritual problems include religious or spiritual questioning, loss of faith or loss of spiritual connection, meditation-related problems, disruptive or distressing mystical experiences, near-death experiences, leaving a spiritual teacher or path, religious or spiritual struggle (divine, intrapersonal, or interpersonal), or spiritual emergencies (Lukoff, 1998). (See chapter 6 for more on this topic, including descriptions of religious or spiritual struggles and types of spiritual emergencies.)

As discussed in chapter 6, it can be difficult to disentangle religious or spiritual problems from other forms of psychopathology, and in that chapter we provided some screening questions to help you differentiate between the two. Here are some general guidelines from David Lukoff:

> There is considerable overlap among the criteria proposed by different authors for making the differential diagnosis between psychopathology and spiritual emergencies. These constants include: (1) cognitions and speech thematically related to spiritual traditions or to mythology; (2) openness to exploring the experience; [and] (3) no conceptual disorganization (Buckley, 1989; Grof & Grof, 1989; Lukoff, 1985; K. W. Watson, 1994). Lukoff (1985) suggested using good prognostic signs to help distinguish between psychopathology and spiritual emergencies, including: (1) good pre-episode functioning; (2) acute onset of symptoms during a period of three months or less; (3) stressful precipitants to the psychotic episode; and (4) a positive exploratory attitude toward the experience. (1998, para. 52)

Once you've made a provisional determination that a client is presenting a religious or spiritual problem, you can address it as such in therapy.

✳ Clinician's Diary

A colleague told us about a client named George, whom she had worked with for several years. Initially, George presented with mild psychotic symptoms that included unusual magical beliefs and odd perceptions. He had a vivid imagination that made him feel quite separate from his friends and work colleagues, and he feared that if others knew about his fantasy life, they'd think he was crazy. As his therapy evolved, several spiritually oriented fantasies came out. Rather than being random tangential snippets, these fantasies were long, involved stories more akin to dreams.

As our colleague worked with George, several themes emerged, including discriminating right from wrong and having faith in the unknown. George felt that he was becoming telepathic and developing an ability to heal others. As the therapy progressed, our colleague focused on grounding and normalizing George's fantasies by discussing the importance of imagination. She also addressed the influence of George's Catholic upbringing and how it had dampened his ability to deal with these fantasies, which had originated when he was a child. She helped George discover his own spirituality, leading him through the process of active imagination (a method used in Jungian psychology) to explore figures in his dreams and fantasies. She referred him to spiritual practitioners she thought might be able help him explore this realm; for example, she recommended that George consider working with a shaman to help him learn about journeying and spirit guides. She also encouraged George to take yoga classes to help him ground himself in the physical realm, and meditation to help him observe his thought patterns. The work she did with George in therapy sessions, combined with his spiritual development outside of therapy, helped George find new ways of managing his imagination as a resource, rather than a detriment.

Although George's presenting symptoms had caused him to feel alienated in his social and work life at the outset of therapy, they were eventually recognized as a call to acknowledge and develop his unique spiritual identity. This development of a spiritual framework helped him contain and understand his imagination, and he utilized what he learned through the various traditions to better integrate the spiritual aspects of his psyche. Ultimately, George chose to change his career and pursue a line of work much more meaningful to him. He also made new friends and developed better relationships with his family.

Working with Religious and Spiritual Problems

Specific approaches to working with religious and spiritual problems are too numerous to describe in this chapter, but the following four-step process will help you determine which approach may be most beneficial for a given client:

1. Learn more about the problem.

2. Identify the source of the problem.

3. Look for imbalances and potentially helpful counterbeliefs.

4. Acknowledge and witness the client's process.

Learn More About the Problem

First, learn more about the religious or spiritual problem the client is encountering, including any general theories and research that exist on the topic. Since the field of psychology is only beginning to address religious and spiritual issues, the empirical data may be sparse. You might find it helpful to broaden your search for information to religious studies or anthropology literature.

You can also gain information about the problem by directly consulting with a clergyperson, teacher, or advisor who's experienced in the spiritual or religious domain that's troubling the client. If you're impressed by this person's understanding, it may be helpful to explicitly collaborate on the client's treatment plan or refer your client for direct guidance. If not, you can at least learn more about how the clergyperson or spiritual advisor typically deals with this issue when it arises in a religious or spiritual setting. Of course, often you can best learn about the problem by exploring it in depth with the client, with curiosity and compassion, even if the clients holds a somewhat biased perspective on it.

Identify the Source of the Problem

Try to identify the source of the religious or spiritual problem, such as an unhelpful belief or thinking pattern, a trigger (which could be a person, symbol, place, or practice), or a conflict with another person or a tenet of the religious or spiritual tradition. If you can determine the source, you may be able to gently encourage the client to remove the source, perhaps only temporarily. For example, if a client begins to experience agitation whenever she does the rosary, you might consult with a priest about what practice could replace that, at least for a while. If a client has a panic attack during sitting meditation, maybe substituting walking meditation could be useful. If problems seem to arise after a client visits a place of worship, you might encourage her to temporarily use nature as her cathedral. Sometimes certain beliefs and practices become so ingrained that people simply don't consider alternatives.

For some religious and spiritual problems, you can use basic cognitive behavioral approaches, such as reframing or choosing to engage in positive activities while avoiding distressing activities. However, some problems are resistant to these kinds of approaches and require deeper existential exploration.

Look for Imbalances and Potentially Helpful Counterbeliefs

Examine the extent to which a client may be valuing one aspect of his religious or spiritual teachings over another. To right the balance, emphasize less troubling and more positive elements of his religious or spiritual tradition. These may serve as antidotes while also helping the client mature spiritually. The key here is to help clients find their own countering beliefs, rather than providing them yourself. With your help and gentle exploration, clients can often find their own more positive ways of interpreting their situation.

Acknowledge and Witness the Client's Process

Finally, and this cannot be emphasized enough, you can simply acknowledge and witness the client's process using the OARS approach mentioned in chapter 11 or something similar. (As a reminder, OARS stands for open-ended questions, affirmation, reflective listening, and summaries.) Do so without being obsequious, and with an eye toward helping the client (and yourself) reach a place of greater understanding. This kind of process often facilitates insights that naturally lead to resolution. The key is to demonstrate genuine interest, authentic openness and compassion, and a desire to break through to a more complete level of understanding. When approaching religious and spiritual issues, humility is crucial. In a sense, you stand shoulder to shoulder with clients, lending them support as they explore some of the most profound questions people face.

A Note About Medications

When you're trying to differentiate between a psychiatric disorder such as depression, anxiety, or psychosis and a religious or spiritual experience, it's important to remember that psychosis can often be effectively treated with one of the many prescription medications available. Psychotropic medications can be very helpful for people suffering from debilitating symptoms. We have both seen various clients benefit enormously from medications, though this often involves a period of trial and error to find the right medication and dosage.

Clients experiencing religious or spiritual problems with symptoms of depression, mania, anxiety, or psychosis may also benefit from medications. However, be aware that a religious or spiritual experience may be hampered by medications, making it less likely that a person will integrate such experiences into her life story in a healthy way. As Stan and Christina Grof (1989), two of the world's leading experts on spiritual emergencies, note, "The concept of spiritual emergency integrates findings from many disciplines, including clinical and experimental psychiatry, modern consciousness research, experiential therapies, anthropological field studies, parapsychology, thanatology, comparative religion, and mythology. Observations from all these fields suggest strongly that spiritual emergencies have a positive potential and should not be confused with diseases that have a biological cause and necessitate medical treatment" (p. x). (See chapter 6 for more on spiritual emergencies.)

That said, if there is a risk to a client's health, severe impairment of functioning, inability to manage mood, or persistent disruptions to sleeping or eating patterns, that client may benefit from medication as she works to integrate her religious and spiritual issues within herself.

An Alternative View of Religious or Spiritual Problems

You might recall from chapter 6 the story of our collaborator David Lukoff, who had a mystical experience that interrupted his functioning for several months but eventually led him to become a pioneer in working with religious and spiritual problems in therapy. After his experience of grandiosity and mania subsided—with the help of friends and without medication—David began the long process of integrating that experience into his life. He moved to Cape Cod, where he had a recurrence of Crohn's disease that left him exhausted and in pain, yet he continued searching for answers, turning particularly to books by Carl Jung and Joseph Campbell.

While walking on the beach one day, he heard a "voice" telling him to become a healer. So he moved to his parents' house and started his own healing process by trying alternative eating regimens, while also learning to facilitate healing practices such as Gestalt therapy, transactional analysis, primal therapy, bioenergetics, massage, and psychodrama. After three years, he entered a doctoral clinical psychology program. He learned there that his experience would have been diagnosed as a schizophrenic episode, and in a different set of circumstances he would almost certainly have been hospitalized and medicated.

Upon finishing his doctorate in 1980, he became a faculty member at the Clinical Research Center for Schizophrenia at the UCLA Neuropsychiatric Institute. As a staff member of the Ojai Foundation, started by Joan Halifax, he began to learn about shamanism and came to see that a psychotic break was one way of explaining what had happened to him, but another way to explain it was through the lens of shamanic initiation, with its key themes of elevation into an upper world, followed by descent into a lower world, dismemberment, and then rebirth (Eliade, 1951/1964). Through shamanic practices, he learned how to exercise voluntary control over his entry into and out of ecstatic states and how to keep them contained in social contexts where they might be inappropriate (Lukoff, 1990b).

David's experience is an example of how viewing psychological symptoms from a different perspective can result in a positive outcome. In this case, his experience encouraged him to be of service to others in similar situations, and in some ways this has defined his life's work. In fact, such events often lead people to choose a healing profession (Achterberg, 1988, p. 20). From this perspective, these kinds of spiritual and religious experience are seen not as problems, but as a necessary and beneficial process that orients people toward their true life purpose.

Although this is a very different perspective from the conventional Western mental health care paradigm, it does provide the valuable insight that sometimes it may be counterproductive to prematurely eradicate symptoms or interrupt a process of religious or spiritual development. Integrating an anomalous experience is often a long journey, sometimes lasting a lifetime. The difference between a spiritual or religious journey versus psychopathology is that the former enriches a person's life and the lives of others as the person searches for meaning and life purpose, whereas the latter detracts from life, relationships, and making meaning of life. As an effective clinician, make sure that, in your quest to reduce symptoms, you don't prevent a deeper process of growth or transformation from unfolding. In these situations, your job may be to witness the process and provide a safe container.

Another example of this occurred years ago when Shelley participated in the thirty-day silent meditation retreat we described in chapter 13, which had a very demanding schedule. As the days of rigorous practice went on, Shelley noticed that the behavior of another member of the retreat was becoming increasingly strange, until finally the administrators of the retreat removed that member from the group. For the next few days, the participant was never left alone by staff even to sleep; she ate heavier foods (meat and other proteins), rested, was accompanied on slow walks, and was evaluated by a psychiatrist for possible intervention with medication. After a few days, she returned to her normal state and was asked to leave the retreat. The intense schedule of the retreat had overwhelmed her normal defenses, which can happen in certain cases. The retreat center did a good job of evaluating her and eventually removing her for her own benefit and for the benefit of others on retreat. Later, the woman was able to practice brief periods of meditation, under less extreme conditions, to good effect.

When encountering a spiritual emergency or less severe religious or spiritual problem in clients, you might take the same kind of "containment" approach, ideally enlisting the client's family members or friends to help her navigate her difficulties. This may involve removal of religious or spiritual triggers, close observation, shared meals, gentle walks, and providing a safe haven. If the symptoms don't resolve, more intensive mental health interventions may be required. But if risks to the safety of the client are minimal, a gentler approach can be much more useful than focusing on immediate eradication of symptoms.

Conclusion

If a client presents with significant distress or disruption of functioning due to a religious or spiritual problem that's unfamiliar to you, the best course of action is to collaborate with a clergy member or spiritual teacher who's familiar with the problem at hand, to consult with a spiritually oriented therapist who's familiar with the issue, or to refer the client to a clinician who's skilled in dealing with these issues. If the distress or disruption is milder, if you feel somewhat familiar with the issue, or if you feel capable of addressing the issue in your own clinical practice, you can proceed with treatment in much the same way you might approach other Z code problems, such as parent-child relational problems or occupational or academic problems. Obviously, the content of the interventions will differ for each of these issues, but the process of assessment, exploration, treatment planning, and implementation of a treatment plan will be the same.

As you formulate the problem and determine which interventions might be useful, consider running them by a colleague, supervisor, or clergyperson or spiritual teacher from your client's tradition. Through a process of trial and error, you can find interventions that work for the client, discard those that don't work, and ideally, help the client either resolve the issue or develop coping skills to deal with it on an ongoing basis.

Your choice of interventions should rely on your clinical expertise, the expertise of any experts you consult, the client's knowledge of what's helpful and what isn't, and, ideally, the theoretical and research literature on the topic. To help you with the latter, the next chapter focuses on staying up-to-date with the research on religious and spiritual issues in clinical work.

Chapter 15

STAYING UP-TO-DATE

I n the world of clinical practice, we have the good fortune of having an ever-expanding and improving array of protocols, medications, theories, and options available to us. This allows us to help our clients increasingly effectively and also keeps us invigorated in our perspective. We can add new paradigms, practices, and styles of working as we grow as practitioners, helping us stay engaged and interested and even staving off burnout, which is a very real possibility for mental health practitioners.

COMPETENCY 15: Psychologists stay abreast of research and professional developments regarding spirituality and religion specifically related to clinical practice and engage in ongoing assessment of their own spiritual and religious competency.

Just as in other arenas of effective clinical practice, new theories and discoveries are constantly emerging in regard to spiritual and religious issues. To remain competent in addressing this aspect of diversity, it's essential to stay current on best practices. In this chapter, we'll outline some of the key ways of doing so.

Pursue Continuing Education

Because of the sheer number of ongoing important developments in psychology and mental health care, licensing boards have established requirements for continuing education over the course of clinicians' careers to ensure that they continue to learn, grow, and develop their knowledge and skills. In addition to this formal continuing education, you're also expected to engage in informal and ongoing professional development. It can be challenging to stay up-to-date with all aspects of the field, so professionals typically focus on their own specialty or patient population.

Given that this is the case, there are a few simple ways you can stay competent and continue to develop your attitudes, knowledge, and skills in relation to SRBPs in clinical practice. Consider dedicating some of your required continuing education to topics that are relevant to spiritual and religious practices and beliefs or to forms of therapy that include elements drawn from spiritual and religious traditions, such as mindfulness-based therapies. At professional conferences, you might choose to attend a session or two addressing SRBPs. If you don't typically attend professional conferences, many of them now live stream their content, allowing you to access presentations by the top experts in the field from the comfort of your home, often free of charge.

Follow the Literature

Make it a practice to review the table of contents of psychology and mental health journals dedicated to religious, spiritual, transpersonal, or consciousness studies. Examples include the American Psychological Association's *Psychology of Religion and Spirituality* and *Spirituality in Clinical Practice*, as well as *Journal of Transpersonal Psychology*, *International Journal of Transpersonal Studies*, and *Transpersonal Psychology Review*. For Jungian studies, journals include *Spring: A Journal of Archetype and Culture*, *International Journal of Jungian Studies*, *Journal of Analytical Psychology*, *Jung Journal*, and *Psychological Perspectives*. Religious journals include *Religious Studies*, *Religion and American Culture*, *Reviews of Science and Religion*, and *Journal of Religious History*. When you come across articles that catch your interest, read the abstract, and if it seems particularly relevant to your specialty or client population, read the full article.

Utilize the Internet

Another potential source of informal continuing education is online massive open online courses (MOOCs) or other courses that are streamed online or have been archived. Some of these are presented by leading scholars at the top universities in the world and are available at no cost.

You can set a Google alert to automatically e-mail you when articles are posted on the Internet about specific topics, using Boolean operators. For example, if you set a Google alert for "religious or spiritual" and "psychology or psychotherapy," you'll periodically receive a list of links to articles or videos that have recently been posted on the intersection of religion or spirituality with psychology or psychotherapy. If you work with a specific group, you can specify further by adding, for example, "and psychosis" or "and adolescents." You can scan through the headlines to get a sense of what people are talking about online in this domain and follow the links that interest you. You might also find it illuminating to follow the links that make you feel uncomfortable or provoke you. Some Internet content may seem or be inaccurate or silly, but it could also reveal your sore spots or weak points in relation to spirituality and religion, and therefore be worth exploring.

Consider Informal Approaches

Another way to make yourself increasingly comfortable and effective in discussing spiritual and religious issues with clients is to practice talking about these issues outside of the clinical context. For example, say you're at a social gathering and someone mentions being a Sikh. You might then share that you're a mental health professional and ask something like, "I'm curious. How is mental illness viewed in your spiritual tradition?" or "If I were working with a Sikh client, what would be one important thing for me to remember to be more effective or sensitive?" Given that religion and spirituality are often avoided by academics and professionals, you may be surprised to find that people really enjoy discussing these questions.

Even more informally, you can learn from books, films, online videos, and other media. When you encounter such media addressing the topic of religion and spirituality, reflect on how what you observe or learn could be applied in your practice. In the resources section at the back of the book, recommended materials for further developing the sixteen competencies sometimes include films, books, and other popular media resources that might be useful for this exploration. Such sources can be a more entertaining and engaging way to learn about different SRBPs than reading scholarly theory and research, but do keep in mind that they aren't submitted to peer review or necessarily checked for accuracy, and the information they provide is often strongly biased. However, such stories can be a powerful way to explore spirituality and religion in a more "right-brain," emotional way.

When using media to explore SRBPs, be cognizant of stereotypes and memes that are reinforced by the media and by the culture at large, such as the stereotype of the neurotic Jewish person, the guilt-ridden Catholic, or the hippie who meditates and chants. Ask yourself, "If I'd been represented this way throughout the culture and media, in cartoons, movies, books, plays, television, and so on, because of my religious or spiritual background, heritage, or affiliation, how would that have affected my psychological and emotional well-being?" Imagine how this kind of cultural reinforcement might affect clients and their willingness to share their religious or spiritual ideas in therapy. Your job is to be cognizant of generalizations related to clients' SRBPs while also approaching each client as a unique individual and inquiring about her specific SRBPs as though you were encountering them for the first time. This is one of the paradoxes of all forms of cultural competency.

Engage in Ongoing Self-Assessment

Becoming competent and effective in dealing with religious and spiritual issues in your clinical practice is an ongoing process, not an event. Be sure to assess your own spiritual and religious competence from time to time. You might even take a moment to rate yourself on each of the competencies presented in this book. For example, to assess competency 12, ask yourself, "Am I routinely remembering to include religion and spirituality when I take a history with my clients?" To assess competency 8, ask yourself, "Have I explored the potential spiritual and religious resources this client may have access to that could help with planning his treatment?" And to assess competency 7, ask yourself, "Have I asked this client lately how his SRBPs have changed, if at all, over the past few months?" Also see the training guidelines in this book's appendix.

If you find yourself inadvertently avoiding spiritual and religious issues, you might consider engaging in one of the professional development activities discussed earlier in this chapter, or you might seek consultation with a trusted colleague. As you continue to grow as a clinician—hopefully a never-ending process!—you can grow more comfortable and effective in engaging with clients around religious and spiritual topics. Exploration, training, and continuing education can all be useful in this regard. Then, the fact that you're more comfortable with these issues will help your clients feel comfortable discussing religious issues when relevant, creating a more robust and effective therapeutic alliance.

Conclusion

New developments in the field of psychology offer so many opportunities to discover and learn. Just as every new client keeps us fresh and growing, we always have access to new theories or tools that can invigorate our professional practice. This is a wonderful attribute of our field. And at the same time, the areas of religion and spirituality continue to expand and diversify, calling on us to be more tolerant and aware. By staying abreast of new developments in the areas of religion and spirituality, you can provide an environment of openness and curiosity in which clients feel free to discuss their experiences in these areas of their lives.

Even when you've taken the initiative to learn about SRBPs that may be important to your clients, through one or all of the methods outlined in this chapter, there will likely be times when you encounter religious and spiritual issues that are outside your expertise. The next chapter discusses recognizing your limits and what to do when the material being presented is beyond the scope of your practice.

Chapter 16

ACKNOWLEDGING YOUR LIMITS

We have now reached the last of our competencies. Hopefully your understanding of religious and spiritual issues in therapy, and of competence in this area, has increased a great deal since you first opened this book. You've had a chance to review your own history of spiritual and religious beliefs and practices—not just for your own benefit, but to help you better serve your clients. This increased awareness places you in a minority among the population of clinicians, at least according to those who completed our 2014 survey (Vieten et al., 2014). We sincerely hope that a trend toward greater awareness firmly takes hold in our field. After all, as mental health practitioners, we must be dedicated to benefiting our clients to the best of our ability.

However, we all have our limits. None of us knows so much about this realm that we can easily move forward, without hesitation, into any clinical situation. Indeed, even therapists who are trained to be proficient in religious or spiritually informed therapy sometimes encounter clinical material that they aren't qualified to address. (We'd go as far as to say that if this never happens in your career, you may be doing something wrong—or at least not paying attention.) Always bear in mind that it is a good thing, not a failure, to recognize the limits of your competence and, if warranted, to seek consultation or further training or make a referral. Hence, this final competency.

COMPETENCY 16: Psychologists recognize the limits of their qualifications and competence in spiritual and religious domains, including their responses to clients' spirituality or religion that may interfere with clinical practice, so that they (1) seek consultation from and collaborate with other qualified clinicians or spiritual or religious sources (priests, pastors, rabbis, imams, spiritual teachers, and so on), (2) seek further training and education, and/or (3) as appropriate, refer clients to more qualified individuals and resources.

The Principle D ethics code for psychologists not only entitles "all persons to access and benefit from the contributions of psychology and to equal quality in the processes, procedures, and services being conducted by psychologists," but also calls upon psychologists to "ensure that their potential biases, the boundaries of their competence and the limitations of their expertise do not lead to or condone unjust practices" (American Psychological Association, 2010, pp. 3–4).

So here's the challenge: You most certainly have your own SRBPs, even if those consist of not holding to any beliefs or engaging in any practices. Clients have their own individual sets of beliefs and practices. Professionally, can you hold these sets separately? Are you able to discern your own tendencies and keep them in check for the well-being of clients? If you realize that you cannot, which is an admirable level of discernment, are you comfortable referring clients out to someone more in tune with their spiritual or religious beliefs or practices—even if it may be financially undesirable for you to lose such a client?

Limits of Competence

Of course, in addition to being comfortable with the material clients present, you need to have the competence necessary to address that material. Competence is determined by education, training, and supervised clinical experience (Yarhouse & Johnson, 2013, p. 59). As mental health practitioners, we have to ensure that we receive adequate education initially, that we are well trained in working with clients, and that we have supervised clinical experience. The latter two can be done while in school or during internship as a matter of course, or with continuing education units if you are already licensed.

Keeping up your expertise is critical, especially because psychology is an ever-shifting field, with emerging scientific insight informing our work. For example, Shelley was officially trained to do eye movement desensitization and reprocessing (EMDR; F. Shapiro, 2002) as a trauma protocol at an internship site in San Francisco in the late 1990s. However, she voluntarily chose to repeat the training a few years ago in order to ensure she was still following the protocol correctly, and she has also attended various seminars (for continuing education credits) over the years, focusing on updated information on trauma, with experts in the field. The science of psychology is changing daily, and as competent clinicians, it is our duty to stay abreast of current findings.

Recognizing When Your Limits Are Exceeded

You may wonder how you can identify when you've encountered material that's outside your scope of practice. Here are a few signs you might notice:

- You find yourself emotionally upset or reactive, whether during a session or afterward, in response to religious or spiritual material presented in session, or you find yourself ruminating about the session rather than simply reflecting on it.

- A client shares with you, either explicitly or nonverbally (crying, shouting, shutting down, or not showing up to the next session), that your response to the religious or spiritual material she presented has upset her.

- You, your client, or both of you experience an empathic failure, clinical rupture, or failure of attunement as a result of your response to what the client has shared.

- You encounter in yourself a strong bias, judgment, or opinion about something a client has shared that makes it difficult for you to continue to listen or respond empathically.

- You simply don't know what to do or say in response to what a client has shared and are unsure what steps to take next.

Seeking Consultation

Have you ever sought consultation on a case or been in an ongoing case consultation group? When you're grappling with cases that are puzzling, beyond your usual scope of practice, or downright challenging, seeking help from a qualified professional may be the best choice. All therapists occasionally face cases that just aren't clear, yet speaking with a colleague or associated professional (including MDs, clergy members, and others) may prove helpful. For example, it can be quite difficult to make a differential diagnosis on a client presenting with psychotic features that include religious themes, such as seeing ghosts, feeling threatened by the devil, encountering dark evil, and so forth. Because psychiatrists also handle this type of differential diagnosis, conferring with a psychiatrist may be useful.

Another choice for consultation may be a religious or spiritual leader or expert who is better qualified to cover the issue a client has presented.

As a reminder, if you aren't sure about something, there's no shame in consulting another professional who might know more. In addition to being wise, it's also the most ethical behavior. Especially in this era, when we can Skype, e-mail, peruse the Internet, or use our cell phones to contact experts around the country, or even around the globe, with a little research we can easily access the assistance needed.

※ Clinician's Diary

Shelley worked with a couple who initially presented with a relationship problem. After working with them for a few sessions about a relatively simple issue, it came to the fore that the two had radically differing views on their shared religion. While the husband was more liberal in his views, the wife was more conservative on all fronts, politically and religiously. She was devout, attending services several times a week, volunteering at the church, and staunchly supporting the worldview that their pastor set forth. The husband, however, had come from a more liberal religious background and was becoming increasingly uncomfortable with her worldview as it shifted to fit their church.

Theirs was a large church, and Shelley didn't have much experience with their church community and the difficulties they were facing. Although she tried to understand their world, it quickly became apparent that it was radically different from Shelley's. In addition, this issue had become a pivotal point in the therapy. Shelley determined that this was really a case for their pastor. She asked if the couple would be willing to transfer their religious issues to their pastor because they were beyond her scope of practice. They agreed to do so, and Shelley left the door open for them to return anytime to address issues that were more purely "psychological" in nature. This seemed to work, as the pastor later informed Shelley that the couple was attending sessions and working out their church-related issues.

When to Refer

When is it appropriate to refer out? Regarding religious issues, Richards (2009) enumerated a number of circumstances in which pastoral professionals felt it would be appropriate for mental health professionals to refer to them (adapted with permission from Richards, 2009, pp. 390–391):

- You (the mental health professional) are struggling to understand the religious beliefs or thought world of a religious client or feel confused by it.

- You are wondering whether a client's religious beliefs are healthy and normative or unhealthy and idiosyncratic.

- You believe a client's religious beliefs may be keeping him emotionally stuck.

- A client expresses feelings of guilt that seem to originate in violations of her religious beliefs and values.

- A client expresses a desire to reconnect with previously held religious beliefs and community.

- A client raises questions about God, a higher power, or other sources of hope.

- A client expresses a desire to participate in or experience a religious ritual or inquires about spiritual or religious resources.

- A religious client is severely depressed and socially isolated.

- A religious client is suffering from serious illness, loss, or grief.

As you may have noticed, Shelley's difficulty in the case above is covered by the first point. Also, be aware that all of these suggestions apply equally to clients who identify as spiritual but not religious. And to that list, we'd like to add that if you're inexperienced with something of a religious or spiritual nature that a client describes, asks about, or is involved with and the topic makes you uncomfortable, it's wisest to refer out and have the client work with someone more qualified.

Referring to a Medical Practitioner or Psychiatrist

Sometimes it may be best to seek medical or psychiatric help for a client. After listening carefully to people's stories regarding spiritual and religious experiences, Shelley has sometimes referred clients to psychiatrists who are open-minded but also have expertise in medications. As discussed in earlier chapters, at times, people do need psychotropic medications to help them get through a tough transition. In fact, they may have experienced a psychotic break with religious features. If in doubt, the wisest choice is to get further help from a qualified professional.

Referring to an Alternative Practitioner

Sometimes you might consider referrals to alternative practitioners, such as licensed acupuncturists (Chinese medicine practitioners), naturopaths, nutritionists, Ayurvedic practitioners, shamans, or even energy healers (if they exist in your area and are truly gifted). Shelley maintains a list of qualified, grounded alternative practitioners in her area who do types of work for which she's not qualified or trained. In addition, when appropriate, it may be helpful to recommend physical practices such as yoga, hiking in nature, swimming, biking, or other gentle forms of exercise, especially for people who are experiencing challenging symptoms. That said, if a client has any sort of medical problem, always refer to a qualified physician before making any recommendations, even for exercise, however mild they may seem to you.

Conclusion

As a final reminder, the principle of beneficence guides psychologists, as well as other mental health practitioners, to "strive to benefit those with whom they work and take care to do no harm" (American Psychological Association, 2010, Principle A, p. 3). If you follow basic ethical guidelines—remembering to practice within your area of competence, asking for consultation help if you need it, and referring to another professional if a case is beyond your competency or comfort level—you will be practicing in an ethical manner. By doing so, you ensure clients' safety and well-being and your own sense of peace about doing your work well and to the best of your ability, while also maintaining your professional demeanor and license.

CONCLUSION

The primary purpose of this book has been to help you, as a mental health professional, achieve competence in addressing the domains of religion and spirituality, which are important aspects of cultural diversity and are involved in most people's psychological and emotional well-being. At the very least, competence involves avoiding discrimination or prejudice based on religious or spiritual background, heritage, or affiliation. But as we've set forth, true competence goes much farther. Ideally, a therapist competent in the domains of religion and spirituality should possess each of the sixteen competencies presented here.

Competence means being able to demonstrate empathy, compassion, and respect for clients from any spiritual or religious background, and having the skills to effectively conduct therapy with them. It means understanding how your own religious and spiritual background might affect your perceptions, formulations, and behaviors as a clinician, including in ways that you may not always be aware of.

It bears repeating: spirituality and religion are as important as race, ethnicity, gender, sexual orientation, and other forms of human diversity. Competence involves being aware that many forms of religious and spiritual diversity exist. It means taking the time to actively explore aspects of religious and spiritual diversity that are important to your clients.

As a therapist with this competence, you recognize that religion and spirituality are overlapping yet distinct constructs and know that increasing numbers of people identify as spiritual but not religious. You are cognizant that spiritual and religious beliefs and practices, now more than ever before, can change significantly over people's life span, and you routinely inquire about religious and spiritual background when taking client histories.

You know that certain religious or spiritual experiences can sometimes be difficult to distinguish from symptoms of psychopathology, and vice versa. You also understand that spiritual and religious strengths and resources can support psychological well-being, and you are able to employ strategies for helping clients access and take advantage of resources to enhance treatment effectiveness. You have a sense of how to recognize when SRBPs are harmful and how to identify whether clients are experiencing religious or spiritual problems. You are aware that, in extreme cases, legal and ethical issues related to SRBPs may arise. You stay up-to-date with current evidence and theory regarding the intersection between spirituality or religion and therapy. And, importantly, you understand your own limits, including limits of competence, and make referrals when indicated.

Sixteen competencies is a lot. Cultivating all of them at once is a tall order. You may wonder where to focus your efforts initially. In our research, the psychologists and mental health professionals we surveyed rated all of these competencies as important to include in training and continuing education, but some were generally perceived as more important than others. The three items that received the highest importance ratings were as follows, in order of importance:

Competency 1. Psychologists demonstrate empathy, respect, and appreciation for clients from diverse spiritual, religious, or secular backgrounds and affiliations.

Competency 11: Psychologists are able to conduct empathic and effective therapy with clients from diverse spiritual or religious backgrounds, affiliations, and levels of involvement.

Competency 3: Psychologists are aware of how their own spiritual or religious background and beliefs may influence their clinical practice and their attitudes, perceptions, and assumptions about the nature of psychological processes.

If you are unable to include all of the competencies in your own training, or if you are a clinical supervisor, professor, or training program director, be sure to include these three as a matter of course, including for all supervisees and clients.

At the core of these three most important competencies lies our fundamental hope for this book: that it has helped you cultivate an innate sensitivity and effectiveness in interacting with clients with respect to their religious or spiritual backgrounds, beliefs, and practices, or lack thereof. A genuine respect and regard for the variety of SRBPs you'll encounter through the course of your career will enrich your practice and deepen your connection with your clients. You role is to appreciate and be curious about religious and spiritual differences, rather than thinking you can simply be blind to them, so as to avoid repeating the same mistake that was made for many years in the arena of racial diversity.

As you become increasingly aware of any explicit and implicit biases you hold about spirituality and religion—or atheism or agnosticism for that matter—you'll be better able to put aside assumptions and empathize with each client's unique experience. You also may engage in a revealing process of self-exploration that can help you clarify your values and learn more about your own worldview.

There is a difference between a competent clinician and a master clinician. Cultivating the attitudes, knowledge, and skills encompassed by the sixteen competencies in this book will enhance your sophistication and clinical prowess. If you are like most mental health professionals, your training has probably focused primarily on reducing cognitive, emotional, and behavioral problems. In recent years, positive psychology has encouraged us to focus on enhancing clients' strengths, values, and positive emotions at least as much as we attend to ameliorating their difficulties. Greater attention is being paid to physiology, genetics, nutrition, exercise, and sleep—all of which are fundamentally linked to psychological health. The domains addressed by psychology and mental health care are expanding, and rightly so. Our clients are sure to benefit from a more whole-person approach to cultivating their psychological well-being. This includes incorporating the spiritual and religious dimensions of their lives.

Pay attention to clients' beliefs about God or the divine. Inquire into what they hold sacred, what they believe happens after death, and how they relate to their own spirit or consciousness. Do this in the same way you would with other arenas of their lives, such as work, family, or hopes and fears. Even with clients who have no formal SRBPs and don't identify as spiritual or religious in any way, you can inquire about what holds most meaning for them in life. What are their orienting principles? When do they feel most at peace? What internal resources do they rely on in difficult times?

Remember, developing the sixteen competencies we've presented doesn't mean you'll become a spiritual or religious therapist, and it doesn't require that you have any SRBPs of your own. It means that you're comfortable exploring all arenas of clients' lives that may have a bearing on helping them find relief from cognitive and emotional pain and assisting them in moving toward psychological thriving. Your best friends in this exploration are genuine curiosity and sensitive inquiry.

Engaging clients in this way will bring a deeper sense of meaning and value to your sessions. No matter what therapeutic orientation you hold, allowing yourself to move from what Carl Jung described as the small "s" self to the big "S" self from time to time in your clinical work can bring a larger perspective to your practice. Much of the work therapists do with clients focuses on exploring and improving symptoms, thinking patterns, perceptions, reactions, and relationship and work issues, often repeatedly and painstakingly over time. For clients who have told you that they're religious, you can bring new perspective to certain issues by asking questions such as "How would your religious tradition view this issue?" Likewise, for a client you know to have a spiritual practice, you could ask, "If you look at this from a spiritual perspective, what would you say about it?" For those who identify as being neither religious nor spiritual, you might say, "If you take a few steps back from this, like a bird's-eye view, what do you think is the overall meaning of this situation? At the larger level, what do you think is really going on here?"

Taking the time every once in a while to make this kind of shift can allow wisdom and presence to illuminate the clinical encounter. It can help you learn more about clients' views of the world and provide space to breathe and reflect together. In this way, you can be trusted to walk beside clients through all aspects of their experience, without shying away or inelegantly stumbling through. We hope this book has provided guidance that will help you navigate this particular portion of the terrain with ease and sensitivity.

Appendix

PROVISIONAL TRAINING GUIDELINES

If you are involved in educating, training, or supervising mental health professionals, how can you assess their progress in cultivating the religious and spiritual competencies we've presented in this book? Below we provide observable and measurable guidelines for assessing the extent to which trainees or clinicians are competent in each domain.

This set of guidelines may also be helpful if you're creating a syllabus or series of didactic materials for teaching religious and spiritual competencies or wish to include any of them as goals for your training program. This list provides another way for you to assess your own competency as a clinician. The development of multicultural competencies is a process rather than an event, and they can be assessed periodically throughout your training and your career.

Competency 1: Clinicians demonstrate empathy, respect, and appreciation for clients from diverse spiritual, religious, or secular backgrounds and affiliations.

- Clinicians demonstrate an attitude of empathy, respect, and appreciation toward spiritual and religious material presented by their clients.

- Clinicians can define the terms "empathy," "respect," and "appreciation" with regard to spiritual and religious beliefs and practices.

- Clinicians are willing to address and explore spiritual and religious issues presented by clients and not avoid them.

- Clinicians can describe three methods for increasing empathy, respect, and appreciation with regard to clients' spiritual and religious beliefs and practices.

- Clinicians can identify when their empathy, respect, or appreciation of religious or spiritual issues has been challenged and seek consultation or supervision when needed.

Competency 2: Clinicians view spirituality and religion as important aspects of human diversity, along with factors such as race, ethnicity, sexual orientation, socioeconomic status, disability, gender, and age.

- Clinicians can describe the reasons why it's important to pay attention to spiritual and religious diversity in therapy, similar to other elements of human diversity, including race, ethnicity, sexual orientation, socioeconomic status, disability, gender, and age.

- Clinicians can describe how some people have experienced prejudice, discrimination, assumptions, or unfair generalizations due to their spiritual or religious beliefs.

- Clinicians avoid generalizations based on their clients' religious and spiritual background, affiliation, beliefs, and practices.

Competency 3: Clinicians are aware of how their own spiritual or religious background and beliefs may influence their clinical practice and their attitudes, perceptions, and assumptions about the nature of psychological processes.

- Clinicians can describe how individual and cultural spiritual and religious beliefs and practices may influence how people make meaning of the world, including thoughts on free will, personal responsibility, ethics, and morals.

- Clinicians are able to identify how their personal spiritual and religious beliefs and practices may cause them to have explicit and implicit biases, assumptions, or prejudices.

- Clinicians can identify how their personal spiritual and religious beliefs and practices may affect how they formulate cases and the way they interact with clients.

- Clinicians have explored their own current and historical religious and spiritual beliefs and practices and have actively reflected on how these may have influenced their current worldview.

Competency 4: Clinicians know that many diverse forms of spirituality and religion exist, and explore spiritual and religious beliefs, communities, and practices that are important to their clients.

- Clinicians can identify sensitive ways to ask clients about spiritual and religious beliefs and practices (SRBPs) that may be important to them.

- Clinicians can identify ways, outside of therapy sessions, to inform themselves about SRBPs that are important to their clients.

- Clinicians take the time to learn about SRBPs that they encounter in their clinical practice with which they are unfamiliar.

- Clinicians explore clients' lived experience with respect to their SRBPs.

Competency 5: Clinicians can describe how spirituality and religion can be viewed as overlapping yet distinct constructs.

- Clinicians can define the terms "religion" and "spirituality."

- Clinicians are able to describe how religion and spirituality are distinct from one another yet can overlap to varying degrees.

- Clinicians ask clients about their religious and spiritual beliefs and practices, current and past.

Competency 6: Clinicians understand that clients may have experiences that are consistent with their spirituality or religion, yet may be difficult to differentiate from psychopathological symptoms.

- Clinicians can identify religious or spiritual experiences that may mimic psychological disorders.

- Clinicians can define the terms "mystical experience" and "spiritual emergency," and describe some forms of each.

- Clinicians are able to describe several factors that can help differentiate a spiritual emergency or religious struggle from psychopathology.

- Clinicians recognize that spiritual and religious problems and psychopathology are not mutually exclusive and can be present simultaneously.

- Clinicians seek consultation, collaborate with clergy or spiritual teachers, or make referrals when they find it difficult to distinguish psychopathology from religious or spiritual issues.

Competency 7: Clinicians recognize that spiritual or religious beliefs, practices, and experiences develop and change over the life span.

- Clinicians are able to describe ways that SRBPs can change over the life span.

- Clinicians ask clients not only about their SRBPs but also about how those SRBPs have changed over time.

- Clinicians acknowledge clients' religious and spiritual development as part of their overall psychological development.

Competency 8: Clinicians are aware of clients' internal and external spiritual or religious resources and practices that research indicates may support psychological well-being and recovery from psychological disorders.

- Clinicians can access current research literature to learn about religious and spiritual resources that may be helpful to clients.

- Clinicians are able to describe examples of inner and outer religious and spiritual resources that may be available to their clients.

- Clinicians can describe examples of positive and negative religious coping.

- Clinicians demonstrate the ability to discover what religious or spiritual resources may be available to their clients.

- Clinicians encourage clients to access spiritual and religious resources that may support their treatment for, recovery from, or coping with psychological disorders.

- Clinicians can identify psychological interventions that include or draw from religious or spiritual traditions or practices.

Competency 9: Clinicians can identify spiritual and religious experiences, practices, and beliefs that may have the potential to negatively impact psychological health.

- Clinicians can describe forms of SRBPs that may be associated with poorer psychological health, such as negative religious coping, religious scrupulosity, overinvolvement in SRBPs, belonging to a cult or group with cultlike characteristics, unresolved religious and spiritual struggles, and inability to integrate spiritual or peak experiences.

- Clinicians can identify several factors that differentiate potentially maladaptive SRBPs from other SRBPs, and that differentiate cults from other religious or spiritual groups.

- Clinicians are able to describe different types of religious and spiritual struggles.

- Clinicians demonstrate willingness and the ability to consult or collaborate with clergy members or spiritual teachers when attending to clients' religious or spiritual struggles.

Competency 10: Clinicians can identify legal and ethical issues related to spirituality and religion that may surface when working with clients.

- Clinicians are able to describe the legal and ethical guidelines for avoiding discrimination and prejudice based on religious and spiritual diversity.

- Clinicians can describe legal or ethical issues that may arise in the domain of religion and spirituality.

- Clinicians are able to recognize the limits of their competency and stay within their scope of practice in the treatment of religious and spiritual issues.

Competency 11: Clinicians are able to conduct empathic and effective therapy with clients from diverse spiritual or religious backgrounds, affiliations, and levels of involvement.

- Clinicians demonstrate the ability to sensitively address religious or spiritual diversity in therapy.

- Clinicians don't ignore or avoid religious or spiritual material in therapy.

- Clinicians are able to describe some of their biases regarding SRBPs and can identify when those biases are interfering with effective therapy.

- Clinicians demonstrate the ability to sensitively inquire about and listen to clients' diverse experiences of religion and spirituality.

- Clinicians have methods for dealing with their own negative reactions to clients' religious or spiritual beliefs and practices.

Competency 12: Clinicians inquire about spiritual and religious background, experience, practices, attitudes, and beliefs as a standard part of understanding a client's history.

- Clinicians gather information about clients' current and past SRBPs as a standard part of conducting an intake or assessment.

- Clinicians are able to implement several methods for assessing clients' spiritual and religious SRBPs.

Competency 13: Clinicians help clients explore and access their spiritual and religious strengths and resources.

- During initial assessment and periodically thereafter, clinicians identify inner and outer religious and spiritual resources that may be available to support clients' psychological well-being.

- Clinicians can describe examples of inner and outer religious and spiritual resources and tools.

- Clinicians sensitively encourage clients to explore and access those inner and outer resources.

- Clinicians avoid acting as spiritual advisors and act ethically as well as cautiously if recommending new religious or spiritual practices to clients.

Competency 14: Clinicians can identify and address spiritual and religious problems in clinical practice and make referrals when necessary.

- Clinicians explicitly inquire about whether clients' SRBPs are causing them any concerns or problems.

- Clinicians demonstrate the ability to identify religious or spiritual problems such as loss of faith or loss of spiritual connection, meditation-related problems, disruptive or distressing mystical experiences, near-death experiences, leaving a spiritual teacher or path, religious or spiritual struggles, or spiritual emergencies.

- Clinicians acknowledge and address spiritual or religious problems in therapy and consult or collaborate with outside experts if indicated.

- Clinicians can describe the *DSM 5/ICD 10* category Z65.8 "Religious or Spiritual Problem."

- Clinicians acknowledge that religious and spiritual problems are sometimes normative aspects of religious and spiritual development and personal growth.

Competency 15: Clinicians stay abreast of research and professional developments regarding spirituality and religion specifically related to clinical practice and engage in ongoing assessment of their own spiritual and religious competency.

- Clinicians can describe several ways to stay up-to-date on current thinking about the intersection of religion/spirituality and clinical practice, such as

186

advanced training, continuing education, review of current literature, and seeking consultation or supervision.

- Clinicians can describe methods for periodically assessing their own comfort and competence in addressing spiritual and religious issues in therapy.

Competency 16: Clinicians recognize the limits of their qualifications and competence in spiritual and religious domains, including their responses to clients' spirituality or religion that may interfere with clinical practice, so that they (1) seek consultation from and collaborate with other qualified clinicians or spiritual or religious sources (priests, pastors, rabbis, imams, spiritual teachers, and so on), (2) seek further training and education, and/or (3) as appropriate, refer clients to more qualified individuals and resources.

- Clinicians can identify several signs that would indicate that they've reached the limits of their religious and spiritual competence.

- Clinicians admit their limits in working with certain clients and, when this occurs, seek consultation, supervision, or additional training, or make referrals.

RESOURCES

This list of resources provides you with a diverse assortment of materials—books, articles, videos (including lectures), and websites—to help you to explore the many diverse aspects of religion and spirituality in our culture. Although many of them are educational, we've purposely included thought-provoking resources that can serve as catalysts for you to examine your assumptions and expand your attitudes, knowledge, and skills in these domains. We have intentionally included materials that are provocative and controversial, as well as others that are more mainstream. We don't endorse any of the points of view represented here; rather, we recommend that you use them as jumping-off points for reflection and discussion. For the most part, this list excludes items that appear in the list of references cited (which, of course, includes many excellent resources).

General Resources

Books

Brownell, P. M. *Spiritual competency in psychotherapy.*

Hood Jr., R. W., Hill, P. C., & Spilka, B. *The psychology of religion: An empirical approach.*

Paloutzian, R. F., & Park, C. L. (Eds.). *Handbook of the psychology of religion and spirituality.*

Pargament, K. I. (Ed.). APA *handbook of psychology, religion, and spirituality, Volumes 1 and 2.*

Websites

American Association of Pastoral Counselors. http://www.aapc.org.

This website offers psychologically informed counseling tools for spiritual and religious counselors.

New York Zen Center for Contemplative Care. http://www.zencare.org.

This organization provides continuing education to licensed caregivers, particularly medical professionals, using Buddhist contemplative practices to support mindful, compassionate, interfaith medical care.

Competency 1: Demonstrating Empathy, Respect, and Appreciation

Books

Brownell, P. M. *Spiritual competency in psychotherapy.*

Matlins, S. *How to be a perfect stranger: The essential religious etiquette handbook.*

Rogers, C. *The Carl Rogers reader.*

Articles

Emore, H. Religious and cultural sensitivity. http://www.gatheringoffaiths.com/wp-content/uploads/Religious-and-Cultural-Sensitivity.pdf.

Videos

TED (Director & Producer). *His Holiness the Karmapa: The technology of the heart.* http://www.ted.com/talks/his_holiness_the_karmapa_the_technology_of_the_heart.
Ogyen Trinley Dorje, the seventeenth Gyalwang Karmapa, discusses the technology of the heart within the context of Buddhist teachings.

TED (Director & Producer). *Jeremy Rifkin: The empathic civilization.* http://www.ted.com/talks/jeremy_rifkin_on_the_empathic_civilization.
Rifkin discusses the ways in which empathy has evolved and influenced culture.

TED (Director & Producer). *Krista Tippett: Reconnecting with compassion.* http://www.ted.com/talks/krista_tippett_reconnecting_with_compassion.
Journalist Krista Tippett relays stories about compassion and suggests a new way to conceptualize and define it.

Wagner, P. M. (Director & Producer). *The wisdom of faith: A Bill Moyers special with Huston Smith* [5-part PBS special].
Comparative religions scholar Huston Smith discusses his ideas on faith and religion in interviews with Bill Moyers.

Competency 2: Appreciating Religious and Spiritual Diversity

Books

Armstrong, K. *The case for God.*

Eck, D. *A new religious America: How a "Christian country" has become the world's most religiously diverse nation.*

Frankel, J., & Mendelsohn, E. (Eds.). *The Protestant-Jewish conundrum: Studies in contemporary Jewry, volume XXIV.*

Kirby, T. (Producer). *The story of God: A personal journey in to the world of science and religion* [3-part documentary].

Robert Winston explores the history of God across continents and cultures.

TED (Director & Producer). *Wade Davis: Dreams from endangered cultures.* http://www.ted.com/talks/wade_davis_on_endangered_cultures?language=en.

Anthropologist and photographer Wade Davis discusses many indigenous cultures and their religions.

Websites

Association of Religion Data Archives. http://www.thearda.com.

A learning resource for teachers and students of any level, with copious statistics on US and world religions.

Encyclopedia of Religion and Society. http://www.hirr.hartsem.edu/ency/index.htm.

This site offers definitions for hundreds of religious terms.

Library of World Religions and Faith Traditions. http://www.patheos.com/Library.

This website offers peer-reviewed, encyclopedic information to help readers learn about the origins, history, beliefs, rituals, and ethics of a wide variety of religions.

Religions. http://www.bbc.co.uk/religion/religions.

This archived BBC website provides general information on world religions.

The World Factbook. https://www.cia.gov/library/publications/the-world-factbook/fields/2122.html.

This CIA website describes the primary characteristics of world religions, including origins, populations size, and current status.

Competency 5: Understanding Spirituality and Religion as Different but Overlapping

Books

Churchward, A. *The origin and evolution of religion.*

Daniel, L. *When "spiritual but not religious" is not enough: Seeing God in surprising places, even the church.*

Fuller, R. C. *Spiritual, but not religious: Understanding unchurched America.*

Kripal, J. J. *Esalen: America and the religion of no religion.*

Singer, M. A. *The untethered soul: The journey beyond yourself.*

Videos

Swyer, A. (Director). *Spiritual revolution.*
    This documentary describes the influx of Eastern spirituality into America.

Competency 6: Knowing the Difference Between Spirituality and Psychopathology

Books

Borchert, B. *Mysticism: Its history and challenge.*

Clarke, I. (Ed.). *Psychosis and spirituality: Consolidating the new paradigm.*

Gale, J., Robson, M., & Rapsomatioti, G. (Eds.). *Insanity and divinity: Studies in psychosis and spirituality.*

Khalsa, G. K., et al. *Kundalini rising: Exploring the energy of awakening.*

Moore, T. *Dark nights of the soul: A guide to finding your way through life's ordeals.*

Videos

Elrod, J. & Crespi, C. (Directors), & Hutensky, S. (Producer). *Wake Up.*
    This documentary tells the story of a man who inexplicably developed the seeming ability to access other dimensions.

Olsson, S. (Director & Producer), CEM Productions & Link Media (Producers). *Global spirit: The mystical experience.* https://www.linktv.org/series/global-spirit.
    In this episode in a series on spiritual practices, Phil Cousineau explores diverse forms of mysticism.

TEDxTeachersCollege (Director & Producer). *Depression and spiritual awakening: Two sides of one door.* http://tedxtalks.ted.com/video/Depression-Spiritual-Awakening.
    Lisa Miller discusses a personal event in her life that caused a deep depression and how spirituality helped her understand the meaning of the experience.

TEDxUMKC (Director & Producer). *Psychosis or spiritual awakening: Phil Borges at TEDxUMKC.* http://tedxtalks.ted.com/video/Psychosis-or-Spiritual-Awakenin.
    Phil Borges discusses the experience of spiritual awakening and how it looks like psychosis to people in some circles.

Websites

Spiritual Competency Resource Center. http://www.spiritualcompetency.com.
    This website created by David Lukoff provides access to online resources for enhancing the cultural sensitivity of mental health professionals, including online courses, audiovisual resources, and articles.

Competency 7: Recognizing Life Span Development

Books

Fowler, J. W. *Stages of faith: The psychology of human development and the quest for meaning.*

Gilbert, E. *Eat, pray, love: One woman's search for everything across Italy, India, and Indonesia.*

Hesse, H. *Siddhartha.* (H. Rosner, Trans.).

Rinpoche, S. *The Tibetan book of living and dying.* (P. Gaffney, Ed.).

Salzberg, S. *Faith: Trusting your own deepest experience.*

Smith, G. T. *Beginning well: Christian conversion and authentic transformation.*

Tomer, A., Eliason, G. T., & Wong, P. T. (Eds.). *Existential and spiritual issues in death attitudes.*

Videos

Ki-duk, K. (Director). *Spring, summer, fall, winter...and spring.*
This story of a young boy who studies at a monastery floating on a lake is noted for its cinematography.

Lee, S. (Director), & Worth, M. (Producer). *Malcolm X.*
This 1992 biographical drama depicts the life of Malcolm X, who converted to Islam in prison and became a civil rights leader.

Leeman, L., & di Florio, P. (Directors), & Rader, P. (Producer). *Awake: The life of Yogananda.*
This unconventional biographical film tells the story of Paramahansa Yogananda, who brought Hindu spirituality to America in the 1920s.

Robbins, B. (Director). *A thousand words.*
Eddie Murphy stars in this comedy about a literary agent who tries to stretch the truth with a spiritual guru.

Competency 8: Learning About Clients' Spiritual and Religious Resources

Books

Kalsched, D. *Trauma and the soul: A psycho-spiritual approach to human development and its interruption.*

Lamott, Anne. *Traveling mercies: Some thoughts on faith.*

Videos

Brown, K. (Producer). *Trauma and recovery: A Cambodian refugee experience.*

This documentary explores the convergence of Western mental health care approaches and Buddhist traditions among a community of Cambodian refugees living in Massachusetts.

TED (Director & Producer). *Andy Puddicombe: All it takes is 10 mindful minutes.* http://www.ted.com/talks/andy_puddicombe_all_it_takes_is_10_mindful_minutes ?language=en.

Meditation expert Andy Puddicombe discusses how ten minutes of meditation can be helpful for the heart, creativity, and emotional well-being.

Telonidis, Taki (Director). *Healing the warrior's heart.*

This documentary examines the impact of war on soldiers, primarily members of the Blackfeet tribe, through the lens of Native American traditions and ceremonies.

Websites

Duke University Center for Spirituality, Theology and Health. http://www.spiritualityandhealth.duke.edu.

The center conducts research, offers training, and contributes to field building; resources available on the website include articles, newsletters, and workshops.

Palouse Mindfulness, Online Mindfulness-Based Stress Reduction. http://palousemindfulness.com/selfguidedMBSR.html.

An online mindfulness-based stress reduction (MBSR) course based on the MBSR program begun by Jon Kabat-Zinn at the University of Massachusetts Medical School.

Mindful.org. http://www.mindful.org/resources.

The resources page for Mindful, an initiative dedicated to bringing mindfulness to the public. Includes links to mindfulness courses, mindfulness centers, mindfulness programs in schools, and audio of various meditation practices.

Sounds True's MBSR Online Course. http://www.soundstrue.com/store/the-mbsr-online-course-3226.html.

An eight-week MBSR training course available for purchase; includes CE credits for US customers.

Mindful Schools, Mindful Fundamentals. http://www.mindfulschools.org/training/mindfulness-fundamentals/.

A six-week online mindfulness course.

Competency 9: Recognizing Harmful Involvement

Books

Arterburn, S., & Felton, J. *Toxic faith: Experiencing healing from painful spiritual abuse.*

Kramer, J., & Alstad, D. *The guru papers: Masks of authoritarian power.*

Langone, M. D. (Ed.). *Recovery from cults: Help for victims of psychological and spiritual abuse.*

Videos

Gandhi, V. (Director), & Carmel, B., & Colthurst, B. (Producers). *Kumare.*
This film documents a social experiment in which the director poses as a guru in an effort to undermine blind faith, with surprising results.

Nelson, S. (Director & Producer). *Jonestown: The life and death of Peoples Temple.*
This documentary explores how cult leader Jim Jones persuaded over nine hundred members to commit mass suicide.

TED (Director & Producer). *Diane Benscoter: How cults rewire the brain.*
http://www.ted.com/talks/ex_moonie_diane_benscoter_how_cults_think?language=en.
Diane Benscoter describes her experience as a "Moonie" and provides insight into extremist movements.

Competency 10: Being Aware of Legal and Ethical Issues

Books

Maroukis, T. C. *The peyote road: Religious freedom and the Native American Church.*

McEwan, I. *The Children Act.*

Websites

BBC: Religion and Ethics. http://www.bbc.co.uk/religion.
This website covers several contemporary issues pertaining to religions and ethics.

ReligiousTolerance.org. http://www.religioustolerance.org/conflict.htm.
This website tracks different religious controversies without bias or promotion of a single point of view.

Clinical Lawyer. http://www.clinicallawyer.com.
A website dedicated to providing legal information for mental health practitioners.

Competency 11: Working with Religious and Spiritual Diversity

Books

Armstrong, K. *A history of God: The 4,000-year quest of Judaism, Christianity and Islam.*

Chopra, D. *God: A story of revelation.*

Dawkins, R. *The god delusion.*

Kornfield, J. *A path with heart: A guide through the perils and promises of spiritual life.*

Mabry, J. R. (Ed.). *Spiritual guidance across religions: A sourcebook for spiritual directors and other professionals providing counsel to people of differing faith traditions.*

Smith, H. *Why religion matters: The fate of the human spirit in an age of disbelief.*

Tolle, E. *The power of now: A guide to spiritual enlightenment.*

Competency 12: Taking a Religious and Spiritual History

Books

Fitchett, G. *Assessing spiritual needs: A guide for caregivers.*

Hodge, D. R. *Spiritual assessment: Handbook for helping professionals.*

McLennan, S. *Finding your religion: When the faith you grew up with has lost its meaning.*

Roehlkepartain, E. C., King, P. E., Wagener, L., & Benson, P. L. *The handbook of spiritual development in childhood and adolescence.*

Wagler, I. *Growing up Amish: A memoir.*

Videos

Farmiga, V. (Director). *Higher ground.*

This film about a tight-knit spiritual community explores the intersection of faith and doubt and how people recover their relationship to faith.

Competency 13: Helping Clients Access Their Religious and Spiritual Resources

Books

Chödrön, P. *When things fall apart: Heart advice for difficult times.*

Cloninger, C. R. *Feeling good: The science of well-being.*

198

Keating, T. *Open mind, open heart: The contemplative dimension of the Gospel.*

Pargament, K. I. *The psychology of religion and coping: Theory, research, practice.*

Piver, S. (Ed.). *Quiet mind: A beginner's guide to meditation.*

Plante, T. G. *Spiritual practices in psychotherapy: Thirteen tools for enhancing psychological health.*

Walsh, R. N. *Essential spirituality: The 7 central practices to awaken heart and mind.*

Wilber, K., Patten, T., Leonard, A., & Morelli, M. *Integral life practice.*

Yacoboni, C. (Ed.). *How do you pray? Inspiring responses from religious leaders, spiritual guides, healers, activists, and other lovers of humanity.*

Competency 14: Identifying Spiritual and Religious Problems

Books

Bragdon, E. *The call of spiritual emergency: From personal crisis to personal transformation.*

Articles

Nye, C. Possession, Jinn, and Britain's backstreet exorcists. *BBC News UK.* http://www.bbc.com/news/uk-20357997.

Videos

Barber, G. (Producer), & Shadyac, T. (Director). *Bruce Almighty.*
  Jim Carrey stars in this movie about a man who, despite (or maybe in spite of) his alienation from God, is given omnipotent powers.

Competency 15: Staying Up-to-Date

See chapter 15 for a list of journals that can help you stay up-to-date in this field.

Additional Thought-Provoking Resources

Books

Cheong, P. H., Fischer-Nielsen, P., Gelfgren, S., & Ess, C. (Eds.). *Digital religion, social media, and culture: Perspectives, practices and futures.*

Frawley-O'Dea, M. G. *Perversion of power: Sexual abuse in the Catholic Church.*

Harvey, J. F. *Homosexuality and the Catholic Church: Clear answers to difficult questions.*

Videos

Cronk, H. (Director). *God's not dead.*

This movie about a Christian college student who must debate his college philosophy teacher about the existence of God explores the conflict between philosophical and religious beliefs.

Ewing, H., & Grady, R. (Directors). *Jesus camp.*

This provocative documentary tells the story of kids who participate in a religious summer camp in hopes of one day emulating Billy Graham.

Herek, S. (Director). *Holy man.*

Eddie Murphy portrays a television evangelist who tries to turn shopping into a religious experience.

Maher, B. (Director). *Religulous.*

From his iconoclastic stance, Bill Maher interviews a wide array of people, from a variety of traditions around the globe, about their views on their faith.

Ouroboros, Evison, R., & Velez, R. (Directors). *Stepping into the fire.*

This documentary tells the story of three professional people who turned to shamanistic practices to address the sense of dis-ease they felt in their lives.

Schmidt, D. (Director). *Inner worlds, outer worlds.*

This documentary explores meditation.

TED (Director & Producer). *Aicha el-Wafi and Phyllis Rodriguez: The mothers who found forgiveness, friendship.* http://www.ted.com/talks/9_11_healing_the_mothers _who_found_forgiveness_friendship.

This video tells the story of two mothers, one with a son who was killed in the September 11 attacks, and the other with a son who was convicted of having a role in the attacks. Through reconciliation meetings, they overcome their differences and form a lasting friendship.

TED (Director & Producer). *Zak Ebrahim: I am the son of a terrorist. Here's how I chose peace.* http://www.ted.com/talks/zak_ebrahim_i_am_the_son_of_a_terrorist _here_s_how_i_chose_peace?language=en.

Zak Ebrahim tells the story of his father, a terrorist, and how he coped after discovering his father's religious and social choices.

References

Abramowitz, J. S., Huppert, J. D., Cohen, A. B., Tolin, D. F., & Cahill, S. P. (2002). Religious obsessions and compulsions in a non-clinical sample: The Penn Inventory of Scrupulosity (PIOS). *Behaviour Research and Therapy* 40(7): 825–838. doi:10.1016/S0005-7967(01)00070-5.

Abramowitz, J. S., & Jacoby, R. J. (2014). Scrupulosity: A cognitive-behavioral analysis and implications for treatment. *Journal of Obsessive-Compulsive and Related Disorders* 3(2): 140–149.

Achterberg, J. (1988). The wounded healer: Transformational journeys in modern medicine. In G. Doore (Ed.), *Shaman's path: Healing, personal growth, and empowerment* (pp. 115–126). Boston: Shambhala.

Adamczyk, A., & Hayes, B. E. (2012). Religion and sexual behaviors: Understanding the influence of Islamic cultures and religious affiliation for explaining sex outside of marriage. *American Sociological Review* 77(5): 723–746. doi:10.1177/0003122412458672.

Allport, G. W., & Ross, J. M. (1967). Personal religious orientation and prejudice. *Journal of Personality and Social Psychology* 5(4): 432–443.

American Psychiatric Association. (1994). *Diagnostic and statistical manual of mental disorders* (4th ed.). Washington, DC: Author.

American Psychiatric Association. (2013). *Diagnostic and statistical manual of mental disorders* (5th ed.). Washington, DC: Author.

American Psychological Association. (2002). *Guidelines on multicultural education, training, research, practice, and organizational change for psychologists.* Washington, DC: Author.

American Psychological Association. (2007). Guidelines for psychological practice with girls and women. *American Psychologist* 62(9): 949–979.

American Psychological Association. (2008). Resolution on religious, religion-based, and/or religion-derived prejudice. *American Psychologist* 63(5): 431–434.

American Psychological Association. (2009). *Multicultural competency in geropsychology: A report of the APA Committee on Aging and its working group.* Washington, DC: Author.

American Psychological Association. (2010). *Ethical principles of psychologists and code of conduct with the 2010 amendments adopted February 20, 2010.* Retrieved November 26, 2014, from http://www.apa.org/ethics/code/principles.pdf.

American Psychological Association. (2012). Guidelines for psychological practice with lesbian, gay, and bisexual clients. *American Psychologist* 67(1): 10–42.

American Psychological Association. (2013). *Guidelines and principles for accreditation of programs in professional psychology.* Washington, DC: Author.

Ammerman, N. T. (2010). The challenges of pluralism: Locating religion in a world of diversity. *Social Compass* 57(2): 154–167.

Ano, G. G., & Vasconcelles, E. B. (2005). Religious coping and psychological adjustment to stress: A meta-analysis. *Journal of Clinical Psychology* 61(4): 461–480.

Aronoff, J., Lynn, S. J., & Malinoski, P. (2000). Are cultic environments psychologically harmful? *Clinical Psychology Review* 20(1): 91–111.

Arredondo, P., Toporek, R., Brown, S. P., Jones, J., Locke, D. C., Sanchez, J., et al. (1996). Operationalization of the multicultural counseling competencies. *Journal of Multicultural Counseling and Development* 24(1): 42–78. doi:10.1002/j.2161-1912.1996.tb00288.x.

Astin, J. A. (1997). Stress reduction through mindfulness meditation: Effects on psychological symptomatology, sense of control, and spiritual experiences. *Psychotherapy and Psychosomatics* 66(2): 97–106.

Association of American Medical Colleges. (1999). *Contemporary issues in medicine: Communication in medicine*. Washington, DC: Association of American Medical Colleges.

Baer, R. (Ed.). (2010). *Assessing mindfulness and acceptance processes in clients: Illuminating the theory and practice of change*. Oakland, CA: New Harbinger.

Barnett, J. E., & Johnson, W. B. (2011). Integrating spirituality and religion into psychotherapy: Persistent dilemmas, ethical issues, and a proposed decision-making process. *Ethics and Behavior* 21(2): 147–164. doi:10.1080/10508422.2011.551471.

Batson, C. D., & Ventis, W. L. (1982). *The religious experience: A social-psychological perspective*. New York: Oxford University Press.

Bergin, A. E., & Jensen, J. P. (1990). Religiosity of psychotherapists: A national survey. *Psychotherapy* 27(1): 3–7.

Betty, S. (2012). The growing evidence for "demonic possession": What should psychiatry's response be? *Journal of Spirituality and Paranormal Studies* 35(1): 23–40.

Bingaman, K. (2011). The art of contemplative and mindfulness practice: Incorporating the findings of neuroscience into pastoral care and counseling. *Pastoral Psychology* 60(3): 477–489. doi:10.1007/s11089-011-0328-9.

Black, D. S., Milam, J., & Sussman, S. (2009). Sitting-meditation interventions among youth: A review of treatment efficacy. *Pediatrics* 124(3): 532–541.

Blanton, P. (2005). How to talk to Christian clients about their spiritual lives: Insights from postmodern family therapy. *Pastoral Psychology* 54(2): 93–101. doi:10.1007/s11089-005-6197-3.

Bledsoe, T. S., Setterlund, K., Adams, C. J., Fok-Trela, A., & Connolly, M. (2013). Addressing pastoral knowledge and attitudes about clergy/mental health practitioner collaboration. *Social Work and Christianity* 40(1): 23–45.

Bonelli, R. M., & Koenig, H. G. (2013). Mental disorders, religion, and spirituality 1990 to 2010: A systematic evidence-based review. *Journal of Religion and Health* 52(2): 657–673. doi:10.1007/s10943-013-9691-4.

Borchard, T. J. (2014). The dark night and clinical depression. *Beyond blue* (blog). Retrieved January 26, 2015, from http://www.beliefnet.com/columnists/beyondblue/2009/05/the-dark-night-and-clinical-de.html.

Bowling Green State University. (2012). Defining religion and spirituality. Retrieved December 10, 2014, from http://www.bgsu.edu/arts-and-sciences/psychology/graduate-program/clinical/the-psychology-of-spirituality-and-family/relational-spirituality/defining-religion-and-spirituality.html.

Bragdon, E. (1988). *A sourcebook for helping people in spiritual emergency*. Los Altos, CA: Lightening Up Press.

Brawer, P. A., Handal, P. J., Fabricatore, A. N., Roberts, R., & Wajda-Johnston, V. A. (2002). Training and education in religion/spirituality within APA-accredited clinical psychology programs. *Professional Psychology: Research and Practice* 33(2): 203–206.

Brewerton, T. D. (1994). Hyperreligiosity in psychotic disorders. *The Journal of Nervous and Mental Disease* 182(5): 302–304.

Buckholtz, A. (2005, December 6). Help from above. *Washington Post.* Retrieved November 24, 2014, from http://www.washingtonpost.com/wp-dyn/content/article/2005/12/02/AR2005120202287.html.

Buckley, K. (1989). *Mechanical man: John Broadus Watson and the beginnings of behaviorism.* New York: Guilford.

Cahn, B. R., Delorme, A., & Polich, J. (2013). Event-related delta, theta, alpha, and gamma correlates to auditory oddball processing during Vipassana meditation. *Social Cognitive and Affective Neuroscience* 8(1): 100–111.

Cahn, B. R., & Polich, J. (2006). Meditation states and traits: EEG, ERP, and neuroimaging studies. *Psychological Bulletin* 132(2): 180–211.

Campbell, D., & Putnam, R. (2012). God and Caesar in America: Why mixing religion and politics is bad for both. *Foreign Affairs,* March–April: 34–43. Retrieved October 1, 2014, from http://www.foreignaffairs.com/articles/137100/david-e-campbell-and-robert-d-putnam/god-and-caesar-in-america.

Campbell, N., Stuck, C., & Frinks, L. (2012). Spirituality training in residency: Changing the culture of a program. *Academic Psychiatry* 36(1): 56–59. doi:10.1176/appi.ap.09120250.

Carlson, L. E., & Garland, S. N. (2005). Impact of mindfulness-based stress reduction (MBSR) on sleep, mood, stress and fatigue symptoms in cancer outpatients. *International Journal of Behavioral Medicine* 12(4): 278–285.

Carlson, L. E., Speca, M., Patel, K. D., & Goodey, E. (2003). Mindfulness-based stress reduction in relation to quality of life, mood, symptoms of stress, and immune parameters in breast and prostate cancer outpatients. *Psychosomatic Medicine* 65(4): 571–581.

Cashwell, C. S., Bentley, P. B., & Yarborough, J. (2007). The only way out is through: The peril of spiritual bypass. *Counseling and Values* 51(2): 139–148.

Cochran, J. K., Chamlin, M. B., Beeghley, L., Harnden, A., & Blackwell, B. (1996). Religious stability, endogamy, and the effects of personal religiosity on attitudes toward abortion. *Sociology of Religion* 57(3): 291–309.

Collins, D. (2014, November 14). There's a new mainstream out there—and you're probably part of it. *Huff Post GPS for the Soul.* Retrieved January 6, 2015, from http://www.huffingtonpost.com/dianne-collins/theres-a-new-mainstream-o_b_6146988.html.

Coon, D. J. (1992). Testing the limits of sense and science: American experimental psychologists combat spiritualism, 1880–1920. *American Psychologist* 47(2): 143–151.

Corbett, L. (1996). *The religious function of the psyche.* London, UK: Routledge.

Corbett, L. (2007). *Psyche and the sacred: Spirituality beyond religion.* New Orleans, LA: Spring Journal Books.

Corbett, L. (2011). *The sacred cauldron: Psychotherapy as a spiritual practice.* Wilmette, IL: Chiron Publications.

Cornah, D. (2006). *The impact of spirituality on mental health: A review of the literature.* Retrieved November 24, 2014, from http://www.mentalhealth.org.uk/content/assets/PDF/publications/impact-spirituality.pdf?view=Standard.

Cortright, R. (1997). *Psychotherapy and spirit: Theory and practice in transpersonal psychotherapy.* Albany: State University of New York Press.

Council for Accreditation of Counseling and Related Educational Programs. (2009). *Council for Accreditation of Counseling and Related Educational Programs (CACREP) 2009 standards.* Retrieved November 24, 2014, from http://www.cacrep.org/wp-content/uploads/2013/12/2009-Standards.pdf.

Cox, J., Campbell, A., & Fulford, B. (2007). *Medicine of the person: Faith, science, and values in health care provision.* London: Jessica Kingsley.

Cragun, C. L., & Friedlander, M. L. (2012). Experiences of Christian clients in secular psychotherapy: A mixed-methods investigation. *Journal of Counseling Psychology* 59(3): 379–391. doi:10.1037/a0028283.

Crook-Lyon, R. E., O'Grady, K. A., Smith, T. B., Jensen, D. R., Golightly, T., & Potkar, K. A. (2012). Addressing religious and spiritual diversity in graduate training and multicultural education for professional psychologists. *Psychology of Religion and Spirituality* 4(3): 169–181.

Cruz, M., Schulz, R., Pincus, H. A., Houck, P. R., Bensasi, S., & Reynolds, C. F. (2009). The association of public and private religious involvement with severity of depression and hopelessness in older adults treated for major depression. *American Journal of Geriatric Psychiatry* 17(6): 503–307. doi:10.1097/JGP.0b013e31819d37a9.

Daniel, L. (2014). *When "spiritual but not religious" is not enough: Seeing God in surprising places, even the church.* New York: Jericho Books.

Davis, D. M., & Hayes, J. A. (2011). What are the benefits of mindfulness? A practice review of psychotherapy-related research. *Psychotherapy* 48(2): 198–208. doi:10.1037/a0022062.

Davis, J. A., Smith, T. W., & Marsden, P. V. (2007). *General social surveys, 1972–2006* [Cumulative file]. Inter-university Consortium for Political and Social Research.

Decker, S. E., Nich, C., Carroll, K. M., & Martino, S. (2014). Development of the therapist empathy scale. *Behavioural and cognitive psychotherapy* 42(3): 339–354.

Delaney, H. D., Forcehimes, A. A., Campbell, W. P., & Smith, B. W. (2009). Integrating spirituality into alcohol treatment. *Journal of Clinical Psychology* 65(2): 185–198.

Delaney, H. D., Miller, W. R., & Bisono, A. M. (2007). Religiosity and spirituality among psychologists: A survey of clinician members of the American Psychological Association. *Professional Psychology: Research and Practice* 38(5): 538–546.

Devine, P. G., Forscher, P. S., Austin, A. J., & Cox, W. T. (2012). Long-term reduction in implicit race bias: A prejudice habit-breaking intervention. *Journal of experimental social psychology* 48(6): 1267–1278.

Diallo, A. (2013). Clients' willingness to incorporate religion or spirituality in counseling: A brief report. *Rehabilitation Counseling Bulletin* 56(2): 120–122. doi:10.1177/0034355212439425.

Dura-Vila, G., & Dein, S. (2009). The dark night of the soul: Spiritual distress and its psychiatric implications. *Mental Health, Religion, and Culture* 12(6): 543–559. doi:10.1080/13674670902858800.

Dy-Liacco, G. S., Piedmont, R. L., Murray-Swank, N. A., Rodgerson, T. E., & Sherman, M. F. (2009). Spirituality and religiosity as cross-cultural aspects of human experience. *Psychology of Religion and Spirituality* 1(1): 35–52.

Eastman-Mueller, H., Wilson, T., Jung, A. K., Kimura, A., & Tarrant, J. (2013). iRest yoga-nidra on the college campus: Changes in stress, depression, worry, and mindfulness. *International Journal of Yoga Therapy* 2(2): 15–24.

Easwaran, E. (2008). *Passage meditation: Bringing the deep wisdom of the heart into daily life.* Tomales, CA: Nilgiri Press.

Eliade, M. (1964). *Shamanism: Archaic techniques of ecstasy* (W. Trask, Trans.). New York: Pantheon Books. (Original work published 1951.)

Ellis, A. (2001). *Albert Ellis on REBT* [Video]. Interview by M. Heery. Retrieved January 26, 2015, from http://www.psychotherapy.net/video/albert-ellis-rebt.

Ellison, C. G., Krause, N. M., Shepherd, B. C., & Chaves, M. A. (2009). Size, conflict, and opportunities for interaction: Congregational effects on members' anticipated support and negative interaction. *Journal for the Scientific Study of Religion* 48(1): 1–15.

Ellison, C., & McFarland, M. (2013). The social context of religion and spirituality in the United States. In K. I. Pargament (Ed.), *APA handbook of psychology, religion, and spirituality: Vol. 1. Context, theory, and research* (pp. 21–51). Washington, DC: American Psychological Association.

Emmons, R. A., & Paloutzian, R. F. (2003). The psychology of religion. *Annual Review of Psychology* 54(1): 377–402.

Espinosa, G. (2008). The influence of religion on Latino education, marriage, and social views in the United States. *Marriage and Family Review* 43(3–4): 205–225.

Exline, J. J., Grubbs, J. B., & Homolka, S. J. (2014). Seeing God as cruel or distant: Links with divine struggles involving anger, doubt, and fear of God's disapproval. *International Journal for the Psychology of Religion*, published online November 17.

Exline, J. J., & Rose, E. (2005). Religious and spiritual struggles. In R. F. Paloutzian and C. L. Park (Eds.), *Handbook of the psychology of religion and spirituality* (pp. 315–330). New York: Guilford.

Exline, J. J., Yali, A. M., & Lobel, M. (1999). When God disappoints: Difficulty forgiving God and its role in negative emotion. *Journal of Health Psychology* 4(3): 365–379.

Feder, A., Ahmad, S., Lee, E. J., Morgan, J. E., Singh, R., Smith, B. W., et al. (2013). Coping and PTSD symptoms in Pakistani earthquake survivors: Purpose in life, religious coping, and social support. *Journal of affective disorders* 147(1): 156–163.

Fjorback, L. O., & Walach, H. (2012). Meditation based therapies: A systematic review and some critical observations. *Religions* 3(1): 1–18.

Fowler, J. W. (1981). *Stages of faith: The psychology of human development and the quest for meaning.* New York: Harper and Row.

Frazier, R. E., & Hansen, N. D. (2009). Religious/spiritual psychotherapy behaviors: Do we do what we believe to be important? *Professional Psychology: Research and Practice* 40(1): 81–87. doi:10.1037/a0011671.

Fredrickson, B. L. (2002). How does religion benefit health and well-being?: Are positive emotions active ingredients? *Psychological Inquiry* 13(3): 209–213.

Freud, S. (1961). *Civilization and its discontents* (J. Strachey Ed. and Trans.). New York: W. W. Norton & Company. (Original work published 1930.)

Fry, P. S. (2000). Religious involvement, spirituality, and personal meaning for life: Existential predictors of psychological wellbeing in community-residing and institutional care elders. *Aging and Mental Health* 4(4): 375–387. doi:10.1080/713649965.

Fukuyama, M. A., & Sevig, T. D. (2002). Spirituality in counseling across cultures. In P. B. Pedersen, J. G. Draguns, W. R. Lonner & J. E. Trimble (Eds.), *Counseling across cultures* (pp. 273–295). Thousand Oaks, CA: Sage.

Fuller, R. C. (2001). *Spiritual, but not religious: Understanding unchurched America.* New York: Oxford University Press.

Galanter, M. (2013). Charismatic groups and cults: A psychological and social analysis. In K. I. Pargament (Ed.). *APA handbook of psychology, religion, and spirituality: Vol. 1. Context, theory, and research* (pp. 729–740). Washington, DC: American Psychological Association.

Galanter, M., & Forest, F. (2006). Cults, charismatic groups and social systems: Understanding the behavior of terrorist recruits. In J. J. F. Forest (Ed.)., *The making of a terrorist: Recruitment, training, and root causes: Vol. 2. Training* (pp. 51–70). Westport, CT: Praeger Security.

Gallup. (2012). Religion (poll). Retrieved November 24, 2014, from http://www.gallup.com/poll/1690/religion.aspx.

Gallup, G. H., Jr. (2003, February 11). Americans' spiritual searches turn inward. Retrieved November 24, 2014, from http://www.gallup.com/poll/7759/americans-spiritual-searches-turn-inward.aspx.

Gallup, G. H., Jr., & Bezilla, R. (1994, January 22). More find religion important. *Washington Post*, p. G10.

Germer, C. K., Siegel, R. D., & Fulton, P. R. (Eds.). (2013). *Mindfulness and psychotherapy.* New York: Guilford.

Green, M., & Elliott, M. (2010). Religion, health, and psychological well-being. *Journal of Religion and Health* 49(2): 149–163. doi:10.1007/s10943-009-9242-1.

Greenberg, D. (2013). Religion and mental health: A double-edged sword or a life-giving medicine? *World Psychiatry* 12(1): 40–41. doi:10.1002/wps.20012.

Greenberg, D., & Huppert, J. D. (2010). Scrupulosity: A unique subtype of obsessive-compulsive disorder. *Current Psychiatry Reports* 12(4): 282–289.

Greenberg, D., Witztum, E., & Pisante, J. (1987). Scrupulosity: Religious attitudes and clinical presentations. *British Journal of Medical Psychology* 60(1): 29–37. doi:10.1111/j.2044-8341.1987.tb02714.x.

Grof, C., & Grof, S. (1986). Spiritual emergency: The understanding and treatment of transpersonal crises. *ReVision* 8(2): 7–20.

Grof, S., & Grof, C. (Eds.). (1989). *Spiritual emergency: When personal transformation becomes a crisis.* New York: Penguin Putnam.

Grof, C., & Grof, S. (1990). *The stormy search for the self: A guide to personal growth through transformational crisis.* Los Angeles: J. P. Tarcher.

Hage, S. M. (2006). A closer look at the role of spirituality in psychology training programs. *Professional Psychology: Research and Practice* 37(3): 303–310.

Hanson, R. (with Mendius, R.). (2009). *Buddha's brain: The practical neuroscience of happiness, love, and wisdom.* Oakland, CA: New Harbinger.

Harris, S. (2014). *Waking up: A guide to spirituality without religion.* New York: Simon and Schuster.

Hathaway, W. L. (2008). Clinical practice with religious/spiritual issues: Niche, proficiency, or specialty? *Journal of Psychology and Theology* 36(1): 16–25.

Hathaway, W. L. (2011). Ethical guidelines for using spiritually oriented interventions. In *Spiritually Oriented Interventions for Counseling and Psychotherapy* (pp. 65–81). Washington, DC: American Psychological Association.

Hathaway, W. L. (2013). Pathways toward graduate training in the clinical psychology of religion and spirituality: A spiritual competencies model. In K. I. Pargament (Ed.), *APA handbook of psychology, religion, and spirituality: Vol. 2. An applied psychology of religion and spirituality* (pp. 635–649). Washington, DC: American Psychological Association.

Hathaway, W. L., & Ripley, J. (2009). Ethical concerns around spirituality and religion in clinical practice. In J. Aten & M. Leach (Eds.), *Spirituality and the therapeutic process: A comprehensive resource from intake to termination* (pp. 25–52). Washington, DC: American Psychological Association Books.

Hathaway, W. L., Scott, S. Y., & Garver, S. A. (2004). Assessing religious/spiritual functioning: A neglected domain in clinical practice? *Professional Psychology: Research and Practice* 35(1): 97–104.

Hayes, S. C., Strosahl, K., & Wilson, K. G. (1999). *Acceptance and commitment therapy: An experiential approach to behavior change.* New York: Guilford.

Hempel, L. M., & Bartkowski, J. P. (2008). Scripture, sin, and salvation: Theological conservatism reconsidered. *Social Forces* 86(4): 1647–1674.

Hill, J. (2000). A rationale for the integration of spirituality into community psychology. *Journal of Community Psychology* 28(2): 139–149.

Hill, P. C., Pargament, K. I., Hood, R. W., McCullough, M. E., Swyers, J. P., Larson, D. B., et al. (2000). Conceptualizing religion and spirituality: Points of commonality, points of departure. *Journal for the Theory of Social Behaviour* 30(1): 51–77.

Himle, J. A., Chatters, L. M., Taylor, R. J., & Nguyen, A. (2011). The relationship between obsessive-compulsive disorder and religious faith: Clinical characteristics and implications for treatment. *Psychology of Religion and Spirituality* 3(4): 241–258.

Hodge, D. R. (2005). Spiritual lifemaps: A client-centered pictorial instrument for spiritual assessment, planning, and intervention. *Social Work* 50(1): 77–87.

Hodge, D. R. (2004). Why conduct a spiritual assessment? A theoretical foundation for assessment. *Advances in Social Work* 5(2): 183–196.

Hodge, D. R. (2005). Developing a spiritual assessment toolbox: A discussion of the strengths and limitations of five different assessment methods. *Health and Social Work* 30(4): 314–323.

Hodge, D. R. (2007). The spiritual competence scale: A new instrument for assessing spiritual competence at the programmatic level. *Research on Social Work Practice* 17(2): 287–294.

Hodge, D. R. (2013). Assessing spirituality and religion in the context of counseling and psychotherapy. In K. I. Pargament (Ed.), *APA handbook of psychology, religion, and spirituality: Vol. 2. An applied psychology of religion and spirituality* (pp. 93–123). Washington, DC: American Psychological Association.

Hodge, D. R., & Limb, G. E. (2010). A Native American perspective on spiritual assessment: The strengths and limitations of a complementary set of assessment tools. *Health and Social Work* 35(2): 121–131.

Hofmann, S. G., Sawyer, A. T., Witt, A. A., & Oh, D. (2010). The effect of mindfulness-based therapy on anxiety and depression: A meta-analytic review. *Journal of Consulting and Clinical Psychology* 78(2): 169.

Integrative Restorative Institute. (2013). iRest in current VA or military settings. Retrieved November 24, 2014, from http://www.irest.us/projects/veterans/settings.

James, W. (1988). *William James: Writings: 1902–1910. The varieties of religious experience.* (B. Kuklick, Ed.). Oxford, UK: Oxford World's Classics. (Original work published 1902.)

Joint Commission on the Accreditation of Healthcare Organizations. (2014). *Comprehensive accreditation manual for hospitals: The official handbook.* Oakbrook Terrace, IL: Joint Commission.

Jones, D. E., Doty, S., Grammich, C., Horsch, J. E., Houseal, R., Lynn, M., et al. (2002). *Religious congregations and membership in the United States 2000: An enumeration by region, state, and county based on data reported for 149 religious bodies.* Nashville, TN: Glenmary Research Center.

Josephson, A. M., Peteet, J. R., & Tasman, A. (2009). Religion and the training of psychotherapists. In P. J. Verhagen, H. M. van Praag, J. J. López-Ibor, J. L. Cox, & D. Moussaoui (Eds.). *Religion and psychiatry: Beyond boundaries* (pp. 571–586). Chichester, UK: John Wiley & Sons. doi:10.1002/9780470682203.ch31.

Kabat-Zinn, J. 1991. *Full catastrophe living: Using the wisdom of your body and mind to face stress, pain, and illness.* New York: Delta.

Kahn, P. J., & Greene, A. L. (2004). "Seeing conversion whole": Testing a model of religious conversion. *Pastoral psychology* 52(3): 233–258.

Kapuscinski, A. N., & Masters, K. S. (2010). The current status of measures of spirituality: A critical review of scale development. *Psychology of Religion and Spirituality* 2(4): 191–205.

Karg, R., Bose, J., Batts, K. R., Forman-Hoffman, V. L., Liao, D., Hirsh, E., Pemberton, M. R., et al. (2014). Past year mental disorders among adults in the United States: Results from the 2008–2012 Mental Health Surveillance Study. *Center for Behavioral Health Statistics and Quality CBHSQ Data Review*, October. Retrieved November 24, 2014, from http://www.samhsa.gov/data/sites/default/files/NSDUH-DR-N2MentalDis-2014-1/Web/NSDUH-DR-N2MentalDis-2014.pdf.

Kaslow, N. J. (2004). Competencies in professional psychology. *American Psychologist* 59(8): 774–781.

Kenny, M. A., & Williams, J. M. G. (2007). Treatment-resistant depressed patients show a good response to mindfulness-based cognitive therapy. *Behaviour Research and Therapy* 45(3): 617–625.

King, M., Marston, L., McManus, S., Brugha, T., Meltzer, H., & Bebbington, P. (2013). Religion, spirituality, and mental health: Results from a national study of English households. *British Journal of Psychiatry* 202(1): 68–73. doi:10.1192/bjp.bp.112.112003.

Knox, S., Catlin, L., Casper, M., & Schlosser, L. Z. (2005). Addressing religion and spirituality in psychotherapy: Clients' perspectives. *Psychotherapy Research* 15(3): 287–303. doi:10.1080/1050330 0500090894.

Koenig, H. G. (1997). *Is religion good for your health? The effects of religion on physical and mental health.* Binghamton, NY: Haworth Press.

Koenig, H. G., Hooten, E. G., Lindsay-Calkins, E., & Meador, K. G. (2010). Spirituality in medical school curricula: Findings from a national survey. *International Journal of Psychiatry in Medicine* 40(4): 391–398.

Koenig, H. G., King, D., & Carson, V. B. (2012). *Handbook of religion and health.* New York: Oxford University Press.

Kosmin, B. A., & Keysar, A. (2009). *American Religious Identification Survey (ARIS 2008): Summary report.* Retrieved November 24, 2014, from http://b27.cc.trincoll.edu/weblogs/AmericanReligion-Survey-ARIS/reports/ARIS_Report_2008.pdf.

Kosmin, B. A., Mayer, E., & Keysar, A. (2001). *American religious identification survey 2001.* New York: Graduate Center of the City University of New York.

Kripal, J. (2007). *Esalen: America and the religion of no religion.* Chicago, IL: University of Chicago Press.

Lake, J. (2012). Spirituality and religion in mental health: A concise review of the evidence. *Psychiatric Times* 29(3): 34–38.

Langone, M. D. (2005). Cult awareness groups and NRM scholars: Toward depolarization of key issues. *Cultic Studies Review* 4(2): 146–168.

Lehman, C. (1993). Faith-based counseling gains favor. *Washington Post*, pp. B7–B8.

Leong, F. T., Wagner, N. S., & Tata, S. P. (1995). Racial and ethnic variations in help-seeking attitudes. In J. G. Ponterotto, J. M. Casas, L. A. Suzuki, & C. M. Alexander (Eds.), *Handbook of multicultural counseling* (pp. 415–438). Thousand Oaks, CA: Sage.

Levin, J. S., & Chatters, L. M. (1998). Research on religion and mental health: An overview of empirical findings and theoretical issues. In H. G. Koenig (Ed.), *Handbook of religion and mental health* (pp. 33–50). San Diego, CA: Academic Press.

Lindeman, M., & Aarnio, K. (2007). Superstitious, magical, and paranormal beliefs: An integrative model. *Journal of Research in Personality* 41(4): 731–744. doi:10.1016/j.jrp.2006.06.009.

Lindsey, S. C., Sigillo, A. E., & Miller, M. K. (2013). Attitudes toward parental involvement clauses in minor abortion laws and individual differences in religion, political affiliation, and attribution style among college students. *Individual Differences Research* 11(2): 59–69.

Linehan, M. M. (1993). *Cognitive-behavioral treatment of borderline personality disorder.* New York: Guilford.

Lish, R. A., Fitzsimmons, C. R., McMinn, M. R., & Root, A. M. (2003). Clergy interest in innovative collaboration with psychologists. *Journal of Psychology and Christianity* 22(4): 294–298.

Loewenthal, K. M. (2010). Spirituality and cultural psychiatry. In D. Bhugra & K. Bhui (Eds.). *Textbook of cultural psychiatry* (pp. 59 -71). Cambridge, UK: Cambridge University Press.

Loewenthal, K. M., MacLeod, A. K., Goldblatt, V., Lubitsh, G., & Valentine, J. D. (2000). Comfort and joy? Religion, cognition, and mood in Protestants and Jews under stress. *Cognition and Emotion* 14(3): 355–374.

Lopez, L., Brooks, D. F., Phillips, A., & Hathaway, W. L. (2005). *Preliminary guidelines for addressing practitioner and client religious-spiritual diversity issues.* Paper presented at the annual convention of the American Psychological Association, Washington, DC.

Luhrmann, T. M. (2001). *Of two minds: An anthropologist looks at American psychiatry.* New York: Vintage Books.

Luhrmann, T. M. (2012). *When God talks back.* New York: Alfred A. Knopf.

Luhrmann, T. M. (2013). Making God real and making God good: Some mechanisms through which prayer may contribute to healing. *Transcultural Psychiatry* 50(5): 707–725. doi:10.1177/136346151 3487670.

Lukoff, D. (1985). The diagnosis of mystical experiences with psychotic features. *Journal of Transpersonal Psychology* 17(2): 155–181.

Lukoff, D. (1990a). David Lukoff's experience [part 1]: Talk at Ruth Inge Heinz's annual conference on shamanism. Retrieved January 26, 2014, from http://www.spiritualcompetency.com/se/experiences/exp-lukoff-3.html.

Lukoff, D. (1990b). David Lukoff's experience, part II: Talk at Ruth Inge Heinz's annual conference on shamanism. Retrieved November 24, 2014, from http://www.spiritualcompetency.com/se/experiences/exp-lukoff-final.html.

Lukoff, D. (1998). From spiritual emergency to spiritual problem: The transpersonal roots of the new *DSM-IV* category. *Journal of Humanistic Psychology* 38(2): 21–50.

Lukoff, D. (2007). Spirituality in the recovery from persistent mental disorders. *Southern Medical Journal* 100(6): 642–646.

Lukoff, D., Lu, F., & Turner, R. (1992). Toward a more culturally sensitive *DSM-IV*: Psychoreligious and psychospiritual problems. *Journal of Nervous and Mental Disease* 180(11): 673–682.

Lukoff, D., Lu, F. G., & Yang, C. P. (2011). *DSM-IV* religious and spiritual problems. In R. J. Peteet, F. G. Lu, and W. E. Narrow (Eds.), *Religious and spiritual issues in psychiatric diagnosis: A Research Agenda for* DSM-V. Washington, DC: American Psychiatric Publishing.

Lukoff, D., Turner, R., & Lu, F. (1992). Transpersonal psychology research review: Psychoreligious dimensions of healing. *Journal of Transpersonal Psychology* 24(1): 41–60.

Ma, S. H., & Teasdale, J. D. (2004). Mindfulness-based cognitive therapy for depression: Replication and exploration of differential relapse prevention effects. *Journal of Consulting and Clinical Psychology* 72(1): 31.

Magaldi-Dopman, D., & Park-Taylor, J. (2010). Sacred adolescence: Practical suggestions for psychologists working with adolescents' religious and spiritual identity. *Professional Psychology: Research and Practice* 41(5): 382–390.

Maj, M. (2010). Foreword. In P. J. Verhagen, H. M. van Praag, J. J. López-Ibor, J. L. Cox, & D. Moussaoui (Eds.), *Religion and psychiatry: Beyond boundaries* (pp. xiii-xiv). Chichester, UK: John Wiley & Sons.

Marler, P. L., & Hadaway, C. K. (2002). "Being religious" or "being spiritual" in America: A zero-sum proposition? *Journal for the Scientific Study of Religion* 41(2): 289–300.

Martin, J. (2010, March 11). Spiritual but not religious—Not so fast! Making the case for moving beyond your own personal God. *Busted Halo: An Online Magazine for Spiritual Seekers.* Retrieved November 24, 2014, from http://bustedhalo.com/features/spiritual-but-not-religious-not-so-fast/2.

Martinez, J. S., Smith, T. B., & Barlow, S. H. (2007). Spiritual interventions in psychotherapy: Evaluations by highly religious clients. *Journal of Clinical Psychology* 63(10): 943–960. doi:10.1002/jclp.20399.

Maslow, A. H. (1970). *Religions, values, and peak-experiences.* New York: Viking Press.

Mayers, C., Leavey, G., Vallianatou, C., & Barker, C. (2007). How clients with religious or spiritual beliefs experience psychological help-seeking and therapy: A qualitative study. *Clinical Psychology and Psychotherapy* 14(4): 317–327.

McDonald, N., & Messinger, D. (2011). The development of empathy: How, when, and why. In A. Acerbi, J. A. Lombo, & J. J. Sanguineti (Eds.), *Moral behavior and free will: A neurobiological and philosophical approach* (pp. 333–358). London, UK: IF-Press.

McGuire, M. B. (2008). *Lived religion: Faith and practice in everyday life.* Oxford: Oxford University Press.

McMinn, M. R., Hathaway, W. L., Woods, S. W., & Snow, K. N. (2009). What American Psychological Association leaders have to say about psychology of religion and spirituality. *Psychology of Religion and Spirituality* 1(1): 3–13.

McNamara, P., Burns, J. P., Johnson, P., & McCorkle, B. H. (2010). Personal religious practice, risky behavior, and implementation intentions among adolescents. *Psychology of Religion and Spirituality* 2(1): 30–34. doi:10.1037/a0017582.

McQuaid, J. R., & Carmona, P. E. (2004). *Peaceful mind: Using mindfulness and cognitive behavioral psychology to overcome depression.* Oakland, CA: New Harbinger.

McSherry, W., Gretton, M., Draper, P., & Watson, R. (2008). The ethical basis of teaching spirituality and spiritual care: A survey of student nurses' perceptions. *Nurse Education Today* 28(8): 1002–1009.

Mercadante, L. (2014). *Belief without borders: Inside the minds of the spiritual but not religious.* New York: Oxford University Press.

Mercer, J. (2013). Deliverance, demonic possession, and mental illness: Some considerations for mental health professionals. *Mental Health, Religion, and Culture* 16(6): 595–611. doi:10.1080/13674676.2012.706272.

Merriam-Webster. (2014). Empathy. Retrieved January 26, 2015, from http://www.merriam-webster.com/dictionary/empathy.

Messina, I., Palmieri, A., Sambin, M., Kleinbub, J. R., Voci, A., & Calvo, V. (2013). Somatic underpinnings of perceived empathy: The importance of psychotherapy training. *Psychotherapy Research* 23(2): 169–177. doi:10.1080/10503307.2012.748940.

Miller, C. H., & Hedges, D. W. (2008). Scrupulosity disorder: An overview and introductory analysis. *Journal of Anxiety Disorders* 22(6): 1042–1058.

Miller, G. (1999). The development of the spiritual focus in counseling and counselor education. *Journal of Counseling and Development* 77(4): 498–501.

Miller, L., & Kelley, B. S. (2005). Relationships of religiosity and spirituality with mental health and psychopathology. In R. F. Paloutzian & C. L. Park (Eds.), *Handbook of the psychology of religion and spirituality* (pp. 460–478). New York: Guilford.

Miller, L., Wickramaratne, P., Gameroff, M., Sage, M., Tenke, C. E., & Weissman, M. M. (2012). Religiosity and major depression in adults at high risk: A ten-year prospective study. *American Journal of Psychiatry* 169(1): 89–94.

Miller, L., Wickramaratne, P., Tenke, C., & Weissman, M. (2012). Spirituality and major depression: A ten-year prospective study. *American Journal of Psychiatry* 169(1): 89–94.

Miller, W. R., & Rollnick, S. (1991). *Motivational interviewing: Preparing people to change addictive behavior.* New York: Guilford.

Miller, W. R., & Thoresen, C. E. (2003). Spirituality, religion, and health. *American Psychologist* 58(1): 24–35.

Miller, W. R., Zweben, A., DiClemente, C. C., & Rychtarik, R. G. (1992). *Motivational enhancement therapy manual: A clinical research guide for therapists treating individuals with alcohol abuse and dependence.* Rockville, MD: National Institute on Alcohol Abuse and Alcoholism.

Minor, H. G., Carlson, L. E., Mackenzie, M. J., Zernicke, K., & Jones, L. (2006). Evaluation of a mindfulness-based stress reduction (MBSR) program for caregivers of children with chronic conditions. *Social Work in Health Care* 43(1): 91–109. doi:10.1300/1010v43n01_06.

Mohr, S. (2013). Religion, spirituality, and severe mental disorder: From research to clinical practice. In K. I. Pargament (Ed.), *APA handbook of psychology, religion, and spirituality: Vol. 2. An applied psychology of religion and spirituality* (pp. 257–273). Washington, DC: American Psychological Association.

Mohr, S., Borras, L., Betrisey, C., Pierre-Yves, B., Gilliéron, C., & Huguelet, P. (2010). Delusions with religious content in patients with psychosis: How they interact with spiritual coping. *Psychiatry: Interpersonal and Biological Processes* 73(2): 158–172. doi:10.1521/psyc.2010.73.2.158.

Mother Teresa. (2009). *Mother Teresa: Come be my light: The private writings of the Saint of Calcutta* (B. Kolodiejchuk, Ed.). New York: Random House.

Nagai, C. (2008). Clinicians' self-assessment of cultural and spiritual competency: Working with Asians and Asian Americans. *Community Mental Health Journal* 44(4): 303–309.

Nassif, T. H. (2013). *Examining the effectiveness of mindfulness meditation for chronic pain management in combat veterans with traumatic brain injury.* Washington, DC: American University.

National Institute of Mental Health. (2013). Serious mental illness (SMI) among U.S. adults. Retrieved November 24, 2014, from http://www.nimh.nih.gov/health/statistics/prevalence/serious-mental -illness-smi-among-us-adults.shtml.

Neukrug, E., Bayne, H., Dean-Nganga, L., & Pusateri, C. (2013). Creative and novel approaches to empathy: A neo-Rogerian perspective. *Journal of Mental Health Counseling* 35(1): 29–42.

Newport, F. (2011, June 3). More than 9 out of 10 Americans continue to believe in God. Retrieved November 24, 2014, from http://www.gallup.com/poll/147887/americans-continue-believe-god .aspx.

Newport, F. (2012, December 4). Seven in 10 Americans are very or moderately religious. Retrieved November 24, 2014, from http://www.gallup.com/poll/159050/seven-americans-moderately-reli gious.aspx.

Nooney, J., & Woodrum, E. (2002). Religious coping and church-based social support as predictors of mental health outcomes: Testing a conceptual model. *Journal for the Scientific Study of Religion* 41(2): 359–368. doi:10.1111/1468-5906.00122.

Norenzayan, A., Dar-Nimrod, I., Hansen, I., & Proulx, T. (2009). Mortality salience and religion: Divergent effects on the defense of cultural worldviews for the religious and the non-religious. *European Journal of Social Psychology* 39(1): 101–113.

Norris, P., & Inglehart, R. (2004). *Sacred and secular: Religion and politics worldwide.* Cambridge, UK: Cambridge University Press.

O'Connor, M. (2002). Spiritual dark night and psychological depression: Some comparisons and considerations. *Counseling and Values* 46(2): 137–148.

O'Connor, S., & Vandenberg, B. (2005). Psychosis or faith? Clinicians' assessment of religious beliefs. *Journal of Consulting and Clinical Psychology* 73(4): 610–616.

Oman, D., Hedberg, J., & Thoresen, C. E. (2006). Passage meditation reduces perceived stress in health professionals: A randomized, controlled trial. *Journal of Consulting and Clinical Psychology* 74(4): 714–719. doi:10.1037/0022-006X.74.4.714.

Oman, D., Shapiro, S. L., Thoresen, C. E., Plante, T. G., & Flinders, T. (2008). Meditation lowers stress and supports forgiveness among college students: A randomized controlled trial. *Journal of American College Health* 56(5): 569–578.

Oman, D., & Thoresen, C. E. (2005). Do religion and spirituality influence health? In R. F. Paloutzian & C. L. Park (Eds.), *Handbook of the psychology of religion and spirituality* (pp. 435–459). New York: Guilford.

Oxhandler, H. K., & Pargament, K. I. (2014). Social work practitioners' integration of clients' religion and spirituality in practice: A literature review. *Social Work* 59(3): 271–279.

Pargament, K. I. (1997). *The psychology of religion and coping: Theory, research and practice.* New York: Guilford.

Pargament, K. I., & Sweeney, P. J. (2011). Building spiritual fitness in the army: An innovative approach to a vital aspect of human development. *American Psychologist* 66(1): 58–64.

Pargament, K. I. (2007). *Spiritually integrated psychotherapy: Understanding and addressing the sacred.* New York: Guilford.

Pargament, K. I. (Ed.). (2013). *APA handbook of psychology, religion, and spirituality: Vol. 2. An applied psychology of religion and spirituality.* Washington, DC: American Psychological Association.

Pargament, K. I., Ano, G. G., & Wachholtz, A. B. (2005). The religious dimension of coping: Advances in theory, research, and practice. In R. F. Paloutzian & C. L. Park (Eds.), *Handbook of the psychology of religion and spirituality* (pp. 479–495). New York: Guilford.

Pargament, K., Feuille, M., & Burdzy, D. (2011). The Brief RCOPE: Current psychometric status of a short measure of religious coping. *Religions* 2(1): 51–76.

Pargament, K. I., Koenig, H. G., & Perez, L. M. (2000). The many methods of religious coping: Development and initial validation of the RCOPE. *Journal of clinical psychology* 56(4): 519–543.

Pargament, K. I., Koenig, H. G., Tarakeshwar, N., & Hahn, J. (2004). Religious coping methods as predictors of psychological, physical, and spiritual outcomes among medically ill elderly patients: A two-year longitudinal study. *Journal of Health Psychology* 9(6): 713–730. doi:10.1177/135910 5304045366.

Pargament, K. I., Mahoney, A., Exline, J., Jones, J., & Shafranske, E. P. (2013). Envisioning an integrative paradigm for the psychology of religion and spirituality. In K. I. Pargament (Ed.). *APA handbook of psychology, religion, and spirituality: Vol. 1. Context, theory, and research* (pp. 3–19). Washington, DC: American Psychological Association.

Pargament, K. I., & Raiya, H. A. (2007). A decade of research on the psychology of religion and coping. *Psyke and Logos* 28(2): 742–766.

Pargament, K. I., & Saunders, S. M. (2007). Introduction to the special issue on spirituality and psychotherapy. *Journal of Clinical Psychology* 63(10): 903–907.

Park, C. L. (2005). Religion as a meaning-making framework in coping with life stress. *Journal of Social Issues* 61(4): 707–729.

Park, C. L. (2013). Religion and meaning. In R. F. Paloutzian and C. L. Park (Eds.), *Handbook of the psychology of religion and spirituality* (pp. 357–379). New York: Guilford.

Patterson, C. H. (1984). Empathy, warmth, and genuineness in psychotherapy: A review of reviews. *Psychotherapy: Theory, Research, Practice, Training* 21(4): 431–438.

Pearce, L., & Denton, M. (2011). *A faith of their own: Stability and change in the religiosity of America's adolescents.* New York: Oxford University Press.

Pesut, B. (2008). Spirituality and spiritual care in nursing fundamentals textbooks. *Journal of Nursing Education* 47(4): 167–173.

Pew Forum on Religion and Public Life. (2008). *US religious landscape survey: Religious affiliation: Diverse and dynamic.* Retrieved January 25, 2015, from http://religions.pewforum.org/pdf/report-religious-landscape-study-full.pdf.

Pew Forum on Religion and Public Life. (2009). *Faith in flux* (updated 2011). Retrieved November 24, 2014, from http://www.pewforum.org/2009/04/27/faith-in-flux.

Pew Forum on Religion and Public Life. (2011). *Global Christianity: A report on the size and distribution of the world's Christian population.* Retrieved November 24, 2014, from http://www.pewforum.org/files/2011/12/Christianity-fullreport-web.pdf.

Pew Forum on Religion and Public Life. (2012a). *The global religious landscape: A report on the size and distribution of the world's major religious groups as of 2010.* Washington, DC: Pew Research Center. Retrieved January 26, 2015, from http://www.pewforum.org/files/2014/01/global-religion-full.pdf.

Pew Forum on Religion and Public Life. (2012b). *"Nones" on the rise.* Retrieved November 24, 2014, from http://www.pewforum.org/files/2012/10/NonesOnTheRise-full.pdf.

Phillips, R. (2010). Research: Millennials are spiritually diverse. Retrieved November 24, 2014, from http://www.lifeway.com/Article/LifeWay-Research-finds-American-millennials-are-spiritually -diverse.

Piedmont, R. L., Ciarrochi, J. W., Dy-Liacco, G. S., & Williams, J. E. (2009). The empirical and conceptual value of the Spiritual Transcendence and Religious Involvement Scales for personality research. *Psychology of Religion and Spirituality* 1(3): 162–179.

Plante, T. G. (2008). What do the spiritual and religious traditions offer the practicing psychologist? *Pastoral Psychology* 56(4): 429–444. doi:10.1007/s11089-008-0119-0.

Plante, T. G. (2009). *Spiritual practices in psychotherapy: Thirteen tools for enhancing psychological health.* Washington, DC: American Psychological Association.

Post, B. C., & Wade, N. G. (2009). Religion and spirituality in psychotherapy: A practice-friendly review of research. *Journal of Clinical Psychology* 65(2): 131–146.

Potik, D. (2010). In loving God's spirit: Integrating the 12-step program into psychoanalytic psychotherapy. *Journal of Spirituality in Mental Health* 12(4): 255–272. doi:10.1080/19349637.2010.518829.

Powell, L. H., Shahabi, L., & Thoresen, C. E. (2003). Religion and spirituality: Linkages to physical health. *American Psychologist* 58(1): 36–52.

Powers, M. B., Zum Vörde Sivi Vörding, M. B., & Emmelkamp, P. M. (2009). Acceptance and commitment therapy: A meta-analytic review. *Psychotherapy and Psychosomatics* 78(2): 73–80. doi:10.1159/000190790.

Rambo, L. R. (1993). *Understanding religious conversion.* New Haven, CT: Yale University Press.

Rambo, L. R., & Farhadian, C. E. (1999). Converting: Stages of religious change. In C. Lamb & M. D. Bryant (Eds.), *Religious conversion: Contemporary practices and controversies* (pp. 23–34). New York: Cassell.

Richards, P. S. (2009). Toward religious and spiritual competence for psychologists: Some reflections and recommendations. *Professional Psychology: Research and Practice* 40(4): 389–391.

Richards, P. S., & Bergin, A. E. (2000). Toward religious and spiritual competency for mental health professionals. In P. S. Richards & A. E. Bergin (Eds.), *Handbook of Psychotherapy and Religious Diversity* (pp. 3–26). Washington, DC: American Psychological Association.

Richards, P. S., & Bergin, A. E. (2005). *A spiritual strategy for counseling and psychotherapy* (2nd ed.). Washington, DC: American Psychological Association.

Robertson, L. A. (2010). The Spiritual Competency Scale. *Counseling and Values* 55(1): 6–24.

Robins, C. J., & Chapman, A. L. (2004). Dialectical behavior therapy: Current status, recent developments, and future directions. *Journal of Personality Disorders* 18(1): 73–89.

Robinson, B. A. (2007). How Christians view other religions: Views of Protestant, Roman Catholic, and Eastern Orthodox churches. Retrieved November 24, 2014, from http://www.religioustoler ance.org/chr_othe1.htm.

Rocha, T. (2014). The dark knight of the soul. *The Atlantic*, June 25. Retrieved November 24, 2014, from http://www.theatlantic.com/health/archive/2014/06/the-dark-knight-of-the-souls/372766.

Roesch, S. C., & Ano, G. (2003). Testing an attribution and coping model of stress: Religion as an orienting system. *Journal of Psychology and Christianity* 22(3): 197–209.

Rogers, C. R. (1961). *On becoming a person: A therapist's view of psychotherapy.* Boston: Houghton Mifflin.

Rogers, S. A., Poey, E. L., Reger, G. M., Tepper, L., & Coleman, E. M. (2002). Religious coping among those with persistent mental illness. *International Journal for the Psychology of Religion* 12(3): 161–175. doi:10.1207/S15327582IJPR1203_03.

Rose, E. M., Westefeld, J. S., & Ansley, T. N. (2001). Spiritual issues in counseling: Clients' beliefs and preferences. *Journal of Counseling Psychology* 48(1): 61–71.

213

Rosenfeld, G. W. (2010). Identifying and integrating helpful and harmful religious beliefs into psycho-therapy. *Psychotherapy: Theory, Research, Practice, Training* 47(4): 512–526.

Rosenzweig, S., Reibel, D. K., Greeson, J. M., Brainard, G. C., & Hojat, M. (2003). Mindfulness-based stress reduction lowers psychological distress in medical students. *Teaching and Learning in Medicine* 15(2): 88–92.

Rosmarin, D. H., Bigda-Peyton, J. S., Ongur, D., Pargament, K. I., & Bjorgvinsson, T. (2013). Religious coping among psychotic patients: Relevance to suicidality and treatment outcomes. *Psychiatry Research* 210(1): 182–187.

Ruff, J. (2008). Psychologist bias in implicit responding to religiously divergent nonpatient targets and explicit responding to religiously divergent patients. *Journal of Dissertations* 2(1).

Ruiz, F. J. (2010). A review of acceptance and commitment therapy (ACT) empirical evidence: Correlational, experimental psychopathology, component and outcome studies. *International Journal of Psychology and Psychological Therapy* 10(1): 125–162.

Sandage, S. J., & Moe, S. P. (2013). Spiritual experience: Conversion and transformation. In K. I. Pargament (Ed.), *APA handbook of psychology, religion, and spirituality: Vol. 1. Context, theory, and research* (pp. 407–422). Washington, DC: American Psychological Association.

Sargeant, K. (2000). *Seeker churches: Promoting traditional religion in a nontraditional way.* New Brunswick, NJ: Rutgers University Press.

Saucier, G., & Skrzypinska, K. (2006). Spiritual but not religious? Evidence for two independent dispositions. *Journal of Personality* 74(5): 1257–1292.

Saunders, S. M., Miller, M. L., & Bright, M. M. (2010). Spiritually conscious psychological care. *Professional Psychology: Research and Practice* 41(5): 355–362.

Schafer, R. M., Handal, P. J., Brawer, P. A., & Ubinger, M. (2011). Training and education in religion/spirituality within APA-accredited clinical psychology programs: 8 years later. *Journal of Religion and Health* 50(2): 232–239.

Schlehofer, M. M., Omoto, A. M., & Adelman, J. R. (2008). How do "religion" and "spirituality" differ? Lay definitions among older adults. *Journal for the Scientific Study of Religion* 47(3): 411–425. doi:10.1111/j.1468-5906.2008.00418.x.

Schlitz, M. M., Vieten, C., & Amorok, T. (2008). *Living deeply: The art and science of transformation in everyday life.* Oakland, CA: New Harbinger.

Schneiders, S. M. (2003). Religion vs. spirituality: A contemporary conundrum. *Spiritus: A Journal of Christian Spirituality* 3(2): 163–185.

Schulte, D. L., Skinner, T. A., & Claibom, C. D. (2002). Religious and spiritual issues in counseling psychology training. *Counseling Psychologist* 30(1): 118–134.

Schultz, J. M., Tallman, B. A., & Altmaier, E. M. (2010). Pathways to posttraumatic growth: The contributions of forgiveness and importance of religion and spirituality. *Psychology of Religion and Spirituality* 2(2): 104–114.

Schwadel, P., & Falci, C. (2012). Interactive effects of church attendance and religious tradition on depressive symptoms and positive affect. *Society and Mental Health* 2(1): 21–34; doi:10.1177/2156869312442885.

Sedlmeier, P., Eberth, J., Schwarz, M., Zimmermann, D., Haarig, F., Jaeger, S., et al. (2012). The psychological effects of meditation: A meta-analysis. *Psychological Bulletin* 138(6): 1139–1171.

Segal, Z. V., Williams, J. M. G., & Teasdale, J. D. (2002). *Mindfulness-based cognitive therapy for depression: A new approach to preventing relapse.* New York: Guilford.

Sephton, S. E., Salmon, P., Weissbecker, I., Ulmer, C., Floyd, A., Hoover, K., et al. (2007). Mindfulness meditation alleviates depressive symptoms in women with fibromyalgia: Results of a randomized clinical trial. *Arthritis care and research* 57(1): 77–85.

Shafranske, E. P. (1996). Religious beliefs, affiliations, and practices of clinical psychologists. In E. P. Shafranske (Ed.), *Religion and the clinical practice of psychology* (pp. 149–162). Washington, DC: American Psychological Association.

Shafranske, E. P., & Cummings, J. P. (2013). Religious and spiritual beliefs, affiliations, and practices of psychologists. In K. I. Pargament (Ed.), *APA handbook of psychology, religion, and spirituality: Vol. 2: An applied psychology of religion and spirituality* (pp. 23–41). Washington, DC: American Psychological Association.

Shafranske, E., & Sperry, L. (2005). Addressing the spiritual dimension in psychotherapy: Introduction and overview. In L. Sperry & E. Shafranske (Eds.), *Spiritually oriented psychotherapy* (pp. 11–29). Washington, DC: American Psychological Association.

Shapiro, F. (2002). *EMDR as an integrative psychotherapy approach: Experts of diverse orientation explore the paradigm prism.* Washington, DC: American Psychological Association.

Shapiro, S. L., & Carlson, L. E. (2009). *The art and science of mindfulness: Integrating mindfulness into psychology and the helping professions.* Washington, DC: American Psychological Association.

Shapiro, S. L., Schwartz, G. E., & Bonner, G. (1998). Effects of mindfulness-based stress reduction on medical and premedical students. *Journal of Behavioral Medicine* 21(6): 581–599.

Sharpe, E. J. (2009). The study of religion in historical perspective. In J. R. Hinnells (Ed.), *The Routledge companion to the study of religion*, 2nd edition (pp. 21–45). London: Routledge.

Sherkat, D. E. (2014). *Changing faith: The dynamics and consequences of Americans' shifting religious identities.* New York: New York University Press.

Siddle, R., Haddock, G., Tarrier, N., & Faragher, E. B. (2002). Religious delusions in patients admitted to hospital with schizophrenia. *Social Psychiatry and Psychiatric Epidemiology* 37(3): 130–138.

Singer, M. (2007). *The untethered soul: The journey beyond yourself.* Oakland, CA: New Harbinger.

Smith, H. (2013). The "four forces" of modern psychology and the primordial tradition. Interview by S. D. Sotillos. In S. B. Sotillos (Ed.), *Psychology and the perennial philosophy: Studies in comparative religion* (pp. 87–91). Bloomington, IN: World Wisdom.

Strawbridge, W. J., Shema, S. J., Cohen, R. D., & Kaplan, G. A. (2001). Religious attendance increases survival by improving and maintaining good health behaviors, mental health, and social relationships. *Annals of Behavioral Medicine* 23(1): 68–74.

Sue, D. W., & Sue, D. (2008). *Counseling the culturally diverse: Theory and practice* (5th ed.). New York: John Wiley & Sons.

Sue, S. (1998). In search of cultural competence in psychotherapy and counseling. *American Psychologist* 53(4): 440–448.

Tay, L., Li, M., Myers, D., & Diener, E. (2014). Religiosity and subjective well-being: An international perspective. In C. Kim-Prieto (Ed.), *Religion and spirituality across cultures* (pp. 163–175). Dordrecht, Netherlands: Springer Science.

Teasdale, J. D., Segal, Z. V., Williams, J. M. G., Ridgeway, V. A., Soulsby, J. M., & Lau, M. A. (2000). Prevention of relapse/recurrence in major depression by mindfulness-based cognitive therapy. *Journal of Consulting and Clinical Psychology* 68(4): 615–623.

Tepper, L., Rogers, S. A., Coleman, E. M., & Malony, H. N. (2001). The prevalence of religious coping among persons with persistent mental illness. *Psychiatric Services* 52(5). doi:10.1176/appi.ps .52.5.660.

Thalbourne, M. A. (1991). The psychology of mystical experience. *Exceptional Human Experience* 9(2): 168–186.

Thomas, J. N., & Olson, D. V. A. (2010). Testing the strictness thesis and competing theories of congregational growth. *Journal for the Scientific Study of Religion* 49(4): 619–639.

Thumma, S., & Bird, W. (2009). Not who you think they are: A profile of the people who attend America's megachurches. Retrieved November 24, 2014, from http://hirr.hartsem.edu/mega church/megachurch_attender_report.htm.

Tolle, E. (2004). *The power of now: A guide to spiritual enlightenment.* Novato, CA: New World Publishers.

Toneatto, T., & Nguyen, L. (2007). Does mindfulness meditation improve anxiety and mood symptoms? A review of the controlled research. *Canadian Journal of Psychiatry* 52(4): 260–266.

US Department of Health and Human Services. (2012). Results from the 2012 National Survey on Drug Use and Health: Mental Health Findings. Retrieved November 24, 2014, from http://www .samhsa.gov/data/NSDUH/2k12MH_FindingsandDetTables/2K12MHF/NSDUHmhfr2012 .htm#sec2-2.

Vallurupalli, M., Laurerdale, M. K., Balboni, M. J., Phelps, A. C., Block, S. D., Ng, A. K., et al. (2012). The role of spirituality and religious coping in the quality of life of patients with advanced cancer receiving palliative radiation therapy. *Journal of Supportive Oncology* 10(2): 81–87. doi:10.1016 /J.suponc_2011.09.003.

VanderWaal, C. J., Hernandez, E. I., & Sandman, A. R. (2012). The gatekeepers: Clergy involvement in referrals and collaboration with mental health and substance abuse professionals. *Social Work and Christianity* 39(1): 27–51.

Van Leeuwen, R., Tiesinga, L. J., Middel, B., Post, D., & Jochemsen, H. (2008). The effectiveness of an educational programme for nursing students on developing competence in the provision of spiritual care. *Journal of Clinical Nursing* 17(20): 2768–2781.

Verhagen, P. J., & Cox, J. L. (2010). Multicultural education and training in religion and spirituality. In P. J. Verhagen, H. M. van Praag, J. J. López-Ibor, J. L. Cox, & D. Moussaoui (Eds.), *Religion and psychiatry: Beyond boundaries* (pp. 587–610). Chichester, UK: John Wiley & Sons.

Vieten, C., Amorok, T., & Schlitz, M. (2005). Many paths, one mountain: A cross-traditional model of spiritual transformation. Presented at Science and Religion: Global Perspectives. An International, Interfaith, Interdisciplinary Conference, Pennsylvania.

Vieten, C., Amorok, T., & Schlitz, M. (2006). I to we: The role of consciousness transformation in compassion and altruism. *Journal of Religion and Science* 41(4): 915–932. doi:10.1111/j.1467-9744.2006.00788.x.

Vieten, C., Amorok, T., & Schlitz, M. (2011). Institute of Noetic Sciences' consciousness transformation model. Retrieved November 24, 2014, from http://www.noetic.org/research/transformation _model.

Vieten, C., Scammell, S., Pierce, A., Pilato, R., Ammondson, I., Pargament, K. I., & Lukoff, D. (2014). Competencies for psychologists in the domains of religion and spirituality. Manuscript submitted for publication.

Vieten, C., Scammell, S., Pilato, R., Ammondson, I., Pargament, K. I., & Lukoff, D. (2013). Spiritual and religious competencies for psychologists. *Psychology of Religion and Spirituality* 5(3): 129–144.

Vieten, C., Schlitz, M., & Amorok, T. (2009). A research-based model of consciousness transformation. *Shift: At the Frontiers of Consciousness* 23: 32–34.

Viggiano, D. B., & Krippner, S. (2010). The Grofs' model of spiritual emergency in retrospect: Has it stood the test of time? *International Journal of Transpersonal Studies* 29(1): 118–127.

Vogel, M. J. (2013). *Examining religion and spirituality as diversity training: A multidimensional study of training in the American Psychological Association.* Doctoral dissertation, George Fox University, Newberg, OR. UMI Number 3515671.

Waller, R., Trepka, C., Collerton, D., & Hawkins, J. (2010). Addressing spirituality in CBT. *Cognitive Behaviour Therapist* 3(3): 95–106.

Watson, J. C., Steckley, P. L., & McMullen, E. J. (2014). The role of empathy in promoting change. *Psychotherapy Research* 24(3): 286–298. doi:10.1080/10503307.2013.802823.

Watson, K. W. (1994). Spiritual emergence: Concepts and implications for psychotherapy. *Journal of Humanistic Psychology* 34(2): 22–45.

Weber, S. R., & Pargament, K. I. (2014). The role of religion and spirituality in mental health. *Current Opinion in Psychiatry* 27(5): 358–363. doi:10.1097/YCO.0000000000000080.

Weiss, M. G., & Somma, D. (2007). Explanatory models in psychiatry. In D. Bhugra and K. Bhui (Eds.), *Textbook of cultural psychiatry* (pp. 127–140). Cambridge, UK: Cambridge University Press.

Welwood, J. (1984). Principles of inner work: Psychological and spiritual. *Journal of Transpersonal Psychology* 16(1): 63–73.

Welwood, J. (2000). *Toward a psychology of awakening: Buddhism, psychotherapy, and the path of personal and spiritual transformation.* Boston, MA: Shambhala.

Wenegrat, B. (1989). Religious cult membership: A sociobiologic model. In M. Galanter (Ed.), *Cults and new religious movements: A report of the American Psychiatric Association* (pp. 193–208). Arlington, VA: American Psychiatric Publishing.

Whitley, B. E., Jr., & Kite, M. E. (2010). *The psychology of prejudice and discrimination* (2nd ed.). Belmont, CA: Thomson-Wadsworth.

Wiggins-Frame, M. (2009). The spiritual genogram in family therapy. *Journal of Marital and Family Therapy* 26(2): 211–216.

Williams, M. G., Teasdale, J. D., Segal, J. V., & Kabat-Zinn, J. (2007). *The mindful way through depression: Freeing yourself from chronic unhappiness.* New York: Guilford.

Wittenbrink, B., & Schwarz, N. (Eds.). (2007). *Implicit measures of attitudes.* New York: Guilford.

Wong, Y. J., Rew, L., & Slaikeu, K. D. (2006). A systematic review of recent research on adolescent religiosity/spirituality and mental health. *Issues in Mental Health Nursing* 27(2): 161–183.

Worthington, E. L., & Sandage, S. J. (2002). Religion and spirituality. In J. Norcross (Ed.), *Psychotherapy relationships that work: Therapist contributions and responsiveness to patients* (pp. 383–399). New York: Oxford University Press.

Wulff, D. M. (2000). Mystical experience. In E. Cardeña, S. J. Lynn, & S. Krippner (Eds.), *Varieties of anomalous experience: Examining the scientific evidence* (pp. 397–440). Washington, DC: American Psychological Association.

Wuthnow, R. (2007). *After the baby boomers: How twenty- and thirty-somethings are shaping the future of American religion.* Princeton, NJ: Princeton University Press.

Yarhouse, M. A., & Johnson, V. (2013). Value and ethical issues: The interface between psychology and religion. In K. I. Pargament (Ed.), *APA handbook of psychology, religion, and spirituality: Vol. 2. An applied psychology of religion and spirituality* (pp. 43–70). Washington, DC: American Psychological Association.

Young, J. S., Cashwell, C., Wiggins-Frame, M., & Belaire, C. (2002). Spiritual and religious competencies: A national survey of CACREP-accredited programs. *Counseling and Values* 47(1): 22–33.

Young, S. (2011). The dark night. *Shinzen's blog.* Retrieved January 26, 2015, from http://shinzenyoung. blogspot.com/2011_11_01_archive.html.

Zinnbauer, B. J., Pargament, K. I., Cole, B., Rye, M. S., Butter, E. M., Belavich, T. G., et al. (1997). Religion and spirituality: Unfuzzying the fuzzy. *Journal for the Scientific Study of Religion* 36(4): 549–564.

Zinnbauer, B. J., Pargament, K. I., & Scott, A. B. (1999). The emerging meanings of religiousness and spirituality: Problems and prospects. *Journal of personality* 67(6): 889–919.

Zuk, G. H., & Zuk, C. V. (1998). Projection, double bind, and demonic possession: Some common elements in three theories of psychosis. *Contemporary Family Therapy: An International Journal* 20(1): 15–23.

Cassandra Vieten, PhD, is a licensed clinical psychologist, president and CEO of the Institute of Noetic Sciences, and a scientist in the Mind-Body Medicine Research Group at the California Pacific Medical Center Research Institute. Her research has focused on spirituality and health, development and pilot testing of mindfulness-based approaches to cultivating emotional balance, and transformative experiences and practices. She is coauthor of *Living Deeply* (New Harbinger/Noetic Books 2008) and author of *Mindful Motherhood* (New Harbinger 2009).

Shelley Scammell, PsyD, is a licensed clinical psychologist with a twenty-year practice in the San Francisco Bay Area. She is an adjunct professor at the California Institute of Integral Studies, and has taught psychology at Sonoma State University, as well as at the American College of Traditional Chinese Medicine. Formerly, she was an associate professor of English at New York University, and taught at Baruch College and Mount Holyoke. As copresident of the Institute for Spirituality and Psychology, she was fundamental in developing the sixteen competencies. She has published articles on the competencies in APA journals as well as presented them at several APA national conventions. Her extensive background in Western and Eastern spiritual practices and studies has informed her diagnosis and treatment of clients in spiritual struggles. Her clinical experience has fostered a desire to share this expertise with fellow clinicians.

Foreword writer **Daniel J. Siegel, MD**, is executive director of the Mindsight Institute and associate clinical professor of psychiatry at the University of California, Los Angeles School of Medicine. He is author of *The Developing Mind*, *The Mindful Brain*, and other books, and founding editor of the Norton Series on Interpersonal Neurobiology.

INDEX

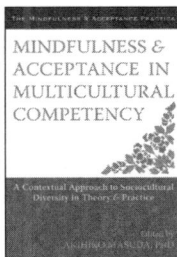

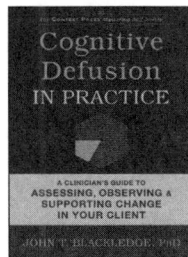

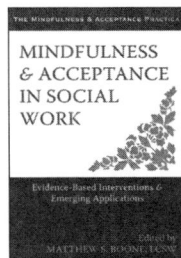